A DISSENTER'S GUIDE TO FOREIGN POLICY

THE EDITOR: Editor of the socialist quarterly *Dissent,* Irving Howe teaches English at Hunter College of the City University of New York, and has also taught at Brandeis and Stanford universities. Among the books he has written or edited are *Politics and the Novel* and *The American Communist Party: A Critical History.*

A DISSENTER'S GUIDE TO FOREIGN POLICY

Edited by
IRVING HOWE

Foreword by
LEWIS COSER

FREDERICK A. PRAEGER, *Publishers*
New York · Washington

BOOKS THAT MATTER
Published in the United States of America in 1968
by Frederick A. Praeger, Inc., Publishers
111 Fourth Avenue, New York, N.Y. 10003

Library of Congress Catalog Card Number: 68-23353

Published by arrangement with Doubleday & Company, Inc.

Printed in the United States of America

Contents

Part III

Part IV

A DISSENTER'S GUIDE TO FOREIGN POLICY

Foreword

Though this book is called a guide, I like to think of it in a somewhat more modest way—as a collection containing a number of signposts which, though by no means always in accord, all point in the same general direction. A more comprehensive and more unified guide might be written sometime in the future, but the time for that has not yet come. The reason for this, I could argue, is twofold; the lack of a left tradition in respect to foreign affairs, and the impact of the Cold War on radical thought.

In domestic affairs, both here and in Europe, the democratic and socialist left has had a fairly consistent point of view. Though there existed, of course, wide divergencies concerning both tactics and strategy, it is relatively easy to discern major lines of agreement on over-all policy and goals. Gradualist and reformist strategies might be countered by "revolutionary" ones, but the main forces on the international left nevertheless converged in their commitment to a struggle for a more humane, fraternal and equalitarian society and in their opposition to exploitation and to all those degrading manifestations of capitalist society which run counter to human dignity. When workers went on strike, it was seen as a matter of course that all otherwise divergent groups on the left would come to their aid. When welfare measures were introduced in a parliament, all tendencies on the left would support them—though they would also claim that they did not go nearly as far as was just and desirable.

The struggle for an extension of civil rights, citizens' rights and civil liberties also found unanimous support in the various sectors of the democratic left. The enhancement of Liberty, Equality and Fraternity, those revolutionary slogans that the labor and socialist left had inherited from its bourgeois democratic forebears, provided major standards to guide the left in its over-all orientation to the domestic scene and to the different political constellations in which left parties were variously placed. But in foreign affairs, no such agreement in principle has been forthcoming.

It could seem at first that the common commitment to a politics of peace among the nations might have served functions similar to the ideas of liberty, equality and fraternity on the domestic scene. But this was by no means the case. The ideal of peace proved so abstract and highly generalized that by itself it was incapable of suggesting specific guidelines to action. And so, from the days of Marx and Engels to our own, the socialist left has been fatefully split in its orientation to foreign policy and international affairs.

When the Franco-Prussian War broke out in 1870, the German Marxists Liebknecht and Bebel abstained from voting for war credits and spoke in the Reichstag against the war and the projected annexation of Alsace-Lorraine. Marx warned the German workers against Bismarck's war aims and stressed that the interests of German and French workers were identical. But in a private letter to Engels, Marx also pointed out that the defeat of Germany, which would have strengthened the French Bonapartist regime and crippled the German workers for many years, might have been even more dismal an outcome than German victory. It would have transferred, he argued, the center of gravity on the socialist left from Berlin to Paris. Yet the German workers were more disciplined and organized than the French and hence could be a stronger rallying point for social democracy than the Frenchmen; the defeat of Bonapartism would remove a major block to progress in Europe. When even so vigorous a thinker as Marx was torn in different directions in regard to issues of war and peace, it is not surprising that his successors and epigones found it even more difficult to agree on common orientations.

Ever since Marx, the socialist and labor movement has been internally torn by major divergencies in the international area. And, as distinct from disagreements about domestic affairs, these divergencies concerned issues of basic substance, not mere tactics. The pre-war Second International managed, at the price of a great deal of ambiguity in its formulations, to present what seemed to outsiders a united front against war; however, as subsequent events showed only too clearly, these pious resolutions did not prevent its major constituent parties from lining up at the outset of World War I behind their respective national governments with practical unanimity. The later reactions against "social patriotism" were, in their turn, far from uniform, ranging as they did from complete pacifism to revolutionary defeatism, from appeals for Negotiations Now to calls for revolutionary strike action.

Nor did matters change basically after the First World War. Though most of the left backed the League of Nations in principle, in practice attitudes toward war still ranged from the pacifism of a George Lansbury to advocacy of militant intervention in the Spanish Civil War or against Nazi Germany; from militant support of the Allies against the German enemy in World War II to commitment to a somewhat vague "Third Camp," opposed to both capitalism and Communism, on the part of the extreme left.

Nor was such disagreement on the left limited to the question of war and peace. Attitudes toward colonialism and national oppression were similarly divided. Marx and Engels fought valiantly in support of Polish and Irish national independence, but when it came to the benighted nations of the Balkan hinterlands they were by no means as positive in their attitude. International socialist congresses might go on record against colonial exploitation, but in practice only a few isolated men on the left concretely envisaged colonial liberation as anything but a distant goal. And both in France and in England socialists served as humane and sometimes not so humane colonial administrators. On the extreme left, on the other hand, there were endless debates on whether national-bourgeois oppositions in the colonial countries deserved support or whether such support should only be granted to (usually non-existent) proletarian movements in colonial countries.

A majority of British Fabians were committed to social imperialism and supported the Boer War, while their latter-day descendant, Lord Bertrand Russell, veered from conscientious objection in the First World War to the advocacy of nuclear attack against the Soviet Union shortly after the Second and back again to a somewhat hysterical anti-American "neutralism" in our days.

It is safe to conclude this sketchy outline by suggesting that there is precious little in the history of the left which suggests consistent orientations and ideas that might serve as a guide for contemporary politics.

Nor are matters more encouraging when one comes to the immediate past of the Cold War confrontation between the United States and the Soviet Union. Since this history is still vivid in our memories and because a number of contributors to this book deal with it in some detail, a few brief pointers should suffice. The non-Communist left tended in the first phases of the Cold War to align itself with a fair measure of agreement in the anti-Soviet camp. Nevertheless, shifting now to the American scene, one notes in the postwar years divergencies in attitudes which ranged from muted or not so muted admiration for the Soviet Union on the part of left authoritarians like Isaac Deutscher or Paul Sweezy to abject surrender of some men on the left to the State Department line.

Many American intellectuals who had previously been committed to a critical stance vis-à-vis American foreign policy, having joined the "American Celebration," now tended to abandon all criticism. Others concluded that capitalism was, after all, the lesser evil. Philip Rahv, a man rather representative of this wing, wrote in 1948:

> Of these forces [Soviet totalitarianism and American capitalism], both hostile, the former is by far the more barbarous and deadly, and for this reason the libertarian socialists have no alternative but to direct their main struggle against it. In this struggle a strategic alliance, chiefly in this country, with bourgeois democracy and to a certain extent even with the bourgeoisie as a class (in so far as its interests coincide, in however temporary a fashion, with those of democracy) becomes unavoidable and in fact indispensable if the struggle is not to be conducted in a quixotic and futile manner. At this time the opportunity for free socialism arises principally out of the conflict between its greater and lesser enemies. This lesser enemy, namely American capitalism, is now plainly in no position to bear down on the non-Communist left at home or abroad. (*Partisan Review,* May 1948).

Others did not choose to express themselves as ponderously

as Rahv, but his sentiments were certainly rather widely shared. Even if recent revisionist efforts at rewriting the history of the Cold War prove correct and it can be shown that Russian expansionism in Europe and elsewhere was not as purposive as had previously been assumed; even if it could be shown that Stalinist foreign policy was reactive rather than deliberate, it remains true that Stalinism was perceived as an immediate threat by the majority of leftist intellectuals. They reacted to this threat in different ways. Some gave up criticism of their home government as they nervously huddled under the protective umbrella of Washington policy-makers; others, with CIA support or for free, became simple propagandists for American foreign policy. Others again, like Norman Thomas and the editors of *Dissent,* while refusing to join the chorus of American yea sayers and maintaining their critical distance from both Western capitalism and Eastern Stalinism, yet in some measure gave critical support to a number of measures of American foreign policy, such as the Marshall Plan, aid for Titoist Yugoslavia and the resistance to the Berlin blockade.

This is not the place to go into details. Suffice it to say that as long as Stalin lived, as long as a monolithic Communist bloc seemed to threaten the Western world and all the human and humane values it had produced in a travail of centuries, foreign policy orientations on the left, no matter how different the motivations behind individual points of view, were dominated by the Cold War confrontation.

Since the middle fifties, and more particularly since the Sino-Soviet split, the incubus of the Soviet threat has largely been lifted. The American left, or so it would seem to me, has now gained a much greater freedom for the rethinking of foreign policy. Moreover, the final breakup of the Soviet camp has been correlative with—I am not saying caused by—a turn toward naked and brutal imperialist ventures on the part of the United States. Men of good will might have differed on the motivations and intentions behind, say, the Marshall plan, yet most of them gave it at least critical support. But the horrible war against the people of Vietnam, the interventions in the Dominican Republic, the CIA-instigated and -financed reactionary coups in Latin America, the overt support for a variety of repressive regimes in the underdeveloped nations, find very few, if any, defenders among men of good will on the left.

While the map of the world was surely never painted in stark blacks and whites, as the Dulleses tried to persuade us, it remains nevertheless colored in morally ambiguous grays to a much greater degree than it was, say, ten years ago. Hence foreign policy attitudes which seemed to have a measure of justification in the days of heightened confrontation with the Soviet Union have now lost it. In fact, they have lost most of their hold on reality. One must distinguish between an anti-Communism which developed as an effort to build a dike against a further invasion of European territory by Russian totalitarianism, and the Rusk-style anti-Communism, a sick fantasy, a gigantic hoax when carried over to the East Asian scene.

It is this changed political situation, I believe, which has led to a new soul-searching on the left. Some writers may be more influenced than others by recent revisionist authors on the origin of the Cold War, such as Gar Alperovitz, but all, save the remaining Cold War diehards who have learned nothing and forgotten nothing, seem now united in the belief that a new look at foreign policy and particularly at America's role on the world scene is on the agenda. When as inveterate a weather vane of trends in left thinking and of the most recent turns of the *Zeitgeist* as the aforementioned Philip Rahv can now quote approvingly the New Left spokesman Carl Oglesby and refer to "the U.S. and its newly acquired empire as 'an imperial house of bondage' " (*The New York Review of Books*, October 12, 1967), then times have indeed changed quite drastically.

Those of us who are now groping toward a new dissenting orientation in foreign affairs are hampered, as I have tried to show, by the unavailability of a secure foreign policy tradition in the history of modern radicalism. We are hampered as well by the fact that the gradual unfreezing of the world scene is only barely ten years old; the Cold War heritage still weighs heavily on us. Moreover, we have to deal with such utterly unprecedented factors as the invention of means of warfare which could annihilate the bulk of the world's population in a few hours or the emergence of literally dozens of new polities in the world of nations. To mention but one of the major factors, we need to come to terms with the stark fact that the differences between the rich and the poor nations of the world, far from decreasing as had been previously hoped, increase each year.

No generation, to be sure, ever faces an intellectual *tabula rasa* upon which wholly novel structures can be erected; the tradition of the past always weighs on the living. Yet I believe that we now face a host of world problems which are totally unprecedented in scope, and which need to be approached with completely new tools of thought. To give just one example: suppose that we were to enter a period in the world economy in which the major nations, far from exploiting colonies or ex-colonies for needed raw materials, will have developed synthetic substitutes for most of them, so that they can simply afford to neglect the have-not nations altogether. What if it came to pass that, as Nathan Keyfitz writes, these countries are "worse than exploited—they are irrelevant." (*Journal of Social Issues*, January 1967, p. 76). Neither Lenin nor Hobson, Schumpeter nor Fanon will help us solve *this* problem.

The essays that follow are far from being written from a commonly agreed perspective. They are groping efforts by a variety of writers on the radical left who hold in common only the conviction that the old shibboleths and the received wisdom of the left are no longer a sufficient guide, if they ever were, to the unprecedented problems of the New World we now face. The reader who would concentrate, say, on pointing out differences and even contradictions between the contributions of Michael Harrington and Philip Green or between Robert Heilbroner and Henry Pachter surely misunderstands our intentions. We were well aware of these differences when we began soliciting manuscripts for this volume. Our idea was to present a collection in which a variety of individual writers, united only by their over-all commitment to a democratic, radical and libertarian vision, attempted in their variant ways to clear some new paths through the underbrush of obsolete ideas.

Let me add just a few sentences about the intellectual style of these contributions. Too often what passes for fresh thinking on the so-called New Left seems full of passionate intensity but fairly short on analytical rigor. But intensity of belief is never a measure of truth. By all means let us have passion and commitment, but let it not be supposed to substitute for hardheaded thinking. This volume provides, I believe, a sample of such rigorous thought. The authors here represented reject the wicked orthodoxies of the Cold War but they are also fairly skeptical of some of the virtuous heterodoxies now becoming the fashion. They are acutely aware of the relevance of Thackeray's dictum, "The wicked are wicked, no doubt . . . but who can tell the mischief which the very virtuous do?" Distant, though not equidistant, from the twin pieties of the Cold War stalwarts and certain New Left champions, they have attempted here to offer some building blocks for a new national perspective on the foreign scene.

I see no reason to discuss here the individual contributions in this book. Efforts along these lines seem always somewhat condescending to the reader, the authors or both. Let the reader judge for himself and let him be aware that each contributor here speaks with his own voice.

Most of the pieces in this volume were written expressly for this book, though many have since been printed in the pages of *Dissent*. Other pieces that have been previously published elsewhere were revised for publication in these pages.

Lewis A. Coser

October 1967

INTRODUCTION

◆

MICHAEL HARRINGTON

American Power in the Twentieth Century

MICHAEL HARRINGTON attended Holy Cross College and the University of Chicago. Formerly associate editor of the *Catholic Worker,* he was also organizational secretary of the Workers' Defense League. Since 1954 Mr. Harrington has been a consultant to the Fund for the Republic and in 1964 was elected chairman of the board of the League for Industrial Democracy. He was consultant to Sargent Shriver in the federal poverty program in 1964 and has lectured extensively on problems of poverty since that time. Books by Mr. Harrington include *The Other America* and *The Accidental Century.*

The democratic left must help finish the creation of the world. The world—and I borrow here from Peter Worsley's imaginative way of speaking—is scarcely begun. The globe has, of course, existed for eons, and humans project their various histories more than 4000 years into the past. But those interrelationships that transcend tribe, nation, and empire, uniting the people of the earth in a common destiny—whether they like it or not—are only a century or so old. The first day of this creation took place when economics, science, and warfare put the planet together. The second day is now, and there might not be a third.

Applying such high-flown biblical imagery to politics strikes most Americans as grandiose; they leave the world to come to the preachers while they pragmatically reconstruct the reality that is. Until World War II the Pacific and Atlantic oceans allowed Americans to disdain foreign entanglements on principle. And being of an anti-imperialist imperialism, a power which usually dominated other lands through the subtlety of money rather than the brutality of force, America burdened its people with an excessively good conscience. For all of these reasons, it is particularly important to insist within the United States that the day-to-day decisions of foreign policy involve the choice of a new order of things for the twenty-first century. So far, America is creating the world very badly—though this need not be.

America is imperialist. To the average citizen, this statement is a patent slander. If the nation has erred, he would say, it has been generous to a fault, and only a Communist could deny the charity and anti-colonialism of its historic record. But the United States has been profoundly imperialist in the decades after World War II (and before, but that is another story). Yet, the United States need not be imperialist. This notion strikes most revolutionists, and not just the Communists, as unpardonably tender-minded. To them, fat, prosperous, capitalist America cannot possibly ally itself with the downtrodden and against the international *status quo*; it is fated to be reactionary, the very headquarters of the world's counter-revolution. This trust in the country's inherent evil is, however, almost as naive as the patriotic faith in its goodness. For given a turn to the democratic left, this nation could play a crucial and positive role in finishing the creation of the world.

Anti-utopia seems more possible than a better world. And yet, there is hope. Although there are tremendous social, political, and economic forces urging the U.S. (and the West, and the rich Communist East) to do wrong, this country could take the lead in making a democratic revolution—in finishing the creation of the world in humane fashion. This fragile hope is my point of departure.

The Progress of the Third World

It has been said so often that the rich nations are getting richer and the poor nations poorer that the very enormity of the fact is lost in cliché.

In the middle of the "Development Decade," proclaimed by the U.N., the Food and Agricultural Organization (FAO) announced that the developing lands were more ill-nourished in 1965 than they had been before World War II, and the Organization for Economic Cooperation and Development (OECD) estimated in 1966 that the nourishment needs in these countries will grow twice as fast as the supply during the remaining years of the century. Also in 1966, the U.N. journal *World Economic Survey* reported that the purchasing power of the Third World had declined while its net outflow of interest and profit to the wealthy powers—the tribute the poor pay to the rich—had increased by 10 per cent. This outrage has been repeatedly denounced by the Secretaries General of the U.N., various Popes, the World Council of Churches, and the U.S. Secretary of Defense.

As Mr. McNamara summarized this anguished prospect in a Montreal speech in 1966, in the year 2000 half of the developing nations will have achieved a per capita income of $170 a year, assuming a continuation of present trends; the American figure would be $4,500. This tragedy is utterly rational according to the economic "laws" of the world the West has carefully created in the last century.

When capitalism conquered the planet, it destroyed or corrupted the indigenous achievements it encountered. Native industry was broken up either by force or because it could not compete with cheap, manufactured goods; direct tribute, and sometimes slave labor, were required; and the "mother" country entered into an alliance with the most reactionary of the local leaders. These cruelties were much more sophisticated and effective than those of the pirates and freebooters; the triumphant entrepreneurs not only stole from their subjects but also integrated them into their economic system.

"You cannot continue to inundate a country with your manufactures," Karl Marx shrewdly observed at the time, "unless you enable it to give some produce in return." Thus, a new economy was created. The colony exported primary products from its fields and mines according to the needs of the metropolitan economy (the profits were shipped out, too). Then, with whatever pittance was left to them, the natives were allowed to buy manufactured goods from their exploiters and so provided them with still another profit. There was, to be sure, some economic progress and modernization in the colony; the

French proclaimed it in most noble terms: they were engaged in *la mission civilatrice*.

According to the rationalizations of the time, the various countries were simply doing what they could do best, submitting to the impersonal laws of economics. People somehow failed to realize that these "laws" were artificial constructions of Western power. Asia, Africa, and Latin America were carefully and systematically denied the benefits of the new industrialism; they were designated the hewers of wood and the drawers of water.

After World War II a new indignity was in store for the Third World. Paradoxically, the new nations suffered because the advanced lands were now less interested in exploiting them. The new mid-century technology no longer required great quantities of traditional raw materials; synthetics now substituted for old imports, and subsidized, protected agricultural sectors took care of about 80 per cent of the need for primary products. Ironically, the very success of the Western welfare state, and particularly of government policies to promote full employment, made profiteering in the backward areas less attractive. For now the wealthy powers had created such stable and enormous markets that they could make more money producing for one another's affluence than by investing in underdeveloped countries.

On the world market, the demand for manufactured goods zoomed while that for primary products declined. The First Committee of the U.N. Trade and Development Conference in 1964 reported the result: between 1950 and 1962 prices paid for the exports of the underdeveloped countries went down by 7 per cent and prices paid for their imports from the industrialized countries went up by 27 per cent. And whenever the Third World managed to attract some public or private capital from the great powers, they paid cash on the barrelhead. The result of these trends has been, in the words of Raùl Prebisch, "a regressive redistribution of income . . . between the developed and developing countries."

Profit, Priorities & Economic "Laws"

As Gunnar Myrdal has pointed out, everyone knows that it is

more profitable to invest in safe projects than in risky ones—in European and American affluence rather than in Third World poverty. Given the political and social outlook of private business, available funds will go to private rather than to public enterprises, and to undertakings in the ex-colonies only when they promote a quick profit rather than balanced growth of the whole society. The priorities so skillfully built into the very structure of the international economy are often a more efficient and subtle way of keeping the world's poor in their unhappy place than were the gunboats and troops of the earlier imperialism. To do incalculable harm to the masses of the Third World, the Western politician or businessman need not be evil, only reasonable and realistic.

The man-made logic of the international division of labor is so compelling that it directs the developing country to embrace the misfortune which has been visited upon it. And this is precisely what the Committee for Economic Development (CED), one of the most sophisticated and liberal business organizations in the U.S., advocated in a 1966 policy statement. The new nations, the CED said, must invest "where the increment in value of product promises to be greatest." This sounds quite sensible, and it leads to the conclusion that priority should be given to those export industries "that can earn substantial foreign exchange if they can compete with effective industries in other countries. . . ." Obviously, fledgling societies cannot compete with the advanced giant industries of Europe and America; it would be a waste to allocate resources to a modern technological sector which would, after all, only duplicate Western factories and at a much higher and noncompetitive cost.

In obedience to the "laws" of the world market, the developing country must find some export specialty that suits the needs of the big powers, for that is the only rational thing to do in a system created by, and for, these big powers. And this logic can easily override consideration of the needs of the people or the requirements for building a balanced, modern economy. But even a country that manages to escape from these inexorabilities of the international economy and invests in an advanced enterprise is victimized by the way the world is organized. Celso Furtado, a brilliant Latin-American economist, has vividly analyzed what this means:

Technology developed "organically" in the West. When the first factories needed semiskilled and unskilled operatives, peasants were expropriated and a working class was created. As mechanical ingenuity advanced, the workers were progressively withdrawn from primary and secondary occupations (agriculture, mining, and mass production) and channeled into the service and white-collar sector. At times, these transitions were accomplished by brute force; at times, mass action won concessions and ameliorations. In either case, economy and society grew up side by side with the machines and the new organization of work.

Thus, Furtado points out, the corporation is designed to fit the needs of profit-making in an advanced economy, and when one tries to transplant its technology to impoverished, developing lands, furious contradictions result. The newest machines save manpower—a blessing in the U.S. and a curse in a country with rampant underemployment. Mass production requires a huge market nonexistent in an archaic agricultural society. So, Furtado concludes, the very structure of economic life in the new nations—forced upon them in the last century—makes it difficult for them to absorb the benefits of scientific and technical progress on those rare occasions when they might have the opportunity to do so.

Thus, the rich nations specialize in activities which make work easier, goods more abundant, leisure more widespread, and living standards higher. The poor nations are left with the grubby tasks of primary production and with a stagnant or declining market; they must sell cheap and buy dear from the booming factories. In such a world, the gap separating the impoverished from the affluent will grow no matter what the U.N. General Assembly decides.

Americans Abroad: Benefactors and Entrepreneurs

The foreign policies of the big powers operate to reinforce the logic of injustice which is part of the world created by the nineteenth-century West. Thus, statesmanship has served to increase the distance between the world's haves and have-nots.

And yet, the average American would argue that the U.S. possesses no colonies; that it has spent tremendous sums in the military defense of freedom around the earth and given away billions of dollars to impoverished nations. In return for all this idealism and largesse, he would conclude, the country has received little but ingratitude; how can the recipients of all this charity call the United States imperialist?

This perplexed and angry view is not described here for purposes of ridicule. No doubt, generosity is a peculiarity of the American national character, and this excellent emotion has provided the political basis for foreign aid from the Marshall Plan to the present. Yet, the results of these efforts have often been at variance with the spirit that motivated them. And this is precisely why it is so important to understand how the U.S., even when it acts out of its best instincts (and is *not* motivated by hysterical anti-Communism, oil diplomacy, and the like), has intensified the very social and economic miseries it deplores.

There is a deep American political tradition which holds that a man who gives away something for nothing is probably effeminate and certainly not fit for public office. Therefore, it is often necessary for the politician to disguise noble impulses in the rhetoric of the counting house. Harry Truman's Leninism in the following statement on Point Four was probably such verbiage, designed to win support from a dubious business community for the do-gooding concepts of Point Four:

> It seemed to me that if we could encourage stabilized governments in underdeveloped countries in Africa, South America, and Asia, we could encourage the use for the development of these areas of some of the capital which had accumulated in the United States. If the investment of capital from the United States could be protected and not confiscated, and if we could persuade the capitalists that they were not working in foreign countries to exploit them, it would be to the mutual benefit of everybody concerned.

From Truman's Presidency to the present, it has been U.S. policy to proceed according to this scenario: to discover some reasonable ex-colonials committed to capitalist development of their lands; to instill some social purpose in American businessmen; then, to have the American government provide the financial framework within which these two groups can make a free-enterprise idyll of peaceful progress. But the contradictory elements in this vision guaranteed its self-defeat. The U.S. indeed honestly felt committed to a democratic alternative to Communist industrialization, to abolition of the world's inequities by means of freedom rather than dictatorship. But this fine aspiration was to be pursued according to the traditional rules of world capitalism—rules which were a major source of the misery that supposedly was to be abolished.

Concretely, American foreign aid and military programs, private investment, and tariff policy were permeated and guided by the principles of the old order they were intended to challenge. While trying to be noble, the U.S. thus, unwittingly but inevitably, made money and, more often than not, worsened the plight of those it had set out to aid and whose support it sought in the Cold War. Dean Acheson, in an important speech in Cleveland, Mississippi, on the direct orders of President Truman, noted that American exports were twice as great as the imports, and that the balance of trade was *too* favorable. Therefore, Acheson concluded, American funds must go to Europe. Now it is clear that the Marshall Plan was not simply designed in order to give businessmen a stable market in the Old World. Political, military, and even cultural considerations led to the decision to defend the continent against what was seen as the imminent threat of Communist insurrection and/or invasion. But American generosity and anti-Communism also had the effect of priming the European pump; it was a type of international Keynesianism creating an effective demand for U.S. products overseas and consequently leading to higher profits.

This self-interest rationale for foreign aid persists to this day. In lobbying for the Administration's 1967 program, the Agency for International Development (AID) told Congress, "In the less developed world today, the AID program is introducing American products and performance standards to some of the great potential markets of the future. . . . The goods and services go overseas, the dollar stays here to pay for them."

In part, this is the same shamming cynicism as Harry Truman's Leninist tough talk, used to conceal decent motives; but it also has another dead serious aspect. For when there is conflict between the needs of the American corporation and those of the impoverished whom we supposedly are helping, the domestic dollar comes first. In March 1966 a Buenos Aires meeting was convened to consider what gains had been made by the Alliance for Progress. There was an immediate uproar when the Latin Americans attacked the policy of "tied" aid— which requires the beneficiary to spend his gift or loan in the United States ("The goods and services go overseas, the dollar stays here to pay for them"). The delegates pointed out that they could often get cheaper goods in Europe or Japan. Lincoln Gordon of the State Department replied for the U.S. His nation, he said, was interested in world-wide trade liberalization but "considerations of national security and structural problems within our own economy have led to the imposition of import restrictions." Plainly, the Latin-American developers were to subordinate their needs to those of the American commitment in Vietnam, the balance of payment problem, and the alleged threat of domestic inflation.

The Varying Uses of Aid

India provides an even better example for the profitable uses of American generosity. This particular case grows out of the fact that there is money to be made in the starvation market. As *Forbes Magazine* (which advertises itself as a "capitalist tool") headlined the cover story in the March 1, 1966 issue: "Feeding the World's Hungry Millions: How It Will Mean Billions for U.S. Business." The American oil companies, *Forbes* said in this article, had got the message and were embarking on fertilizer production. Then followed this frank and revealing anecdote:

> For a long time, India insisted that it handle all the distribution of fertilizer produced in that country by U.S. companies and that it also set the price. Standard of Indiana understandably refused to accept these conditions. AID put food shipments to India on a month-to-month basis until the Indian government let Standard of Indiana market its fertilizer at its own price.

And so, in the 1967 AID proposals, the request for $50 million for fertilizer to India was a "tied" grant and its stated goal was to encourage private enterprise—which is to say American oil corporations—in this area. Oil is, after all, more sovereign than India.

Thus, foreign aid has been an immensely profitable undertaking for the American economy and whenever it shows any sign of becoming a real gift, of requiring more giving then getting, it has been cut back. Here, too, the "rational" approach is to give the largest amount of help to the richest rather than the poorest nations, and this is logical in terms of the world market and the international division of labor. Europe can, after all, absorb more capital than Asia, Africa, or Latin America.

So of the $40 billion spent by AID and its predecessors between 1946 and 1965, $18.5 billion went to restore capitalism in Europe ($13 billion during the brief Marshall Plan period, an extra $2.7 billion to Greece and Turkey, $2.8 billion to Europe after the Marshall Plan). Chiang's "China," Vietnam, and South Korea received another $6 billion. India received more money in the years after the Communist attack in 1962 than in the 15 previous (and largely neutralist) years ($1.4 billion as against $1.022 billion). The funds for Europe were mainly grants, for the poor countries mainly loans. The priorities involved in these allocations, with one major exception, were those that usually motivate investments of a private corporation; aid was directed to the areas of the greatest pay-off. Thus, even benevolence has increased the gap between the rich and the poor.

There was and is, however, a major exception to this rule. In certain cases, the nonprofit logic of military need prevailed over the calculus of the market in the American aid effort. Then a very poor nation could obtain huge sums of money for nothing—although there was usually an unspoken interest rate computed in the numbers of the dead and maimed. This grim exception proved that it was possible, where there was a real political will, to defy the rationality of an artificial world and to favor principles over balance sheets. It is, of course, only one more irony imposed upon the world's impoverished that this burst of idealism took place for purposes of destruction rather than construction.

As a result, the military defiance of economic law accentuated rather than reversed the reactionary priorities at work in the rest of the American aid program. To qualify for this exceptional support, a regime had to be fanatically anti-Communist—and it almost always was opposed to any real democratic social progress as well. Inefficiency, corruption, and instability were tolerated, as in the various governments in Vietnam in the sixties. But, to the military a genuine program for social justice smacked too much of Communism. Indeed, in the postwar period, American military funds for the avowed and practicing opponents of decent change in Asia and Latin America were much more generous than those given to the modernizers.

The U.N. journal *World Economic Survey* in 1965 put the matter succinctly. During that year, it reported, the self-help efforts of the Third World resulted in an increase in savings of 6 per cent (of the surplus deducted from a meager, sometimes starvation-level, consumption). But the outflow to the advanced countries in interest and profit went up by 10 per cent. As a result, the U.N. concluded, the developing countries were sending back to the donors more than half of the funds they had received! The external debt of these nations in 1964 was "on the order of" $40 billion, or roughly equal to the entire postwar American aid program up to 1965.

These figures cover a wide range of societies at different levels of development. The London *Economist* reported in October 1966: "The poorest among them, a former World Bank official has estimated, are now paying more interest and principle on World Bank loans than they are receiving from the World Bank in new loans." Some random cases will demonstrate this fantastic situation: *The New York Times* reported in 1965 that Latin-American "debt payments were as high as the total of all public development loans and grants during the year"; the interest due on past loans to India in 1966, to quote the *Times* again, was equal to 35 per cent of the foreign exchange required for the next five-year plan. And perhaps the most summary and cruel statement of this phenomenon was made by Jacques Ferrandi, Director of the *Fond Européen du Développement*: "We can say without exaggeration that certain recently contracted loans [for "development"] are being used to pay old debts."

So the world's poorest countries have done more to raise the living standards of the affluent than to help their own people. But this monstrous subsidy from the miserable to the fat is, after all, quite logical. With the enormous amounts of money being invested in Europe and America, it is only reasonable that risky, emerging societies should pay dear for whatever they receive. In October 1966 a neutralist "summit" was held at New Delhi and there were reports that Tito, Nasser, and Madame Gandhi were going to protest this tragedy and call for a "freezing" of the debt of all the developing countries. However, the London *Economist* reported, both India and Yugoslavia were fearful that the advocacy of such a radical step would bring the wrath of the U.S. down upon their heads. To protect what financial support they did receive, they refrained from complaining.

But the backward economies export more than money to the industrialized countries; they send their most precious national resource, trained human beings. An Iranian sociologist has reported that Togo sent more physicians and professors to France than vice versa and that, between mid-1950 and mid-1964, Argentina sent 13,800 engineers to the U.S. The president of Cornell University has estimated that in a 12-year postwar period some 43,000 scientists and engineers, "many" of them from developing countries, have migrated to the U.S. As a result, in 1964–65, 28 per cent of the internships and 26 per cent of the residencies in U.S. hospitals were filled by foreigners—and 90 per cent of the students from Asia who came to study in America didn't go home.

But perhaps the most single revealing example of how American policy reinforces the systematic injustices of our artificial economic world is found in the area of tariffs. I am not referring to the straightforward evils of protectionism which were designed to do harm to the poor and benefit the rich. Thus, for example, the "differential" tariff raises the duty on an import according to the degree to which it has been industrially processed. If the backward economy contents itself with the simple—and impoverishing— extraction of raw materials, it is rewarded; but if it develops itself and sends out more sophisticated products, it is penalized. Similarly, the United States admonishes other nations on the importance of free trade and the test of international competition (in the 1960's, India was particularly favored with such lectures). Yet, America scrupulously ignores these pieties where its own corporate interests are involved. Domestic agriculture is subsidized, world oil prices are rigged to suit the needs of Texas millionaires, and so on. In fairness, it must be added that the Common Market agriculturists are adept at the same games.

But more interesting than these routine and self-interested betrayals of our cherished principles are cases when the U.S. does wrong in the name of virtue. Such cases are based on the denial of the very existence of an international order of economic inequity—but they prove the contrary.

Fair Rules for World Trade

To most Americans, the principles behind the rules and regulations for world trade drawn up at a meeting in Havana shortly after World War II and partially embodied in the General Agreement on Tariffs and Trade (GATT), are the essence of fairness itself: the nations would exchange with one another according to a principle of reciprocity; the advanced country would lower its duties on raw materials in response to a reduction of charges on industrial imports in the underdeveloped lands; in this way, all nations would obtain a larger market for whatever they happened to sell and each would be encouraged to specialize in the areas of its particular genius. This was a practical expression of the classic economic faith in free trade and in the benevolent workings of the world market.

This marvelous symmetrical theory assumed that there was free economic exchange among equals; only there were no equals. On the one hand, the advanced countries were making brilliant use of the advantages they had secured by force over the previous two centuries. They were moving into the spheres of super-industrialization, automation, and affluence—making so much money off each other that they were now less interested in exploiting their ex-colonies.

They were, to borrow an irony from George Orwell, becoming "more equal" than ever before. The impoverished lands of the Third World, however, were suffering more and more from their inherited disadvantages. The demand for their raw materials was stagnant, or shrinking, despite their growing need for increased imports in order to feed their expanding population and/or to industrialize. Thus, they were becoming constantly "less equal."

In this setting, the principles of "fairness" laid down at Havana allowed Western capital to increase the world's economic unfairness. As the Secretary-General of the U.N. Trade and Development Conference reported in 1964, reciprocity had actually widened the gap between the rich and the poor. In a pure world of mathematical logic all nations would indeed gain by making equivalent concessions to one another. But in the impure world fashioned in the nineteenth century the impoverished lands were required to give up the possibility of protecting new industries during the first, hesitant phase of development. Meanwhile, the advanced economies were required to make a reduction in duty which was, at most, a minor annoyance.

Under such circumstances, justice would paradoxically require, as Gunnar Myrdal has phrased it, a double standard of international economic morality. In order to compensate for the tremendous disadvantages which have been imposed upon the poor lands for well over one hundred years, they must, in strictest equity, be given special advantages. But this notion was decisively rejected by the Kennedy Round.

The disastrous results of America's seemingly fair policy of tariff reciprocity can stand as a sort of summary symbol of how this nation has made money and harmed the poor of the Third World, even when sincerely trying to do good. For foreign aid, military aid, grants and loans and tariffs were all organized according to the irrational rationality of the world market. And by far and large, postwar American policy reinforced the vicious economic "laws" from which the country benefits so profoundly. Thus, St. Matthew's parable of the rich getting richer and the poor poorer is coming true now on a global scale.

East-West Entente—Rich North Against Poor South?

We have one foot in genesis and the other in apocalypse, and annihilation is always an option. The future could even conform to a half-truth found in the fantasies of Mao Tse-tung: the advanced Communist societies can benefit from international injustice every bit as much as the corporations. This might lead to a deal between well-heeled commissars and executives to end the old-fashioned conflict between East and West, so that the industrialized North could get on with the serious work of exploiting the backward South without regard to race, class, or political creed. An extraordinary potential exists in the world of the late 1960's. The struggle between East and West, Communism and capitalism, which has dominated international politics since the end of World War II, could now come to an end—and be replaced by this conflict between the North, both Communist and capitalist, and the South, which is poor.

The following turgid piece of prose is from an article entitled "Cost Accounting In Economic Relations Between Socialist Countries"; it appeared in the October 1966 issue of the international organ of the pro-Moscow Communists, the *World Marxist Review*:

> The prices for which the socialist countries sell their goods are influenced mostly by the conditions of production in the capitalist lands, and for this reason the exchange proportions are not always commensurate with the proportion of the expenditure of socially necessary labor within the framework of the socialist world economy.

Che Guevara made the same point more bluntly in a 1965 speech:

> We should not speak any more about developing mutually beneficial trade based on prices which are really disadvantageous to the underdeveloped countries because of the law of value and the unequal relations of international trade caused by that law. How can "mutual benefit" mean the selling at world market prices of raw materials that cost the underdeveloped countries unlimited sweat and suffering and the buying at world market prices of machines produced in large, modern, mechanized factories?

There is no way of evading this point. For world prices reflect, precisely, the cheapness of primary products and the great expense of industrial goods. And if the fat Communists use these prices in their relations with the impoverished Communists, then they are getting the same kind of unjust advantage as the fat capitalists.

Guevara followed his logic to its conclusion: "If we establish that type of relationship between two groups of nations, we must argue that the socialist countries are to a certain extent accomplices of imperialist exploitation." And this exactly is admitted in the convoluted phrases of the Russian *World Marxist Review*.

The strange notion of a non- and even anti-capitalist imperialism was first put forward in the 1920's by one of the most brilliant of the Bolshevik economists, E. Preobrazhensky.* His analysis still casts a very real light upon the present relations between the Communists and the Third World. The essence of trade between a capitalist power and a colony, Preobrazhensky said, was that "the figures will always show an inequality in the expenditure of labor on the two masses of goods exchanged as equivalents." In Guevara's terms, sweat is cheap and machines are costly. But, Preobrazhensky continued, this "non-equivalence of exchange" would go on even *after* the victory of socialism in the capitalist countries for it was, in part at least, a function of the backwardness of peasant economies as compared to *any* industrialized economy, capitalist or socialist. Preobrazhensky advocated the abolition of this inequity as fast as possible through the modernization of the retrograde societies.

But the victorious socialist revolution in the "capitalist countries"—that socialism based upon the European working class and technology which all the original Bolsheviks anticipated—never came to pass, and Preobrazhensky's hypothesis was never tested. Yet, it follows from the record of Communist totalitarianism (a system which is neither capitalist nor Communist) that the Bolshevik theorist had divined

* *The New Economics*, by E. Preobrazhensky, translated by Brian Pearce. Oxford, Clarendon Press, 1965.

one of the most important truths of the second half of the twentieth century: that the division between rich and poor, industrialized and backward, North and South can transcend social systems. As the *World Marxist Review* shamefacedly admitted and Guevara boldly asserted, both the fat Communist and the fat capitalist can benefit from the "nonequivalence of exchange" on the world market.

This fact has not escaped the notice of the Third World. Here is Julius Nyerere's observation:

> Socialist countries, no less than capitalist countries, are prepared to behave like the millionaire—to use millions to destroy the other "millionaire," and it need not be a capitalist millionaire—it is just as likely to be a socialist "millionaire." In other words, socialist wealth now tolerates poverty, which is an even more unforgiveable crime . . . don't forget that rich countries . . . may be found on either side of the division between the capitalist and socialist countries.

But this imperialist process on the Communist side was not restricted to profiteering from world market prices; it was political as well. Thus, the pro-Castro editors of the *Monthly Review* in the U.S. rightly noted that Cuba, by specializing in sugar production for the "socialist" market, had become politically dependent on the Russians. There can be little doubt that this client relationship helped cause Fidel to opt for Moscow against Peking in the ideological Sino-Soviet dispute. On the other hand, the East European Communist countries have been openly fighting since 1956 to reject the "socialist" division of labor proposed by the Russians; for under Moscow's system of fraternal exploitation it was suggested that some of the East European states play the classic role of raw-materials and agricultural supplier to the industrialized Big Brother in the Soviet Union.

Acting again in classic capitalist fashion, the Russians have been quite willing to subordinate their ideology in order to make a killing on the international market. In the summer of 1966, for instance, Fidel Castro expressed outrage at the "criminal" idea that Moscow was going to sign a commercial pact with Brazil. Nikolai Patolichev replied for the Soviet Union in the pragmatic phrases of a good businessman who will let nothing interfere with a good deal:

We believe that foreign trade cannot, and should not, acknowledge frontiers or ideology. My government attributes the utmost importance to commercial relations with countries in the course of economic development, like Brazil. . . . The continuous increase of production in the Soviet economy permits us to accelerate the rhythm and volume of our exports. . . .

In this last sentence, the Russian spokesman sounded very much like Harry Truman imitating Lenin. And he clearly implied that his country, as it becomes more industrialized, will take advantage of the exploitative relationships which have been so conveniently designed by world capitalism.

At this point one encounters an element of truth in the Maoist fantasy of international politics and Communist betrayal. Practical reasons have already impelled the U.S. and Russia to a measure of détente—the armament race and the threat of nuclear holocaust. As Russia becomes more modernized, the two social systems seem to some of their proponents less at odds. If these trends continue, the old antagonists of the Cold War might make a *de facto,* worldwide gentleman's agreement in which each tacitly respects the right of the other to exploitation in its own economic and political sphere.

There is a concrete possibility of the development described by the Algerian delegate to the U.N. Economic and Social Council Meeting in Geneva, in July 1966: "Even as the détente in the Cold War has permitted an attenuation of the conflict between blocs with different social systems, one must fear that the East-West opposition will revolve on its axis and become an antagonism of North against South."

Hopeful Omens of Change

There are a few hesitant signs of hopeful change. There is a system to ameliorate the great fluctuations in coffee prices; some of the theoretical justifications of the "Kennedy Round" recognized that tariff reciprocity was profoundly unreciprocal in practice; and the Third World emerged as a cohesive bloc at the U.N. Conference on Trade and Development. But, as the grim figures of failure and retrogression during the first half of the Development Decade show, the basic anti-human trends which distribute more wealth to the rich and more poverty to the poor remain in force. The problem is not to change this or that aspect of American, and Western, policy: a fundamental reorientation is required. Cherished "laws" of the world market must be repealed. The international division of labor must be restructured, and this will go against the old, irrational rationality. To follow the principle of efficiency in world affairs—to insist that resources be allocated and production organized "economically," in the cheapest way—is to condemn the backward to be even more backward. To defy the artificial yet tenacious principles of the present international economy will require that money flow from the rich to the poor until a new and sensible rationality is forged.

If the underdeveloped countries cannot expect any effective aid from the affluent economies, if they can only modernize on the basis of their own impoverished resources, they will be forced to exploit the one thing they have in abundance: human beings. This can hardly be done with the freely given consent of the people, and democracy will therefore be viewed as hostile to economic development and political independence. Many theorists, both in and outside the Third World, describe such terrible necessities as if they were the finest flowering of civilization. Their word for such brutal and forced accumulation of capital is "socialism."

If the West proves incapable of this dramatic about-face (and nothing that has happened in the postwar period gives any basis for optimism), if changes of this character do not take place peaceably, things will continue to get worse—and the earth of the year 2000 will be even more outrageously unjust than it is today and certainly more unstable. Our improbable and only hope is to create a new world to replace the inadequate one in which we now live. That is the task of the democratic left.

Theories on the Fate of Old and New Nations

The theory that the advanced powers are inevitably committed to reaction implies that there is no hope of democracy in the new nations.

The various formulations of America's (or, more precisely, capitalism's) role and fate, from Lenin to Mao, have obvious deficiencies. Yet, it is true that America has displayed a vested interest in at least some of the misery and poverty of the globe, and the defense of such ill-gotten gains could be (and in the past has been) the basis of a world view and foreign policy. There is the tragic possibility that this view might lead America to continue to promote the gap between rich and poor nations. The exploitation of impoverished people, however, is not a necessity for the American economy but only a cruel convenience. The nation could make new international departures without undergoing a sweeping domestic transformation. There would be many motives for such a change, among them enlightened self-interest (the present trends hurry toward more instability and violence which could be disastrous for the wealthy as well as for the hungry)—and that current of democratic idealism which still flows within American society.

So the U.S. embraces an *almost* imperialism. America has the potential of positive change, of helping to create a new world; yet that course would require considerable radicalization of its political life. If, as Aldous Huxley once said pessimistically, a 99 per cent pacifist is a 100 per cent militarist, then one can optimistically hope that an *almost*-imperialist will become anti-imperialist.

Lenin's belief that capitalism's inability to resolve its internal contradiction drove it to seek imperium over the entire world has become one of the most influential ideas of the twentieth century. And not only those who submit to Communist orthodoxy give lip service to this analysis. (As for the Chinese Communists, it is only lip service; for they have made the most sweeping revisions of doctrine, albeit in a spirit of fanatic fundamentalism.) Beyond that, almost all the nationalist, non-Communist revolutionists and reformers of the ex-colonial world have affirmed one or another version of the Leninist thesis. And even in the advanced countries Lenin's idea has had a profound effect upon intellectual life.

On the whole, the postwar experience violates the letter

of the Leninist argument at almost every point—yet leaves much of its spirit intact. Following Marx, Lenin held that capitalism was not simply interested in plunder and booty abroad. The struggle between the various Western powers "for the sources of raw materials . . . and for 'spheres of influence' " was also a fight to avoid crisis at home. Since 1945 and with the single but glaring exception of oil, this assertion has become less true with every passing day. Advances in technology, synthetics, the organization of the market, and a whole host of factors have reduced the importance of the ex-colonies for the big powers; paradoxically, in the short run, the Third World would perhaps be better off if the capitalists were more interested in exploiting it.*

But the heart of Lenin's argument was not the simple assertion that there was a greedy scramble for resources and markets. Lenin believed that capitalism was forced to export its capital because it could not invest it profitably within the limits of the advanced economy. As the system became mature and over-organized, the rate of profit fell, and business was thus driven overseas in search for capital outlets. Thus, imperialism was the distinctive and last historical stage of capitalism itself—a final, desperate attempt to postpone the crisis of the system. However, the same maturity that forced the capitalists to war among themselves over the division of global spoils also heightened the revolutionary consciousness of the working class. World War I signalled the beginning of the epoch of "imperialist war and proletarian revolution."

There is no need here to discuss the complex question of how much this analysis applied to events before 1945. Relevant here is that throughout the postwar period, the trend in the export of capital has been to accentuate investment by the affluent powers *in* the affluent powers, rather than competition among them for opportunities in the ex-colonial world. During this time, American "direct investment" abroad (where business sets up a plant in a foreign country rather

* For relevant figures on the trends in international trade, see *Modern Capitalism,* by Andrew Schonfeld, Appendix I, pp. 428–29. For the most recent government figures, see the September 1966 issue of *Survey of Current Business.*

than exporting American goods to it) more than doubled —and England and Canada absorbed more than 60 per cent of the increase. These movements of capital, leaving the oil industry aside for a moment, accounted for a smaller proportion of the national income than similar exports had for Britain in the nineteenth century.*

In France, by the mid-sixties, this situation had become a key element in Gaullist economic thinking. The failure of the French computer industry had made that country dependent on American corporations—and allowed the U.S. State Department to veto the sale of machines which might have facilitated the development of the *force de frappe*. As a result, the French government launched a state-subsidized merger movement to create a corporate base large enough to sustain a modern computer technology. There were those on the left who criticized de Gaulle for not having acted earlier and more decisively in this area. The socialist Gaston Deferre, for instance, said that "Europe will be colonized by the United States unless we decide to pool our resources in order to create industrial concerns comparable in size to the American ones and able to compete with them on an equal footing." The British Labor government took much the same line when it reopened its bid for entry into the Common Market in 1966.

Now all of this has a familiar, Leninist ring to it and hardly shows that the world market has been turned into a charitable trust. Gigantic corporations, with the conscious political support of their governments, are engaged in a fierce competition for markets. But the setting is not at all Leninist, for the fight is not conducted so much in Asia, Africa, or Latin America as in Europe and America. Thus, Western business has preserved much of its old-fashioned Leninist spirit, though it has profoundly revised the letter of Lenin's law.

But there is a recalcitrant exception to these trends: oil. For the economy as a whole, the raw materials and capital export markets of the Third World have become less and

* See *After Imperialism*, by Michael Barret Brown, p. 206. This is a fascinating book written from a democratic socialist point of view. It makes more contemporary sense out of Lenin than anything I have read.

less important. In economic terms, it is not *necessary* for the U.S. to promote international injustice in order to maintain domestic prosperity. But the huge and politically powerful oil industry thrives on these inequities.

In 1964, there were $44.3 billion of direct U.S. investment overseas, in 1965, $49.2 billion. In both years, net foreign investment was only about 5 per cent of gross private domestic investment (the percentage actually declined a bit from 1964 to 1965). In both years, the distribution of this capital was about the same. In 1964, for instance, 31.2 per cent of the American money had gone to Canada, 27.2 per cent to Europe, 20.1 per cent to Latin America, 6.9 per cent to Asia, and 3.5 per cent to Africa. All these figures support the thesis that exploiting the Third World is a diminishing and non-crucial part of the American economy.

At the same time, however, the petroleum and mining industries accounted for around 40 per cent of this total, about the same portion as that of manufacturing. More to the point, the income in 1964 on $14.3 billion of petroleum investment was more than *twice* as great as that realized on the $16.8 billion of investment in manufacturing ($1.9 billion as against $.876 billion). This obviously is a super-profit and it depends on arrangements with countries that are either poor or rich in a distorted way (Kuwait, which has the second highest per capita income in the world, is a balkanized fief for oil and not, as it should be, a source of wealth for Mideast development generally).

In the process of accumulating this enormous wealth, the oil industry works hand in glove with the U.S. government, and vice versa. The companies benefit, of course, from direct production controls within America—the money made in this rigidly *dirigiste* sector of the economy paradoxically seems to create *laisser-faire* millionaires—and the princely benefits from the 27½ per cent depletion allowance. Import controls are also designed to support the costly, noncompetitive American wells in the manner to which they are accustomed. Indeed, world oil prices are an ingenious and artificial creation; John Strachey once calculated that, were the Arabs to nationalize the petroleum operations in their countries and permit a "market" price to emerge, oil consumers in the West would be able to buy at a much cheaper price than now prevails. However, since a single decision of Royal Dutch Shell was reported by Elizabeth Jager to have affected the balance of payments position of both Britain and Italy, it is unlikely that any such experimentation will be allowed.

But oil politics have also affected American foreign policy. The basic premise was stated in Harry Truman's reminiscences of the 1945 Mideast crisis: "If the Russians were to control Iran's oil, either directly or indirectly, the raw material balance of the world would undergo a serious change and it would be a serious loss for the economy of the Western world."

The oil industry's argument is, of course, that as the producer of a strategic fuel its interests must be protected precisely in the interest of America's common good. Recently, in a Senate speech in May 1966, the late Senator Robert F. Kennedy gave an example of the kind of private self-interest dominating the policy of the nation. In Peru, Kennedy said, President Belaunde had asked for $16 million for a domestic Peace-Corps-type project. The State Department held up these funds in order to "make the Peruvians more reasonable" in the negotiations which they were then carrying on with American oil companies. Kennedy added, "the same was true in Argentina." It should also be noted that when AID threatened to turn off food shipments unless India accepted American price-fixing for fertilizer, it acted as the agent of oil companies.

The oil industry, then, acts according to the classic Leninist scenario. It profiteers in the Third World, supports local reaction, opposes democratic and modernizing movements, and sometimes treats the U.S. government like a hired plant security guard. At almost every point, the result has been to make American foreign policy more reactionary. If the country's international actions were dedicated to reduce the gap between rich and poor nations, the oil industry would suffer. The resultant misery of various millionaires would hardly overturn the American economy; but the catch is, of course, political. Oil is powerful in Washington, therefore any hope of a truly democratic foreign policy would require the defeat of its domestic influence.

With this very important caveat about oil a general and un-Leninist proposition can be restated: the prosperity of the American economy need not depend on the exploitation of the Third World and, to a considerable measure, does not at this moment. The reactionary policies the country has followed in widening the international gap between the rich and the poor are thus not the inexorable expressions of economic and social structure. They are reasonable, businesslike evils perpetrated according to the rules of this world which was so carefully made for us; but these rules could be changed. And that possibility is not to be found in the philosophy of Lenin or his followers.

The Fallacies of Good Intentions

The late Paul Baran, a Marxist sympathetic to the more orthodox brand of Communism, saw how postwar economic trends turned the Cold War into a worldwide paradox. America, he argued, was devoting enormous military and political means to the service of relatively modest material ends. A similar conclusion developed out of quite another point of view. In the mid-sixties Walter Lippmann and other moderate critics of the war in Vietnam held that there simply was no discernible American self-interest to justify the commitment of hundreds of thousands of troops to Southeast Asia. More generally, the flag of American *almost*-imperialism usually did not, during the postwar period, follow the dollar, except in the case of oil. Not only is it statistically possible for U.S. policy to escape from economic determinism; it is already a curious fact.

The Cold War began with a series of crises in Eastern Europe and the Middle East (Poland, Greece, Iran, Turkey). But the real struggle was over the future of Europe. The American commitments were, of course, made in the revered name of centuries of historical, political, and religious ties; but they rested upon a crass substratum of self-interest. I am not suggesting anything subtle or Machiavellian; quite simply, Communist domination of Western Europe or capitalist domination of Eastern Europe would have decisively tipped the international balance of power. Such disequilibrium would have been intolerable enough according to the old-fashioned rules designed for nations within a single social system—but it became utterly impossible when the contending powers represented alternate ways of organizing the globe.

In *Power and Impotence, the Failure of America's Foreign Policy,* Edmund Stillman and William Pfaff wrote, "In effect, the early Cold War was a contest for the control of a prostrate, but fundamentally very rich, continent that had functioned as the center of world politics for three hundred years." There is close correspondence between material self-interest and the political and military commitment on both sides. But once one leaves the initial, European period of the Cold War and turns to the Third World, the disparity between economics and foreign policy becomes manifest.

The historians of the twenty-first century might well conclude that the Korean War was the most curious "accident" of our postwar period. That country had been partitioned in desultory fashion on the basis of proposals made by General MacArthur and sanctioned by Stalin. The Russo-Korean treaty of 1949 did not even contain a mutual assistance provision, and in January 1950 Dean Acheson suggested that both Korea and Formosa were outside of the American defense perimeter. The Chinese Communists did not maintain an ambassador in North Korea and, Robert Guillian speculated in *Le Monde* in 1966, may well have regarded the invasion of the South as a Stalinist adventure. There were even public opinion polls in the United States which showed, in the late forties, that there was no strong popular support for action against Mao. And in August 1946, five months after Winston Churchill's famous "Iron Curtain" speech, President Truman was telling Chiang that, unless he liberalized a bit, "it must be expected that American opinion will not continue its generous attitude toward your nation."

But with the Korean War the ideological hostility which was rooted in the serious conflict of interests in Europe began to take on a life of its own in Asia. The French were then able to involve the U.S. in their Indochina debacle and thus laid the basis for the tragic Vietnamese conflict of the sixties. The issue of who "lost" China began to play a role in American politics, and Chiang's pseudo-China on Taiwan became a centerpiece of the nation's Asian policy. Thus, in the 1950's Chiang, Syngman Rhee, Bao Dai and Diem received a vast outpouring of American aid—and Nehru relatively little. The former group had enlisted in the cause of the "Free World"; the latter was, of course, a neutralist.

John Foster Dulles officially gave the Cold War its ideological cast: the struggle between the United States and the Soviet Union was turned into a titanic conflict between good and evil in which any challenge, no matter how remote, had to be met. A far-flung network of alliances and treaty organizations was established; it was based on conservative and reactionary powers and excluded the modernizers, non-Communist revolutionaries, and neutralists. This approach accentuated the gap between the rich and the poor, for it meant that American donations were effectively militarized and usually assigned to the indigenous friends, rather than the foes, of backwardness.

In the period of the post-European Cold War the U.S. was ruled by domestic conservatism. A Republican, business-oriented Administration held office for two terms, the Dixiecrat-Republican coalition prevailed in Congress, and McCarthyism made it difficult to even have a debate. These were the internal reasons for the nation's reactionary foreign policy. American leadership, unable to see the need for reform at home, was of course bewildered by a world in revolutionary transition. Since the Administration—and the people—genuinely believed in their own benevolence, the only possible explanation for nationalist and anti-American movements abroad seemed to them subversion, spying, infiltration. And these demons are fought with guns and counterespionage, not with social programs. If democratic reformers came to power, the argument went, they would only create instability, a breakdown of order, and conditions which would lead to a Communist take-over. Therefore, the only true friends of the "Free World" were on the right. In the fifties, this logic brought American support to Batista, Jiminez, Trujillo, and their like.

But this emphasis on the ideological aspect of the Dulles policy should not lead to the conclusion that justice would have been served if the nation simply had stuck to its material self-interest. In 1945, as de Gaulle bitterly recounts the fantastic incident in his memoirs, Roosevelt was in favor of independence for Indochina on the basis of the "ideology" of democracy. If the United States had persisted in its policy of cooperating with the nationalist revolutionary movement in that country, there would have been a chance of avoiding the more than two decades of bloodletting which followed the return of French colonialism.

The main point remains: the history of the Cold War shows that American foreign policy need not be the result of economic interest, and much of it has not been. Yet, it is sad to remember that most of our disinterested idealists have been reactionary, as in the case of Dulles. But even this unfortunate example proves that our role in the world need not be determined by cost accountants.

Arms Economy vs. Social Spending

Another important theory seeks to demonstrate that America's reactionary stance in foreign affairs, particularly in the Third World, is an inevitable consequence of the very structure of the society. In this view, the society does not need the Cold War in order to protect its overseas profits, but rather to justify a domestic war economy which is the main bulwark against depression. Thus, the late Paul Baran resolved his paradox about the disparity of the enormous military means which America deployed to protect its relatively modest international economic ends. (At times, Baran veered back to the classic Leninist thesis, as in *Monopoly Capital*, which he wrote in collaboration with Paul Sweezy.) But it was hardly necessary to be a Marxist to understand the tremendous significance of the tens of billions of dollars of annual armament spending. In his farewell message as President, Dwight D. Eisenhower said of the "immense military establishment" which was "new in the American experience," that its "total influence—economic, political, even spiritual—is felt in every city, every state house, every office of the federal government."

If America were to embark upon a genuinely democratic foreign policy, and sought to abolish the gap between rich and poor nations, this vested interest in death would be threatened. For an emphasis on international construction, massive investments of men and money in the Third World, and disarmament would reverse the priorities which have prevailed in the postwar period. Could the American economy tolerate such steps toward peace?

In theory, the answer is yes. In practice, everything depends on politics. Building an arsenal of annihilation is a congenial activity for American society. The mass unemployment of the Depression, it must be remembered, was not ended by the social and economic policies of the New Deal. Indeed, by the end of the thirties, Keynes himself wondered if any peacetime (and capitalist) government would ever intervene on the scale required by his computations. The abolition of joblessness took place during the reign of Dr. Win-the-War, not during that of Dr. New Deal.

There are solid, conservative reasons for the high esteem conferred upon spending for destruction. Government investment in socially useful projects tends to raise disturbing, ideological questions. There is always the danger that some reformer will suggest that monies be appropriated for an undertaking like TVA, and that actually redefines the lines between the public and private sectors.

A vast increase in war spending is usually accompanied by an end to social innovation. The emotion of patriotism unites the entire nation, and class differences are submerged in the common effort. In the case of a shooting conflict, the military obligingly dispenses with competitive principles and adopts uneconomic methods like cost-plus contracts. (When it is necessary in a conservative cause, or in fighting a war, America is always ready to turn its back on the myths of the market economy, but such idealism is almost never applied to truly idealistic projects.) In a cold war, particularly one run by a top executive from the Ford Motor Company, the old rules of efficiency are in force; but then military hardware has the marvelous quality of becoming obsolete almost on the day it becomes operational. The production possibilities are therefore almost infinite.

For these and many other reasons Congress will enthusiastically vote $70 billion for Defense while it haggles over a less than $2 billion appropriation for fighting poverty. It is most dangerous to think that, as peace begins to break out, it would be simple enough to transfer funds from the work of destruction to that of construction. The socialization of death is, thus far, much more generally popular than the socialization of life. And a shift of money from Defense to, say, Health, Education, and Welfare would require a basic turn toward the democratic left within the society.

The crucial question is whether or not it is possible, without a revolution of the system itself, to substitute social for armaments spending. In *Monopoly Capital* Baran and Sweezy curiously treat this most fundamental issue only in a footnote. Writing of the liberals who "postulate . . . a substitution of welfare spending for military spending," they comment: "We must say of such liberals what Marx said of the bourgeois reformers of his day: 'They all want the impossible, namely the conditions of bourgeois existence without the necessary consequences of those conditions.'" This argument, based on a Marxian generality (which arose out of a controversy with Proudhon), is hardly convincing proof of the state and tendency of the American economy in the late sixties and seventies. It is necessary to consult reality as well as authority.

Lenin and Keynes: Past Projections vs. the Present

This can best be done by examining the actual, living fate of a projection very similar to the one urged by Baran and Sweezy. The author was V. I. Lenin, the date, 1916, the text, *Imperialism.*

> It goes without saying [Lenin wrote] that if capitalism could develop agriculture, which today lags far behind industry everywhere, it could raise the standard of living of the masses, who are everywhere still poverty-stricken and underfed; in spite of the amazing advance in technical knowledge, there could be no talk of a superabundance of capital. . . . But if capitalism did these things it would not be capitalism; for uneven development and wretched conditions of the masses are fundamental and inevitable conditions and premises of this mode of production.

Lenin's prediction certainly held up from 1916 to 1945. In the twenties, the purchasing power of the masses of Americans was held down while the productive capacity of the society was vastly increased and there was an eventual collapse. In the thirties, Roosevelt's attempts to follow Keynes and to inject effective demand into the economy were half-hearted and ultimately ineffective. But from 1945 on, every one of the advanced capitalist powers pursued some variant of a full-employment policy. These efforts hardly created utopia; they were consonant with the persistence of great poverty, increasing injustice in the distribution of wealth and, particularly in the U.S., a chronic and scandalous level of unemployment (but not general joblessness of the thirties type). Capitalism had remained capitalism, yet it had learned that improving the lot of the masses could be good business.

There is no point in picturing this development in idyllic terms. The version of Keynesianism embraced by the American businessman of the sixties did not involve the notion that a reduction in defense spending would be compensated by a corresponding, multi-billion-dollar rise in social investments. The "reactionary Keynesians" favored tax cuts which would disproportionately benefit the rich, maximize private consumption, and keep the public sector on starvation rations. If American society has come to a certain consensus that the government must intervene to stave off depression and that intervention would certainly be needed in the case of peace, there is still a fierce debate as to how this shall be done. The conservatives propose to prime the pump by raising the living standard of the wealthy, the liberals and radicals by improving the lot of the poor and of society as a whole.

But the American economy does not correspond to the rigid simplicity of the Baran-Sweezy model. In 1916, Lenin had the excuse that he could not look 30 years ahead into the future; but we have now lived that future and cannot afford to ignore its reality.

Moreover, one cannot speak of a simple substitution of social spending for defense outlays. As John Kenneth Galbraith points out in *The New Industrial State,* the billions for armament go to a very specific sector of the economy, one that requires extensive research and development for the creation of a sophisticated and advanced technology. Some of these machine and human skills could be put to benevolent use—but some could not. There must therefore be, Galbraith argues, a public investment in a peacetime production which is technologically similar to the annihilation industry. Space exploration, he concludes, would meet this requirement.

There is a certain puritanism on the left whenever the question of space comes up. It is the fashion to denigrate spending money on heaven when earth is still so shoddy. But this view ignores two important points. First, if peace were to break out, a massive cutback in the billions for defense plus the normal growth of a full-employment economy would provide sufficient funds for rebuilding America *and* going to the stars. Second, space is not empty of social, scientific, and even aesthetic significance. It could conceivably provide room for human beings, vast new resources for the development of the world, and it will certainly incite a deeper knowledge of both man and the universe. Beyond these pragmatic considerations, there is a moral imperative which requires that humanity live up to the fullness of its powers, and men can rightly boast that they have always experimented and innovated.

There is a general American commitment to government intervention against depressions, and there is the possibility that, with a turn toward the democratic left, this commitment could take the form of a vast social investment which would substitute for the armament sector. Here too, as in the case of overseas exploitation, there are powerful vested interests in the prevailing order of injustice. These will not be easily defeated—but they can be. Cold war, imperialism, the accentuation of the chasm between rich and poor nations, all these are deep trends in both the national and international economy of the U.S. But they are not inexorable fates.

Mao's Thought and Global Good and Evil

No consideration of America's predisposition toward global

good and evil would be complete without reference to the thought of Mao Tse-tung. It would be hard to imagine a more audacious revision of Lenin than Mao's version of Leninist orthodoxy. Mao no longer defines imperialism as the last stage of capitalism but sees it as the united front of the rich, whatever their social system. In his famous essay on "People's War," Lin Piao called North America and Western Europe "the cities of the world"—and Asia, Africa, and Latin America "the rural areas of the world." He delicately refrained from noting that Russia and Eastern Europe were really also part of the "cities of the world"; but the Maoists of the mid-sixties were obviously working on the basis of that deduction. Where Marx and Lenin had seen the working class as the historic agency of social change, the Chinese Communist leader looked to the peasantry—the class Marx had regarded as lumpish, like so many potatoes in a sack.

It is easy to ridicule the fantasy elements in Mao's vision; but it is more important to understand their profound relationship to reality. There is, after all, a basis for a conspiracy of the industrial North, corporations and commissars alike, against the backward South. There even are American liberals who advocate such an arrangement as a way of ending the Cold War. Although the peasants of this world are hardly going to usher in a reign of peace and justice, they could well become the agents of their own enslavement. For the antidemocratic and totalitarian program of modernization which Mao represents is one of the most important trends in the developing lands.

There is a definite reactionary potential in a Soviet-American alliance. Toward the end of World War II, a Republican member of Franklin Roosevelt's cabinet had an intriguing idea of a postwar settlement. Gar Alperovitz has summarized it in this way:

> The essence of Stimson's view was a conservative belief that the postwar power structure in Europe had to be acknowledged so that a *modus vivendi* could be established with Russia. Although he wished to preserve American economic interests in Eastern Europe, he took for granted Soviet special interests in the border countries just as he accepted American special interests in Latin America—the two areas were "our respective orbits."

Secretary of War Stimson's perspective was not adopted; there was a cold war instead. Yet it is important to remember that the Stimson approach was explored by another leading figure in those days: Joseph Stalin. The Russian dictator wrote to Harry Truman:

> The question of Poland has the same meaning for the Soviet Union as the question of Belgium and Greece for the security of Great Britain. . . . I do not know whether there has been established in Greece a truly representative government and whether the government in Belgium is truly democratic. The Soviet Union was not consulted when these governments were established. The Soviet Union did not lay claim to interference in these affairs as it understands the whole importance of Belgium and Greece for the security of Great Britain.

There was some ghoulish humor in this document. When Stalin acknowledged the legitimacy of the British—and imperialist—claim to a sphere of interest in Greece, he was making a not so sly reference to an agreement he had made with Winston Churchill. The Briton and the Russian had coldly divided up Eastern Europe (the details are to be found in Churchill's memoirs of the war), and Greece was given to England. When there was a Communist-led insurrection in Greece, Stalin was as good as his word. He stood by while his comrades were put down in blood. He "knew" very well the character of the Greek government, and he had indeed been "consulted." He was simply advising Truman that he could be counted on to keep a bargain.

But Truman did not take up Stalin's proposal that the Communists and capitalists should recognize each others' spheres of exploitation. The idea, however, did not die out. It was, for example, the program of Presidential candidate Henry A. Wallace in 1948. "The real peace treaty we need now," the former Vice President told a rally in 1946, "is between the United States and Russia. On our part, we should recognize that we have no more business in the political affairs of Eastern Europe than Russia has in the political affairs of Latin America, Western Europe, or the United States."

In the 1950's and 1960's, the atomic balance of terror imposed a *de facto* recognition of power realities somewhat along the lines Stimson, Stalin, and Wallace had proposed. In 1956, the American inability to intervene in Hungary constituted an admission that Communist power in Eastern Europe could not be rolled back. And during the Cuban missile crisis of 1962, Khrushchev was forced to bow to the United States in the Caribbean. No one in Europe any longer believed that they lived under the threat of Soviet invasion, and this was the basis of de Gaulle's attack on NATO.

Mao's Vision: Peasants vs. "Cities of the World"

In terms of world peace, this détente between the nuclear giants was most welcome. But it also gave potential substance to the Maoist vision of the imperialist "cities of the world." An America not inexorably fated to exploit the globe on its own is hardly driven to do so in concert with the Russians; Mao is on to a possibility, not a necessity. Yet, it is particularly important that the democratic left be aware of the element of reality at the center of Mao's often fanciful thought. For the democratic left has understood that peace, in this nuclear age, is the precondition for all progress—but it would be a serious mistake to think that peace is a sufficient condition for that progress. A *pax Sovietica-Americana* is preferable to a holocaust initiated by the two powers, of course; but it is not a genuine vision of justice. It is therefore crucial to be concerned with the far side of disarmament and the kind of a world that must be created.

It is not enough to take Mao's truths seriously. His illusions must also be treated with the utmost respect, for there is a very objective basis for their appeal to despairing masses and aspiring elites. I refer, above all, to the preposterous and powerful notion that the peasants of the Third World are going to build the socialism which the European workers failed to make. For Mao, the contradiction between the rural areas of the world and its cities is the dynamic force in this epoch. The Southern and poor powers are therefore seen as developing a common consciousness of their plight. At first, there will be wars of national liberation and defensive alliances (this is the "democratic" stage of the process). But eventually, the proletarian nations (which are really peasant) will realize that nothing less than socialism can suffice. And, for the indefinite future at least, this drama is to be played out without the intervention of the Western working class, that old Marxian hero, said to be integrated now in imperialist society.

For many reasons this profoundly influential perspective is false. It is racist to assume that the Third World represents a unity, that all the non-whites, all the Southerners and all the poor are like one another. "An African is no Tamil," write Stillman and Pfaff, "a Malay is not a Pathan." More broadly, "Asia is the domain of sophisticated and accomplished civilizations," Africa has "no culture comparable to Asia," and Latin America is an "archaic Western society." There are deep differences within the ex-colonies; sometimes they are even murderous, as the Chinese of Indonesia and the Indians of Africa have learned. Peasants may well be capable of greater political struggle than Marx imagined, but in the ultimate analysis they can only deliver power to the city dwellers who will rule over them. For modern technology is urban and one could almost define a modern nation by saying that it has succeeded in shifting masses from the fields to the factories (and, eventually, to the computers).

But, most important of all, the collectivization of poverty can only produce poverty, not a society of justice and abundance. All the righteousness of the anger of the world's poor cannot will factories and a high level of mass education into existence. Thus, Marx insisted that the socialist future could be more liberating than the capitalist present only because it was to be built upon the material accomplishments of that present.

Therefore, for all of its talk of "freedom," as soon as the Maoist ideology posits a revolution of impoverished peasants going it alone, it must also choose totalitarianism. If the new countries are to accumulate capital, or even keep pace with their expanding populations, and if there is absolutely no hope of genuine aid from the advanced lands— a huge surplus must be extracted from the labor of the people. Yet, neither Western workers nor Third World peasants enjoy sacrificing present consumption to future investment while working harder than ever before. The real meaning of the word "socialism" in the Maoist vocabulary is a forced accumulation of capital more pitiless and systematic than that of Western capitalism.

But the Maoist illusion has great appeal. It can inspire peasants who see no hope in a world order which condemns them to hunger and misery. It reaches out to African nationalists who come to power on the basis of classless, populist movements, and who are therefore suspicious of party democracy which they associate with the ways of imperialism. It speaks to some Western intellectuals who discover in the ex-colonial peasant the miraculous resurrection of The God That Failed.

Maoism also has a message for aspiring elites. For the totalitarian industrialization is not carried out by an impersonal History but by men and women. In theory, the period of monolithic "democracy" which accompanies this accumulation of capital is to be followed by an age of greater political freedom. As the history of Russia demonstrates, the elite which acts in the name of the nation develops common economic privileges and interests, and these eventually come into conflict with the needs of the great mass of the people. After the first stage of totalitarianism there comes, with adjustments and thaws, the second stage of totalitarianism.

There is a strange dialectic of anti-democracy, based on *de facto* cooperation of Western capitalists and Chinese Communists. By maintaining the international order of economic injustice, the West makes it materially impossible for the Third World to advance toward both modernity and freedom. And Maoism (and all the Maoist variants, for the theories of the Chinese Communist are symbolic of a political and intellectual trend found throughout the Third World) makes a choice for totalitarian progress. The democratic left in its commitment to help in the creation of a new world aims at nothing less than at utterly transcending the options which are now available—or at providing a new choice.

Up and On from Almost-Imperialism

America, the *almost*-imperialist, could act to change the imperialist order of things. American (and Western) prosperity does not depend on the evil which is done in the international economy; this country—and the rest of the West—could actually benefit by acting humanely in the world. If the imperialist heritage of economic interest, ideology, and feeling of superiority were rooted in economic necessity, there would be no hope of overcoming it. Since it is not, there is hope—but so far, in the postwar period, this is a most modest and theoretical consolation. The statistical possibilities for doing global good require radicalized politics if they are ever to be realized. An America that cannot even provide decent housing for its own "well-off" poor is hardly going to lead in the bold measures needed to end the threat of starvation forever.

Indeed, non-economic factors might keep America from doing anything decent for the world's poor. In his provocative, thoughtful article on "Counterrevolutionary America" Robert Heilbroner argues that this is necessarily so. In Heilbroner's view, the "social psychology" of the less developed countries is an even greater barrier to modernization than their low levels of production. The ancient ways have to be rooted out, the social structure has to be overturned, and this requires

> some shock treatment like that of Communism. . . . Only a campaign of an intensity and singlemindedness that must approach the ludicrous and the unbearable offers the chance to ride roughshod over the resistance of the rich and the poor alike and to open the way for the forcible implantation of those modern attitudes and techniques without which there will be no escape from the misery of underdevelopment.

Heilbroner concedes that an American economy with $1.3 trillion in corporate assets could afford the loss of $16 billion of capital in Asia, Africa, and Latin America without facing an internal crisis. But he doubts that the U.S. is politically able to tolerate the upheavals, the smashing of the old oligarchies, the violence inherent in the development process. Therefore, he concludes, ". . . Communism, which may indeed represent a retrogressive movement in the West where it should continue to be resisted with full energies, may nonetheless represent a progressive movement in the backward areas where its advent may be the only chance these areas have of escaping misery."

There are two distinct parts of this thesis, one a description, the other a value judgment. The latter asserts that if a coercive and even totalitarian accumulation of capital is the only practical way out of the impoverished past into a more just future, then one reluctantly endorses the "progressive-ness" of this tragic, but unavoidable, transition. There is a perpetual danger that this attitude will lead to a surrender of morality in the name of the "wave of the future." Mussolini made the trains run on time, Hitler "solved" the problem of unemployment, South Africa has the highest per capita income for black men on that continent, and Franco has recently presided over growth rates to be envied by Communist planners. Yet, no one of the democratic left would propose political support for a fascist government, however economically successful.

But even supposing Heilbroner's descriptive analysis is correct and there is no way for developing nations to avoid the agony of totalitarian modernization, democratic leftists still cannot give their support to those who carry out this transformation. Even when a tiny minority whose hour has not yet come—it is those who are struggling for justice rather than growth rates who are the political determinant of what is truly progressive. Sometimes they will even be found within the Communist movement—or in the one, official and single party: wherever they are, these people represent their nation's most precious resource.

But Heilbroner's description is overly pessimistic. The gloomy pattern he outlines is a possibility, perhaps even a probability. But it is not absolutely fated to come true, and by thinking that it is, there is a danger of helping to fulfill a deplorable prophecy.

It is not clear to me that America must react with such hostility to the violence and turmoil of the developmental process. Senator J. W. Fulbright is a conservative in the old, humane and humanist sense of the term; he believes that human nature will eventually assert itself in the Communist world and produce a Thermidor which will make the revolution practical and realistic. He therefore favors a policy of watchful waiting and he is, of course, opposed to American intervention into every upheaval. I disagree with Fulbright's analysis—particularly in discussions of human nature and Thermidor—yet tend to share many of his conclusions. Relevant is the fact that the Senator from Arkansas has long recognized the reality described by Heilbroner and that he has not recoiled from it in horror.

In *Old Myths and New Realities*, Fulbright wrote, ". . . we must be under no illusions as to the extreme difficulty of uprooting long-established ruling oligarchies without disruptions involving lesser or greater degrees of violence. The historic odds are probably against the prospects of peaceful social revolution. . . ." The democratic left could be at least as candid as the conservative Senator; it is not at all precluded that the American people could come to accept these disturbing complexities of international politics.

But it is possible to tamper with the "historic odds" cited by Fulbright (and Heilbroner); for they are, to a degree, man-made. The American policy I have described sets in motion a vicious circle: the market transfers wealth from the poor to the rich—and foreign aid, far from off-setting this tendency, exacerbates it. Thus, the developing countries discover that they must accumulate capital from their own internal resources. They must create a coercive state, whether Communist or not; thus, they suppress the opposition, not simply of the wealthy but of the mass of the people who now must work harder, eat less, and give up the consolation of their ancient superstitions. In the U.S. the attendant violence and impieties are viewed with alarm and their existence becomes one more reactionary argument for pursuing international policies that breed still more violence.

Toward a New World Economy

If, however, the direction of this spiral were reversed, hopeful factors would reinforce one another. If some wealth were actually transferred from the rich nations to the poor, at least some economic compulsion toward coercion and violence would be removed. Consumption could, for instance, be gradually increased without endangering the whole modernization program. And the marvelous fact of ex-colonial people rising out of their poverty should make it politically easier in the U.S. to argue for redoubled efforts. And so, the crucial issue is political, not economic, for trends do not create new societies; they only make them possible.

In undertaking to help complete the creation of a more humane world, one must not expect too much. It will take radical new beginnings to justify modest hopes. This cruel paradox, like everything else about the contemporary international disorder, is a creation of man in history. The developing nations were deprived of capital and skills, and both of these deficiencies can be made up in part by capital and technical assistance from the advanced economies. But a heritage of backwardness is not easily overcome. Native oligarchies, tribalism, anti-modern cultures, and other reactionary trends were vigorously encouraged by the West during its imperial rule. (Africa's Balkanization to suit European needs is an obvious case in point.)

To paraphrase Keynes, the pursuit of a just world economy will guarantee not civilization itself but its possibility. And to follow this unprecedented course of action is our only chance to close the gap between the world's rich and poor.

First, there must be international economic planning which will allocate massive resources to the new nations on the basis of their needs and capacities. To accomplish this, economic aid must be freed from the priorities of generals, diplomats, corporation executives—and commissars. But this cannot be done while appropriations are subject to the vagaries of annual political review in donor countries. The advanced powers will have to agree to some long-term mechanism of international taxation which will automatically provide the required sums—to create a *contrat social* for the planet.

Senator Fulbright put it this way in his *Arrogance of Power*:

> I suggest that we begin to replace bilateral foreign aid, which is analogous to private philanthropy, with an internationalized program based on the same principle of public responsibility which underlies progressive taxation and the social services we provide for our own people. I suggest that we extend the

frontiers of our loyalty and compassion in order to transform our aid to the world's poorer nations from something resembling a private gratuity to a community responsibility.

Second, the present "laws" of the international economy must be repealed and turned upside down. Where the world market of the past century was designed to transfer wealth from poor to rich, we must now devote our ingenuity to the building of mechanisms with the exact opposite effect. This means understanding and applying Gunnar Myrdal's paradox: only a double standard can ensure fairness; for now it is obvious that free and equal trade between unequal nations leads to systematic injustice. In the name of equity and not of charity, trade policies must discriminate in favor of the developing countries.

These new trade and aid programs might come to serve as a substitute for the Cold War. Once again, we must speak of possibilities rather than of utopias. The Cold War has many causes, and the fate of the Third World is not pre-eminent among them. Even if America and Russia have now discovered a common interest in not annihilating one another, they still represent different social systems with conflicting ideas about how to organize the globe. Moreover, the two countries may end their conflict by a gentleman's agreement between rich Northerners to keep the Southerners of the planet poor. Yet, there is hope of combining peace with a modicum of justice which is the aim of these proposals.

For some time, the best Americans have called for a democratic revolution in Asia, Africa, and Latin America, both on grounds of justice and as an alternative to Communism. And yet, this familiar, excellent idea is more radical than its proponents realize. It requires, to use John Kenneth Galbraith's symbolic language, a revolution that would be less than a "Russian" and yet more profound than a "French" revolution. In analyzing why this is so, I hope to develop a long-range perspective on the practical problems of creating a new world.

My point is not to argue for a "Russian" revolution, an imitation of Lenin in 1917, and much less of Stalin in the thirties or of Mao in the fifties and sixties. It is precisely the material and spiritual agony of the totalitarian accumulation of capital initiated by the latter two leaders that must be avoided.

Experiments in Third-World Aid: The Alliance for Progress

To make a democratic revolution here and now, it is necessary to go beyond the French model—to institute extensive economic planning, and to ignore the allocation of resources made by the market. This clearly has anti-capitalist and socialist implications, but not in the ideologically neat way Lenin and Trotsky once imagined; for our time demands a new type of revolution. This means discarding a central assumption of U.S. policy from Harry Truman to the present— that a sophisticated and liberalized free enterprise could provide the economic basis for political democracy in the Third World.

In 1966, the late Senator Robert Kennedy, in a long, probing speech on "The Alliance for Progress: Symbol and Substance," attempted to draw up a balance sheet on this experiment initiated by his brother. The Senator acknowledged that basic issues are at stake for

> a revolution is coming—which will be peaceful if we are wise enough; successful if we are fortunate enough—but a revolution which is coming whether we will it or not . . . large-scale land redistribution necessarily implies major changes in the internal political balance of many Latin-American countries—away from oligarchy and privilege, toward more popular government.

Thus, if literacy is broadened, so are the eligible electors in Brazil; if agricultural credit is made available to the masses, the moneylenders are threatened; if higher education is democratized, the upper-class monopoly of the universities will be broken. And there must be more equitable sharing of wealth to create a large domestic market, and massive investments in education and new industrial and economic infrastructures.

Now this is a call for wide-ranging change (though it falls short of what is needed). Senator Kennedy recognized that neither this dream nor the original ideals of the Alliance are anywhere near accomplishment. He noted that in the first period of the Alliance there was no real increase in per capita agricultural production; North American private capital has not participated in Latin-American development as it was supposed to; and the actual public U.S. aid was much too small and should be immediately doubled. Kennedy also scored the reactionary effect of the oversubsidization of the Latin military, and of the State Department's practice of placing the interest of American oil profits on a higher plane than those of a Peruvian domestic Peace Corps.

Robert Kennedy's criticisms are sound and so are his proposals to double economic aid and cut military subsidies. But on the conceptual level he retains Harry Truman's classic assumptions about Point Four: the government is to create a context in which American businessmen and ex-colonial entrepreneurs can cooperate, to the profit of all, in the work of modernization. As Kennedy stated the premise, "private industry is the primary source of capital in all the underdeveloped regions; it is potentially the major source of development capital . . . private enterprise is also the principal repository of the technical and technological skills which Latin America needs."

This is not true, and a failure to recognize the counter-productivity of private American (or other advanced) capital in Latin America is the basic flaw in Robert Kennedy's candid, genuinely motivated critique of the Alliance. For the market mechanism cannot be the mainspring of Latin-American development in terms either of attracting foreign or allocating domestic capital. There must be, in contradiction to "French" revolutionary principles, conscious economic and social planning, not private enterprise. For the rationality of the profit motive directs the foreign giant corporation to distort the economic structure of the developing nation at best, and to keep it backward at worst. The basic infrastructural needs of the poor nations—roads, education, cheap mass housing, etc.—are simply not profitable investments. No one is really interested in building decent homes for the poverty-stricken *within* the United States, and smart money would shun even more such an undertaking overseas.

In Venezuela, the urban population increased from 35

per cent of the total in 1936 to 63 per cent in 1965, and the 1,632,000 citizens of present-day Caracas total more than all city dwellers in 1941. This situation was precipitated by a foreign-sponsored boom in the oil industry which, with the third largest output in the world, employs only 33,472 workers. Foreign capital, of course, utilized the most modern techniques in order to maximize profit. This helped uproot the old traditions but did not provide new employment, and mass unemployment has been a chronic problem for the post-Jiminez and pro-Alliance governments.

But not only the foreign investor distorts the backward economy; the local oligarch follows the same rationale of profitability. To this day Latin American profits are high in trade, and there is no real incentive to industrialize; the export sector distorts the entire economy. If private industry, as Senator Kennedy suggested, is seen as the primary source of capital in the underdeveloped regions, both foreigners and moneyed natives will have a systematic tendency to invest in the wrong—the highly profitable, distorting, and not so-cially useful—enterprises. As Arthur Schlesinger, Jr., described the conduct of American businessmen in Latin America in the early sixties, they pressured the Alliance "to talk less about social reforms and more about private investment." And these men were quite right to regard social reform and private investment as often antithetical.

One cannot ignore the uncomfortable fact that the West is dominated by business or even argue that there is no role for private corporations in the work of development. But free enterprise can participate in such a process only in a subordinate, never in a primary, role. If, for instance, Eduardo Frei of Chile had followed the advice of the sophisticated executives of the Committee for Economic Development, he would never have "Chileanized" part of the copper industry (a program designed to double output *and* assure partial state ownership). In that case, one of the most hopeful governments on the continent would have lost much of its dynamic and popular support.

The United States must abandon its ideological hostility to the public sector in the developing nations. In saying this, I do not intend to turn the free-enterprise myth topsy-turvy or argue that nationalization is some magic, painless way to modernization. For after recent events in countries like China and Cuba, this view can no longer be seriously maintained. There is no easy road out of underdevelopment, and one must talk pragmatically about some sort of international mixed economy. The Third World cannot simply put its faith in Adam Smith or any of his heirs; for the market mechanism is a cause of, rather than a solution to, its poverty.

Thus, the democratic revolution must build on economic and social foundations unknown, and even antithetical, to those of the great European capitalist transformations of the eighteenth and nineteenth centuries. And the generous vision of Robert Kennedy—and of American liberalism generally—must be amended so as not to depend on private enterprise, either in the U.S. or in the emerging nations, as the prime mover in the modernization process. Yet, even while insisting upon these far-reaching changes in American policy, the political limits of our intervention must be kept carefully in mind.

As John F. Kennedy realized when he initiated the Alliance, there is structural resistance to positive change in the developing lands; the Latin-American oligarchs are the classic case in point. In its original, reformist version, the Alliance sought to meet this problem by making grants contingent on policy changes in the recipient nations, such as the creation of an equitable tax system. Thus, there was hope that a revolution would proceed from the top down. "The leaders of Latin America," President Kennedy said at Bogotà, "the industrialists and the landowners are, I am sure, also ready to admit past mistakes and accept new responsibilities." In retrospect, the President's confidence was either naive or ceremonial. The Latin-American *status quo* is not even prepared to take a position of enlightened self-interest.

Although America must provide massive assistance precisely in order to minimize the potential for bloody conflict within the Third World, there must be an expectation of turmoil and even violence—and the U.S. must find itself sympathetic to armed revolutionists of the left rather than, as so often in the past, to the military dictators of the right. But this most emphatically does not mean that this country should adopt some democratic variant of the Maoist strategy and seek to foment wars of "national liberation" all over the globe. The pretension to omnipotence which led to the tragic commitment in Vietnam is as dangerous in the service of a good policy as of a bad one. And that is why it is so important to specify exactly what is proposed in this activist notion of creating a new world—and what is not proposed.

Paradoxically, one of the most vigorous actions the U.S. could take in support of the democratic revolution simply involves ceasing to do the wrong thing. For during the postwar period, America usually gave political, economic, and military support to the confirmed opponents of social change. The list of recipients is dreary and familiar: Chiang, Rhee, Bao Dai, Diem, Ky, Franco, Batista, Jiminez, Trujillo, and so on. The tragic conflicts of the sixties, as Theodore Draper has pointed out, pitted the United States against popular upheavals—in Vietnam, Cuba, and the Dominican Republic—and were a consequence of previous American policy, such as the support of French imperialism and of Cuban and Dominican dictatorship.

But it is not enough to refrain from doing evil; it is possible to establish political sympathy for revolutionary movements without sending agents to direct them. For all of the failings of the Alliance for Progress, for instance, there is no question that in the period of its inception John F. Kennedy managed to identify his Administration's policy with the aspiration for change in Latin America. And the President's speech in support of Algeria's right to independence was one of the few events of the fifties that demonstrated not all Americans were bent on subordinating democratic and anti-colonial principles to the political needs of the NATO alliance.

Indeed, the U.S. should follow the advice of the Latin Americans who met in Bogotá in August 1966 (Frei of Chile, Lleras Restrepo of Colombia, Leoni of Venezuela) and restore the "Betancourt doctrine" under which this nation refuses to recognize rightist *coups d'état*. In this way, and by refusing to create and finance the armies of Latin America, the U.S. could make an enormous contribution to the cause of democratic revolution without pretending to be omnipotent. Beyond these crucial political and military acts, a public commitment by the United States to make a democratic revolution economically possible will be in itself an incitement to change. Over a century ago, Marx realized that one of the factors which made the bourgeois revolution more dynamic than any previous upheaval was the development of the means of communication; now, of course, this point is a thousand times more relevant. The American word, if it is backed up with the right deeds, could thus become a mighty force. There is the danger that America might adopt a policy of "sentimental imperialism" (the phrase is that of Arthur Schlesinger, Jr.). Instead of assuming that our military technology allows us to intervene everywhere in the world, we would then act as if our social ingenuity and political institutions were universal models. There was more than a hint of this attitude when Lyndon Johnson proposed in 1966 to build a Great Society in Asia (since he had not yet built one in the U.S., the announcement was, at a minimum, premature). Yet, by ceasing to support the rightist opponents of change, by open political sympathy extended to revolutionists (sometimes even violent ones), and, above all, by making political democracy in the Third World an economic possibility, the United States could take a step toward the creation of a new world.

Planning Toward Internationalized Economic Aid

Perhaps the most positive and dramatic action this nation could undertake would be to internationalize its economic aid. This would lay the basis for the global economic planning which alone can make the notion of "democracy between nations" a meaningful reality. For it is now necessary, as Senator Fulbright has said, to "extend the frontiers of our loyalty and compassion."

As the foregoing has shown, postwar aid, whether capitalist or Communist, has been inspired by almost every motive except one of orderly economic development for the earth's poor. In 1963, the Organization for Economic Cooperation and Development (OECD) reported, 84 per cent of aid funds were bilateral—subject to military and political priorities. Thus, France used its disbursements to create a special, and advantageous, relationship with its ex-colonies, and President Kennedy could say, "Our assistance makes possible the stationing of 3.5 million Allied troops along the Communist frontier at one-tenth the cost of main-taining a comparable number of American soldiers." And even when the money was not so blatantly an instrument of the donor's foreign policy, it was regularly tied to the needs of the advanced economy rather than to those of the impoverished economy. And, more recently, the trend has been to loans rather than grants.

For historical reasons normally not of their own making, underdeveloped countries are desperately short on human resources. The tricky political and military vagaries accom-panying postwar aid taxed the capacity of a modern coun-try's computerized planning process—and overwhelmed the shaky planning institutions in the new countries. Obviously, funds must now be allocated on some more rational, pre-dictable basis of need and capacity to use them. The U.N. has already begun the ground work of developing econometric models of the world economy.* If the goal of closing the gap between the rich and the poor is taken seriously, this tentative undertaking must receive massive support and be-come the focus of a system of planned, internationalized aid.

Estimates differ as to how much it would cost were the advanced countries to foot the developing nations' deficiency in capital. In 1966, the Council of Economic Advisers optimis-tically figured that the new nations could only use $3 to $4 bil-lion more than is now available. But there are much higher projections: Jan Tinbergen has set the needed funds at $7 bil-lion, Michael Brower at $12 billion, and the First Committee

* *Studies in Long-Term Economic Projections for the World Econ-omy*, United Nations, 1964. This is an example of the kind of work now being done in this area.

of the U.N. Trade and Development Conference predicted that the "savings gap" would reach $20 billion in 1970.†

However much these computations differ (because of different definitions *and* the fact that so little effort has been devoted to the task), economists consider that there is an objective basis for determining how much capital the developing world needs and how much it can absorb. If massive intellectual and financial resources were invested in the task of such an analysis, rational planning and resources could be allocated on a global scale.

Even if the highest estimate is valid—the U.N.'s prediction of a $20 billion savings gap by 1970—the sum at issue is well within the means of the advanced nations. By 1970, Europe, North America, and Australia will have a total GNP of over $1.5 trillion. A deficit of $20 billion would, in that year, be less than the 3 per cent of American GNP Harry Truman proposed to spend on the Marshall Plan and would approximately equal the extra appropriation Lyndon B. Johnson asked for the Vietnam War in 1967. Such international economic planning could make long-range policies possible. Capital in the developing lands would no longer be at the mercy of the wild fluctuations of the world market in primary commodities or the vicissitudes of a Cold War. Funds would be guaranteed over a considerable period of years, and this would allow local planners to make more efficient use of their resources. But this massive, steady flow of funds could only be assured if foreign aid by the advanced nations were put on a permanent basis.

There have been proposals to commit all wealthy countries to automatically give 1 per cent of their GNP for international economic development. This would be an enormous improvement over the trends of recent years when the ratio has been regularly declining in the U.S. (which possesses more than half of the total GNP of the rich, non-Communist part of the world). This system would yield almost three-fourths of the $20 billion gap the U.N. Conference predicted for 1970.

† Goran Ohlin's study, *Foreign Aid Policies Reconsidered,* Chapter IV (OECD, Paris, 1966), summarizes much of the work already done in computing the capital shortage of the poor nations.

Yet, there is a much better way of appropriating these funds: a progressive income tax:

(1) This notion has an obvious grounding in equity, since the richer a nation (or an individual) the smaller the percentage of income devoted to necessities and the greater the ability to meet social obligations.

(2) Such an approach meets the problem of the gap between rich and poor head-on by proposing (if quite modestly) some redistribution of income shares.

(3) As Senator Fulbright has emphasized, this would take foreign aid out of the realm of charity and philanthropy and make it a matter of right, like U.S. income tax and Social Security.

Experts, like P. N. Rosenstein-Rodan, have already demonstrated that the details of such an international income-tax system can be worked out if there is the political will.*

Aid for Totalitarians?

However, another question in international economic planning is anything but a technicality; this is essentially the same difficulty faced by the Alliance for Progress: what attitude would an international aid agency take toward reactionary governments, toward rightist or Communist dictatorships? Unless this question is answered, the whole enterprise could have the most paradoxical results, and some of these reforms could subsidize local oligarchies, rotten power structures, and economic backwardness. Therefore, some minimal criteria have to be established for these grants.

The U.N., obviously, cannot intervene in the political life of every developing country. Yet it can insist on regional planning in return for its aid; it can disallow dictatorial pyramid-building and old-fashioned thievery; it can insist that nations, and regional groupings, show that there is a "popular consumption criterion" (the phrase is Galbraith's)

* In Rosenstein-Rodan's computation, if all the non-Communist advanced nations with per capita GNP of $600 or more were involved, the United States' share of the burden, on the basis of 1961 figures, would be 65 per cent of the total. P. N. Rosenstein-Rodan, "International Aid for Underdeveloped Countries," in *The Strategy of World Order*, Richard A. Falk and Saul H. Mendlovitz, ed., Vol. IV, p. 517.

in their equations—that projects benefit the present, as well as the future, generation.

It is much simpler, of course, to solve these thorny issues on paper than in practice. Even under the best system of international economic planning there will be waste, funds will be appropriated by the corrupt and the dictatorial, etc. It is not that such an approach will work perfectly; but, if one is serious about closing the gap between rich and poor nations, only something like this approach might work at all. Certainly, the defenders of conventional wisdom and the actual aid-and-trade policies of the postwar period have utterly failed in their professed goal of narrowing the chasm which divides the fat North from the hungry South.

Some American right-wing critics are hostile to the present process of foreign aid for the worst of reasons: they want to turn their backs on the people of Asia, Africa, and Latin America—and they are sympathetic to the world's *status quo* and to military rule. But there are others, and they are much more numerous, who are simply bewildered by the seemingly endless and futile appropriations in Washington. There is no use pretending that these people can be easily convinced to support the regular allocation of even larger amounts of money. But this effort in political persuasion must be made. In the doing it is necessary to explain that past programs failed, not because they were so exceedingly generous, but because they were inadequate and manipulative. And international economic planning should not be proposed as a utopia but as the only *practical* way to reach ends Americans have thought they were supporting for over two decades.

International economic planning and a world system of taxation is the simplest and most direct way of achieving redistribution of wealth, and it has the virtue of creating pressure for structural reform in the recipient countries. A change in trade policies would not require sweeping innovations. It would mean a conscious decision to reverse the present reactionary priorities of the world market, to create a mechanism which would automatically transfer some of the profits of the international economy from the rich to the poor. To accomplish this, the tariff policies of the advanced nations would have to be radically changed. Yet, there would be no need for new institutions—only the old arrangement has to be turned upside down.

Basically, what the developing nations need—and want, for they made these demands on GATT in the summer of 1966—is a transition from tariffs which discriminate *against* them to those which discriminate *for* them. They asked the Kennedy Round negotiators to remove their products from the list of items excluded from tariff reduction; to reduce the rate on goods from developing lands more than rates on goods from advanced countries; to make a maximum reduction of tariffs on tropical foods, and to compensate the developing countries for their loss of tariff preferences when this takes place. These demands were basically turned down.

The U.N. economists have come up with an even broader conception. They have suggested a development insurance fund based on the "willingness of advanced countries to contribute, on the understanding that their direct benefits will not equal their contributions." Under this plan, all nations would pay in to a central fund and each would be compensated if there were a drop in export proceeds. In a series of complicated calculations, the U.N. Committee of Experts which outlined this system concluded that, had it been working between 1953 and 1959, the developing countries' claims would have ranged between $246 and $466 million a year (and the advanced countries would have received between $12 and $142 million a year). Such a program is easily within the bounds of the possible for the rich powers.

It might, however, be difficult to persuade the well-fed to stop making a profit from the hungry. As noted earlier, Nasser wanted the 1966 New Delhi summit meeting to advocate a freezing of the entire debt of the developing countries but, for political reasons, neither Tito nor Mrs. Gandhi could be persuaded to go along with this idea. Yet, there is no possibility of justice so long as India must return about one-quarter of the monies it receives in foreign aid just to service past debts. New Delhi is afraid to protest this outrage because it might then lose the three-quarters of assistance which does come through. The advanced economies hardly require this tribute from the impoverished; the developing countries' debts to the Western powers should be forgiven or else rescheduled and made interest free. Indeed, it is high time that the Western powers reverse the scandalous trend toward loans instead of aid which has been picking up strength throughout the sixties.

This does not mean that the wealthy nations are to choose poverty in order to fulfill a moral obligation to the world's less fortunate. But affluent countries might enrich themselves at a somewhat slower rate and without pushing the majority of the world's population more deeply into misery. This can be done. Sober, intelligent proposals have demonstrated the possibility of creating a new world by simply changing the present injustices of aid and trade. The crucial question is not technical, but political.

The Politics of Hope

There is a sort of international Keynesian argument for the self-interest in America's doing justice in the world. For just as the vast increase in buying power, which developed in the U.S. through the welfare state and the labor movement, has laid the basis for an advance in the prosperity of the entire nation, so a decent life for the peoples of Asia, Africa, and Latin America would be to the economic advantage of the entire world.

There is another paradoxical political case for global decency. For now that the Cold War is, thank God, coming to an end in Europe, it is possible for the first time to realize the decent values which most Americans thought they had been fighting for all along. To clarify this point requires an analysis of the two anti-Communisms.

At the height of the struggle between the Nato West and the Warsaw-Pact East there existed a straightforward version of anti-Communism. It was based on reactionary politics, and it viewed the Soviets as only one manifestation of the godlessness and disorder of a world which had taken leave of its fundamental values. From this point of view, anti-Communism was one, and only one, way of defending a *status quo*. The alliances with rightist dictators were, in this perspective, acts of virtue, not of necessity. And lacking any sense of the economic, political, and social roots of both nationalism and Communism, these rightist anti-Communists saw the enemy as a conspirator, a subversive, an agent who drove otherwise contented workers and peasants to revolt.

The American symbol of this one-dimensional and paranoid anti-Communism was, of course, Senator Joseph McCarthy. And it was no accident that McCarthy's heyday coincided with Stalin's last, demented years, and with the Korean War. The American people were bewildered and fearful in the presence of a megalomaniacal dictator, and involved in a frustrating shooting war only five years after World War II had ended in Tokyo Bay. In this political atmosphere McCarthy rocketed to prominence.

But there was, and is, another anti-Communism. It sought some alternative both to Communism and to the *status quo*, for it recognized the right and necessity of revolution but thought it should be democratic, not totalitarian. The views of Galbraith and Robert Kennedy are obviously in this tradition. Indeed, this attitude regularly supplied the official rhetoric for American development in the Cold War itself. "The seeds of totalitarian regimes," Harry Truman said in March 1947, "are nurtured by misery and want. They spread and grow in the evil soil of poverty and strife. They reach their full growth when the hope of a people for a better life ahead has died."

The words were fine enough—but the President uttered them in defense of the Truman Doctrine in Greece, where the United States placed its enormous power at the disposal of conservative forces fighting a popular movement whose leadership had been won over by the Communists. This was typical of the Cold War. Many Americans were committed to the fight against Communism for excellent reasons of democratic principle and hatred of injustice. Yet, by far and large, the U.S. could not possibly fulfill the hopes of these decent people; for the essential conservatism of the American economy in this artificially unjust world subverted most of the nation's progressive political aspirations.

In practical terms, as long as America's economic and social policies frustrated its political visions, the country regularly turned to the authoritarian right even as it talked in the words of the democratic left. Thus, the militarization of American foreign policy and its association with so many dictators and anti-democrats is not the result of a particular malevolence of this or that politician, but it is related to massive structural trends both within the U.S. and in its dealings with the world.

In this setting, to put an end to the Cold War allows America to recover its vision, to demilitarize its outlook. A massive commitment to international development does not provide simply an economic substitute for the arms economy. It might serve as an emotional and political substitute for the reactionary passions of rightist anti-Communism; it is the one way to implement peacefully the decent values which motivated the anti-Communism of the democratic left. However, and most emphatically, this proposal is not primarily "anti." It cannot be, for a new world cannot be constructed out of hostility. One wants to save the workers and peasants of the Third World from the horrors of totalitarian capital accumulation, to be sure, and, in a social and economic sense, that is an anti-Communist program. But in an enterprise which requires such far-ranging construction, the stress must be positive and the. challenge is, in Fulbright's moving phrase, "to extend the frontiers of our loyalty and compassion."

The United States and the Soviet Union, having brought mankind to the brink of nuclear holocaust, could simply walk away from the Cold War, retreat into their separate self-interests, and respect each other's injustices. Or, America could take the lead in a gigantic international effort to finish the creation of the world. There are economic arguments for such a course, and they must be stated. But ultimately, if this is to be done it will happen because the buried, deep-running force of American idealism bursts out of the channels to which the generals and the executives have confined it, to take its own direction. That will be the politics of hope.

———◆———

PART I

ARNOLD S. KAUFMAN

The Cold War in Retrospect

ARNOLD S. KAUFMAN is an associate professor of philosophy at
the University of Michigan and spent a year at the Center for
Advanced Study in the Behavioral Sciences. He is on the editorial board of *Dissent,* and is the author of *The Radical Liberal:
New Man in American Politics,* as well as many articles in *The
Nation, Socialist Commentary, Dissent,* and various scholarly
journals.

Four Views of the Cold War

Thē Cold War may be a geopolitical conflict, but it is also,
and importantly, *religious* in tone and intensity. Anne O'Hare
McCormick expressed the deep, simple conviction of millions
of Americans when she wrote that "the crux of the Soviet battle is not primarily for physical things . . . It is for dominion
over the soul. For the first time a powerful adversary not only
rejects our civilization but fights to destroy everything we
value."[1]

Perhaps ideological fervor was whipped up by calculating
politicians who wished to secure support for essentially geopolitical aims. It does not matter. For once aroused, such passions come to live a life of their own; rebounding on the
calculating politicians, reshaping their minds and spirits in unanticipated ways.

The world has undoubtedly changed since President Tru-

[1] In "Faith for a Troubled Christmas Time," *New York Times Magazine,* December 2, 1950.

man announced the doctrine that bears his name. But the
florid rhetoric he used to justify his Cold War commitments
persists in high places. Truman assured the American people
that his decision to combat Communism in Greece and Turkey
was forced by the need to choose between alternative ways of
life:

> One way of life is based upon the will of the majority, and is
> distinguished by free institutions, representative government,
> free elections, guarantees of individual liberty, freedom of
> speech and religion, and freedom from political repression.
> The second way of life is based upon the will of a minority
> forcibly imposed upon the majority. It relies upon terror and
> oppression, a controlled press and radio, fixed elections, and
> the suppression of personal freedoms.

Almost two decades later, in May of 1966, Secretary of State
Dean Rusk reminded the American public of Truman's words:

> It is as important to defeat this type of aggression in Southeast
> Asia now as it was to defeat it in Greece nineteen years ago.
> The aggression against Greece produced the Truman Doctrine,
> a declaration of general policy of assisting other free peoples
> who are defending themselves against attacks or threats.

And lest any American be left in any doubt about the parallel
Rusk was drawing, he continued:

> The underlying crisis of our times arises from [a] fundamental
> conflict: between those who would impose their blueprint on
> mankind and those who believe in self-determination—between
> coercion and freedom of choice.[2]

As if to punctuate the Secretary of State's restrained language
with an inimitable exclamation point, Vice President Humphrey more recently poured his soul onto the (luncheon) table
for the Democratic National Committee, exclaiming:

> Don't run from this issue [Vietnam]. God only knows that
> war is what Sherman said it is—Hell. But I will tell you what's
> worse, Tyranny![3]

Things have not, unhappily for American policy-makers,
worked to democracy's advantage in Greece. In any event the

[2] The *New York Times,* May 25, 1966.
[3] Remarks by Vice President Hubert H. Humphrey before the Democratic National Committee luncheon, Washington, D.C., March 9, 1967.

present rulers of Greece have informed the world that Greek freedom requires the overthrow of parliamentary government, control of the Greek Orthodox Church, censorship of the press, suppression of political opposition, and a ban on mini-skirts and, for a brief period, on beards. It all sounds like a program for totalitarian control of Greek life. Undoubtedly, however, the more rabid architects of America's Cold War policies will find some way to convince the American people that tyranny is freedom and military dictatorship is democracy.

The millions of Americans who think of the Cold War entirely in religious terms have little difficulty accepting the assurances of Greek and South Vietnamese dictators alike. For, in truth, they are after bigger game than forces opposed to freedom and democracy. They are after Satan himself. They mean to eliminate Evil. They believe that the only defensible aim of American policy is personal salvation for the millions who would otherwise be damned by Communism to eternal perdition. They may acquiesce in a policy of containment; spiritually, they favor liberation. In them, Prudence and God-liness engage in a gigantic spiritual struggle. One may claim that those who have such views do not make American policy. But they are the ones who most passionately, firmly and publicly support the men who do shape Cold War policy. And they infest centers of military power.

By contrast, some view the Cold War as totally unjustified and wrong from the start, a sinister conspiracy against the have-nots of this country and of the world. They think the Cold War is entirely explicable as an expression of Western corporate greed and lust for power. From their point of view, Communist nations have reacted with reasonable tactical restraint to Western efforts to roll back power the Communists had won during World War II. And they even think that Communist states, especially Russia, have been too obliging in the face of American counterrevolutionary activity everywhere around the globe. Those who favor this strong opposition to U.S. policies—which for purposes of convenience I label "the New Left Opposition"—regard the entire history of American Cold War action as morally obscene.

I am not implying that the two polar opposite positions described are intellectually equivalent. For the New Left Opposition normally base their views on reasoned argument, on scholarly investigation that probes deeply into the origins and nature of the Cold War. By contrast, those who adopt the religious view are, by and large, mindless and bigoted, displaying little respect for the human capacity to reason and to learn the truth.

Nevertheless, it is convenient to contrast the two positions. For by so doing, it is easier to define two intermediate assessments of the Cold War that have gradually gained prominence, and that express the rapidly widening split within American liberalism.

The first of these intermediate positions is held by those I shall call "Moderate Cold Warriors." They argue that the Cold War was, in its initial stages, fully justified by geopolitical considerations. Russian hegemony among Communist states made it plausible to claim that the Red world was monolithic. Moreover, the facts of Stalinist tyranny buttressed the American moral position.

But the Moderate Cold Warriors acknowledge, even insist, that since those early days of conflict basic changes have occurred within the Communist world. Revisionism has resulted in internal changes that have pacified and liberalized many Communist states. These internal developments have combined with the gradual emergence of two great, but conflicting, power centers to produce what has come to be called *the polycentric Communist system*. The Moderate Cold Warrior no longer regards a Sino-Soviet war as a fantastic possibility. For many it is, indeed, a probability fraught with incalculable terrors. These inter- and intra-state changes have in turn strengthened centripetal tendencies within the Western camp. NATO is sick. The United States is virtually isolated in Southeast Asia. The Third World plays off major coalitions of conflicting powers against one another. And these transformations combine to make the ideological dimensions of Cold War conflict decreasingly relevant to the shaping of sound American foreign policy.

At the same time, the geopolitical dimensions of conflict persist and are of great importance. And the ideological issues, while of diminished and subordinate importance, are still significant. The Moderate Cold Warriors continue to believe that the United States is obligated not only to shield societies in which freedom and democracy have stable institutional roots, but to carry these ideals to less hospitable climes. To a considerable extent they identify America's vital national interests with the protection and prudent propagation of freedom and democracy, and they regard those who oppose their viewpoint as "neo-isolationist." Thus, Moderate Cold Warriors generally favor the American intervention in Vietnam, but anxiously urge the President to exercise restraint. They base their support on a combination of geopolitical and ideological considerations which are each necessary and jointly sufficient to justify American policy.[4]

More specifically, Moderate Cold Warriors concede that the tensions and dangers of Cold War conflict, viewed even in exclusively balance-of-power terms, have rapidly receded in those parts of the globe where Russian power is concentrated. But the rise of an aggressive, powerful China has intensified tensions and dangers in Asia. The Vietnamese intervention was required, not only in order to stabilize power relations by containing China, but also to prove to the Chinese that the Russian policy of peaceful coexistence is correct. Moderate Cold Warriors are not opposed to revolutionary movements *per se*. They acknowledge that gradualism can be a dogma and that revolution may be justified. But in practice they tend to oppose revolutionary movements, because in a world in which great powers contend for .position, revolutionary disorder normally upsets the precarious geopolitical balance. Stability must always take precedence over the potential

---

[4] Paul Seabury, in his recently published book *The Rise and Decline of the Cold War* (Basic Books, New York and London: 1967), articulates this general point of view exceedingly well. C. L. Sulzberger, *New York Times* columnist, is another sophisticated proponent of this position. Strongly in support of Johnson's policies in Southeast Asia, he nevertheless had this to say about polycentric tendencies within the Communist world: "Moscow and East Europe now openly favor ideological co-existence—despite the harsh reactions of Peking . . . The menaces to peace today are founded less upon political philosophy than on outright power rivalries and strategic positioning. The old Communist Humpty Dumpty has fallen off the Iron Curtain and shattered into pieces which Moscow can't put together again." (*New York Times,* May 21, 1967.)

benefits of revolution. Hence, from their point of view, American policy-makers should operate on the basis of a presumption against revolutionary movements.

The second intermediate position, the one I defend in this essay, starts from the admission that American Cold War policies had considerable justification at their inception. Though vastly exaggerated by many Americans, the ideological aspect was present and legitimate. Russian expansion was a hypothesis fully warranted by the available evidence. The Marshall Plan was on balance a creative, constructive, and responsible application of American resources to the problems of European reconstruction. NATO provided an indispensable shield for weakened parliamentary democracies.

Nevertheless, even at the outset there was exaggerated American emphasis on military response, and relatively niggardly release of our vast economic resources for more peaceful purposes. Moreover, both kinds of power have often been used in ways that undermine liberal values. In Korea, the decision to cross the 38th parallel was a wholly unjustified application of military power. And our China policy has been nothing but a political ransom paid to the most fanatical and unreflective portions of the American public.

Successive U.S. governments have consistently underestimated the potentialities of Communist systems for change and diversification. Since the death of Stalin and the conclusion of the Korean War there has been no ideological and little geopolitical reason to refrain from embarking on a whole range of initiatives for reducing the tensions of the Cold War.

Though wary of unilateral commitments, it should be fully acknowledged that the country's vast economic resources thrust inescapable responsibilities upon the United States. America must learn to apply this wealth so as to reduce the already dangerous and unjust, but still widening, gap between industrial nations and the impoverished nations of the Third World. But in any and all circumstances the United States must try to deploy its affluence in ways that strengthen the scope and authority of multilateral and supranational agencies. The neo-isolationist charge is true if those who make it mean to imply that Radical Liberals ask the United States progressively to reduce its unilateral commitments to the vanishing point, and at each stage to reinforce the power and authority of supranational bodies. But to call such a view "neo-isolationist" is to abuse the language.

Moreover, such Radical Liberals believe that the Vietnam tragedy magnifies a fact that was evident to all detached observers during Joseph McCarthy's heyday—that the United States is underdeveloped morally and intellectually, and therefore politically; and that possession of the vastest material resources ever entrusted to one nation in the history of mankind makes *America,* and not the Soviet Union or China, the chief threat to world peace today. Admitting all defects, American institutions are, in general, morally superior to Communist institutions. But the incredible concentration of U.S. power enlarges her potential for international mischief many times over. It is not principally arrogance that makes the United States so dangerous, but the fusion of immaturity and vast power that exists here. Small errors, which would have negligible consequences when made by weaker nations, are capable of producing nuclear catastrophe when made by the United States.

In the sections that follow I shall develop these lines of argument, comparing them throughout with two of the other three positions briefly described in this section: those held by Moderate Cold Warriors and by the New Left Opposition. By contrast, the view that the Cold War is a titanic struggle for the redemption of mankind, though enormously important in American politics, is so lacking in moral and intellectual merit that it is not worthy of serious examination. That those who share this belief are politically powerful is one of the principal measures of our social immaturity.

Competition, Capitalism, and the Cold War

Americans supported Cold War policies that evolved after the Truman Doctrine was proclaimed in 1947 because they believed Russia was expanding aggressively. They believed Russia's imperial ambitions threatened both vital national interests and cherished moral values. The men who inspired our early actions thought primarily in terms of geopolitical considerations. But once President Truman announced that the contest was between the free world and a world enslaved, ideological rather than great-power considerations increasingly dominated popular and, to a lesser extent, governmental attitudes about the Cold War.

The thrust of American moral concern was, however, quite ambiguous. Everyone emphasized protection of freedom and democracy. But those who, in some degree, supported the American position disagreed sharply about what "freedom and democracy" meant. In particular, while some virtually identified these ideals with defense of the free enterprise system, others thought that the American private property system was not worth a limb of a single American soldier. Unless this divergence is recognized, early support for American Cold War policies cannot be fairly assessed, the widening split among American liberals cannot be understood.

My own view is that American security was indirectly threatened, our vital national interest seriously jeopardized, only during the brief period of post-World War II Russian expansionism. America's Korean intervention was a partially defensible episode. And an increase in the military threat to American security was virtually absent during the Cuban missile crisis.[5] By contrast to almost all previous crises, the Vietnam intervention actually impairs vital American interests and threatens to undermine her security.

Furthermore, the only things about American capitalism that are, from a moral point of view, worth protecting with American lives are its competitive market mechanisms. For these alone contribute to the growth of liberal institutions; these alone are important in stimulating creative, productive effort. But on these points, thoughtful individuals of every political persuasion are revisionist.

Marx's early attacks on capitalism were based on his profoundly Christian belief that institutionalization of human conflict in a competitive market is evil. He was convinced that private ownership of capital is the necessary and sufficient

---

[5] For example, Arthur Schlesinger, Jr., writes that at the time of the crisis, because the United States had a "2 to 1 superiority in nuclear power targeted against the Soviet Union, the shift in military balance of power would be less crucial than that in the political balance" (*A Thousand Days*, p. 796). It seems to me that this kind of preponderant power made the additional military threat nonexistent.

condition of a competitive market economy. Hence, he viewed capitalism as a great engine for inflicting harm on human beings. He sought to replace an industrial system based on conflict by a system based on Christian love. But he believed, quite rightly, that this redemptive aim cannot be achieved by means of moral education; revolutionary reconstruction of existing institutions is required.

Marx's conviction that private ownership of the means of production, distribution, and exchange is an *essential* condition of competitive institutions is important. For though he developed an analysis of monopolistic capitalism, Marx was certain that an *international* capitalist system could never master what he called "the anarchy of production"—the internal dynamic that resulted in increasingly violent booms and busts. Few thoughtful, knowledgeable individuals, East or West, accept any of these doctrines any longer.

In all the relatively developed Communist states aversion to competitive market mechanisms is disappearing; Yugoslav thinking and initiatives are gaining acceptance. Thoughtful Communists increasingly believe that without economic competition intolerable inefficiencies persist—and that the worst moral consequences of competition, those to which Marx so prophetically called attention, can be eliminated by democratizing industry.

Moreover, reflective Communists reject Marx's doctrine of *immiserization*—i.e., the view that the working classes within capitalist societies are inevitably reduced to a subsistence level of existence. They recognize that capitalist systems can eliminate the anarchy of production without abolishing private ownership of the instruments of production. They admit that Keynesian manipulation of key economic levers can, when combined with welfare programs, mitigate the worst forms of social discontent, thereby reducing the danger of violent revolution to the vanishing point.

Conversely, even Americans who most devoutly believe in the virtues of the free enterprise system admit that Communist states can create free market economies without reintroducing much, if any, private ownership of capital. As Gilbert Burck recently described it in *Fortune* magazine,

Both the Soviet Union and East Europe are in the arduous process of reforming their economies by introducing market forces, and in the bargain they are vouchsafing their citizens increased personal liberty . . . [T]aking the movement as a whole, it is one of the most important events in world affairs since the end of World War II, and one of the most important economic happenings since the Bolshevik revolution itself.

Burck goes on to make a claim which would be surprising when found in any magazine, and is astonishing when it appears in one of the leading journals of American capitalism:

Yugoslavia may yet boast more of a market economy, as Adam Smith broadly conceived of a market economy, than any other nation on earth.[6]

Moreover, as Michael Harrington has pointed out, the history of the Cold War demonstrates that American foreign policy need not bow to economic interests. The Marshall Plan strengthened the area of the world that competes most vigorously with American business. It is absurd to suppose that the CIA-sponsored Guatemalan coup was engineered by United Fruit, or that our interventions in Cuba and the Dominican Republic are principally to be understood as efforts to protect American economic interests. Moreover, even to conceive American policy in Southeast Asia on the model of economic imperialism is to engage in Cold War metaphysics hardly less absurd than that practiced by fanatics of the Right. U.S. military expenditures in South Vietnam are, conservatively, running at the rate of over $2 billion a *month*. The annual gross national product prior to the escalation in South Vietnam was about $1.7 billion a *year*.[7] If the United States government had used the sums it has spent to pursue the war on a program of peaceful pacification, it could probably have bought all the land in South Vietnam at full value, distributed it equitably among the peasants, and had enough left over to resettle and provide pensions for any landlords and political masters whose lives might be endangered by the consequent reconstitution of South Vietnamese political life. The idea that affected

[6] "East Europe's Struggle for Economic Freedom," *Fortune*, May 1967, p. 125.

[7] Computed from statistics available in the *United Nations Statistical Year Book, 1966*.

American corporations dominate Cold War policy through imperialist calculations of economic interest is blatant nonsense.

I am not claiming that American corporate interests are either benign or uninfluential. The oil industry still exerts decisive influence on certain aspects of American policy. And in South America, Central America, South Africa, and elsewhere around the globe business interests influence our actions in significant ways. But neither protection of oil, nor protection of these other interests, are essential conditions of the health of the American economy.[8] Corporate interests have not been nearly as influential in the shaping of American foreign policy as some members of the New Left contend. Liquidation of American interests abroad would produce only minor dislocations in the American economy.

Though many on the New Left argue as if they believed that the conscious aim of American officials is to defend American economic interests abroad, and that this intention decisively determines Cold War policies, there is another, more sophisticated analysis that deserves further consideration. Some members of the New Left contend that American policy can be *explained* in terms of the protection and promotion of corporate interests, in much the way that the demolition of an airplane by a Sidewinder missile can be explained.

Whatever particular causes may operate at a given time, and however often other missiles may miss their mark, the constant and decisive determinant of the path of a Sidewinder is the functional goal for which it is constructed—to destroy targeted aircraft. Similarly, whatever mixture of causes may operate at any particular time, the constant and decisive de-

[8] In 1964 the sum of $44.3 billion was invested directly overseas; in 1965, $49.2 billion. In both years foreign investment was only about 5 per cent of gross domestic investment. Of this total investment abroad, 60 per cent went to Canada and Europe. Of the entire amount, oil and mining accounted for about 40 per cent. Assuming that most of this portion of the total went to areas outside Canada and Europe, it becomes clear that an enormous percentage of the small investments that went to the Third World were made by oil and mining industries—principally oil. Cf. Elizabeth Jager, in "Survey of Current Business," *The Federationist,* September 1966. Referred to by Michael Harrington in "American Power in the Twentieth Century," *Dissent,* September–October 1967, pp. 643–44.

terminant of American foreign policy is the aim for which our entire decision-making apparatus was constructed—to protect and promote American economic interests. Occasionally policy may miss its mark. Benevolent men may participate in operating the policy-making apparatus. None of this affects the basic explanatory point—that the functional goal of the entire mechanism is to serve those who control the American economic system. (I should add here that I have encountered this point of view, not only among members of the New Left, but also among small-business men to whom I have occasionally spoken about the war in Vietnam.)

The explanatory scheme just described easily handles apparent counterexamples, such as the Marshall Plan, opposition to the Suez invasion, the Point Four program, President Kennedy's withdrawal after the Bay of Pigs disaster, the Peace Corps, support of the Viet Minh against French colonialism in the early stages of the Indochina tragedy, and many other Cold War episodes. For careful analysis reveals that each apparent counterinstance is actually explainable in terms of the functional aim posited in the theory. Thus the Marshall Plan was meant to forestall a massive threat to the entire system of free enterprise. Opposition to the Suez adventure was not only consistent with protection of American oil interests in the Middle East, it actually promoted those interests by casting the United States in an unfamiliar and attractive role. Kennedy refused to invade Cuba because an invasion would have destroyed the fledgling Alliance for Progress which was designed to serve larger corporate aims. And so on.

Now it is futile to argue each particular case. I want instead to make a more general theoretical point. The theory the New Left Opposition puts forward is so resourceful that it can be made to explain any apparent counterexample. But, more importantly, it is so amazingly fertile that it also could have been made to explain the opposite of what happened. Thus, had Kennedy authorized the invasion, had we not tried to stop the Suez invasion, had we not proposed the Marshall Plan, had we not developed the Peace Corps, had we not tried to cut our losses in Korea—all this and more would have been even more easily explained in terms of the promotion of corporate interests. Indeed, the New Left can argue that American middle-class policy is dictated by old-fashioned imperial ambition. (But *whose* ambition: the oil industry with its vital stake in Kuwait, Iraq, and other Arab countries?) *And a theory that explains every possibility explains nothing.* A theory that strong is empty. And this is my basic objection to the interpretation of the Cold War proposed by the New Left Opposition—it is at best a useful heuristic, a guide to the search for *one* of the important determinants of American foreign policy. But, as often deployed, even by very scholarly individuals, the interpretation is vacuous because it explains too much. It lacks intellectual basis because it destroys all significant distinctions.

Freedom, Democracy, and American Incompetence

American intervention in Europe at the beginning of the Cold War did serve the cause of freedom and democracy. Russia was aggressive and expansionist. Stalinist tyranny was cruel and oppressive. The argument that Russia was motivated solely by desire to establish defensive buffers has a peculiarly scholastic flavor. Nor does it matter whether, in the perspective of history, Russia or the United States was more to blame for the rapid build-up of tensions. The important question is whether Western statesmen were, *at the time, warranted* in believing that the U.S.S.R. was dangerous. On the evidence available *at the time* the conviction that the Soviets threatened the territorial integrity of sovereign European states was amply justified. Any doubts political leaders may have entertained evaporated when Communists overthrew the regime of Beneš and Masaryk in Czechoslovakia.

While it is probably true that the invention of the atomic bomb helped precipitate Truman's strong response to the Greek rebellion, it is also true that the ruthless use of Russian power in Czechoslovakia—a nation with a strong parliamentary tradition, the second highest per capita income in prewar Europe, and one that had become a symbol of appeasement—was the crucial factor in convincing all European nations not already overrun by Russian armies that they had to take defensive measures. Sweden, Norway, Belgium, the Netherlands, Denmark, as well as Britain, France, Italy, and the

United States, reacted swiftly and strongly. Stalin had over-played his hand; it would have been foolish for the leaders of any parliamentary democracy to have concluded that Russia had no further aggressive designs. Whatever the actual inten-tions of historical actors may be, statesmen must base their policies on reasonable presumptions, not wishful thinking. The United States did not have to coax NATO into existence; member states developed the defensive alliance with enthusi-asm. They welcomed the Marshall Plan with equal warmth.

But even Stalinism and the facts that supported the hypothe-sis of Russian aggressiveness were not sufficient to justify the American claim to be defending freedom and democracy. Also necessary was the further fact that, by and large, the countries we were aiding *were parliamentary democracies in which liberal institutions had already been brought to a rea-sonably high pitch of development.* In other words, the United States was not in a position of having to nourish tender shoots of freedom, or to pacify and teach the population of, for ex-ample, Great Britain, how to be free and democratic. The point is absolutely fundamental in understanding why Cold War policies in Europe were mainly justified, but have proved absolutely disastrous almost everywhere else on this globe.

In Europe American efforts met with considerable success. We did help revitalize German and Italian democracy. We did help the established parliamentary democracies in Great Britain, France, the Benelux countries, Denmark, and Nor-way to recover from the brutal punishment that had been in-flicted on them during World War II.

But the simple fact is that our efforts succeeded almost ex-clusively in those countries *that already had the institutional and economic base essential to the nourishment of liberal insti-tutions and values.* And even Japan had forged the economic base for a functioning democratic order. Elsewhere in the world, U.S. intervention may have staved off Communism, but it has not had notable success in building liberal commu-nities. And the main reason for these failures is, I believe, that American power is not matched by the necessary competence or wisdom. The United States is itself a morally and politically underdeveloped society. In most of the countries of Europe which we aided we had much to learn and little to teach about the processes of liberal society.

Consider, by way of contrast, our record in Vietnam. The other war, the effort to "pacify" the countryside, is, after eleven years and many billions of dollars, still "at the beginning of a beginning"—to quote Senator Mike Mansfield's words. Imagine the outcry if the U. S. Army was to be put in charge of flagging Head Start programs in Mississippi and Alabama. The decision to transfer authority over pacification efforts to the American military command in South Vietnam is no less ludicrous. Men engaged in a shooting war, exposed to a totally different cultural experience, are being asked to teach the Vietnamese how to achieve stability, freedom, and democracy. The notion that their efforts hold any promise of success is nonsense on stilts.

Would American civilians fare better? First, the best of them are needed to complete the work of building a decent society right here in the United States. Second, the typical civilian is ill-equipped to understand the problems of a proud Asian people who have had a totally different cultural experience. Finally, even if civilians had the will, the skill, and the cultural sensitivity to do an effective job, their efforts would be undercut at every juncture by a military force understandably preoccupied with military tasks. Indeed, that is precisely what happened during the nine futile years prior to escalation. We sent many men of good will and superior competence to Vietnam as members of the AID mission; they failed, utterly and completely. The reason for the shift of authority from civilians to army in Vietnam is not that anyone really believes military men are likely to do a superior job. It is simply that the military command wants to eliminate any source of conflict with their armed struggle against the National Liberation Front. They want to get on with their main job—which is to crush, not pacify, the rebellion in the South. And Vietnam only reveals in a particularly crude and outrageous form the incompetence and insensitivity of American efforts to convey freedom and democracy to peoples around the globe. While the Rusks and Humphreys proclaim opposition to tyranny, U.S. actions destroy prospects for political self-determination. The only protection any society has had against our blundering incompetence has been the resilience and integrity of its own national institutions, the pride and the courage of its own members.

Nor should it surprise anyone that the United States, which has after a hundred years failed to bring the blessings of freedom and democracy to the overwhelming majority of its citizens liberated from slavery, should also fail to bring those blessings to societies much less ready to receive them. The arrogance of our policies is, in this respect, surpassed only by the ignorance of those charged with implementing them.

Stability and Revolution

Even if Moderate Cold Warriors are inclined to accept the view that the United States is not competent to *promote* freedom and democracy in societies that lack institutional prerequisites, they may feel—and rightly—that the spine of their general position has not been fairly revealed. For they believe that maintenance of a stable international system should be the central aim of American foreign policy. And they believe also that, though the United States may falter in particular situations, prospects for political democracy are closely identified with American national interests. Hence, failure of American "stability-operations" are setbacks for liberal causes. Thus most Moderate Cold Warriors support the Administration's Vietnam intervention because they believe that it is necessary to deliver a stabilizing rebuff to China and, thereby, to serve the larger cause of political freedom.[9]

Because stability is the Moderate Cold Warrior's fundamental concept and central goal, it is important to examine his views about this subject very carefully. For I am convinced

[9] For example, Paul Seabury thinks that stability in Asia depends on our convincing the Chinese that the Soviet convictions about peaceful coexistence are right. He writes: "In Vietnam, were the outcome of conflict to include the extension of Chinese power in Asia and among revolutionary movements there, this would not simply signify a defeat for America (and for the larger cause of political freedom); it would serve also as a disastrous refutation of Soviet theories and policy, and would further undermine its already challenged legitimacy within the 'Socialist camp.'" (Op. cit., p. 151.)

that it is here that one finds the nerve of disagreement that today divides American liberals in foreign policy matters.

As the Moderate Cold Warrior sees it, American security is ultimately dependent on the stability of the international system; that is, on the effective balancing of powerful coalitions. He believes that this has, in fact, been the greatest accomplishment of America's Cold War containment policy. All around the globe, powers were brought into stable balance. The chief constructive outcome of the Cold War in Europe for example, has been the reduction of traditional intra-European strife. Only in Asia is the precarious balance that was achieved seriously threatened by a fanatically aggressive China. Both Russia and the United States have a vital interest in reestablishing the fragile stability there threatened by irrational Chinese leaders.

It is the maintenance of stability that justifies the bilateral and multilateral treaties into which America has entered with over forty nations. Only through the firm defense of the present balance can underdeveloped nations be saved from falling under the domination of Communist tyrannies. Wars of national liberation must be opposed, not primarily because they are intrinsically bad, but because they jeopardize international stability. Anyone who refuses to acknowledge the basic soundness of this analysis, who is willing to permit those who control liberation movements to win by default, in effect counsels that the United States abandon historic responsibilities. They are, therefore, properly labeled "neo-isolationists."

The position just described has the ring of cool objectivity, prudence, realism. It is, however, immoral and ultimately imprudent. For the emphasis placed on stability leads in practice to counterrevolutionary action; worse still from the point of view of stability-seekers, in the long run it results in international chaos. At least, these are the conclusions that I shall defend in this section and the last.

The functional meaning of "stability-operations" for the industrially underdeveloped world is counterrevolution. Consider the policy pattern the United States typically pursues in its efforts to maintain international stability.

A revolutionary movement, almost inevitably containing some Communists, moves to take power. The proportion of

Communists in the revolutionary force may be tiny, as it was in the Dominican Republic, or significantly large, as it is in South Vietnam. The *possibility* that the Communists will take power causes the United States to view these revolutionary developments as a threat to international stability. American policy-makers reason that to permit these forces to triumph in a new area of the globe will whet the appetite of major Communist powers for further "aggression." Thus, willingness to permit revolutionary triumph is tantamount to appeasement on the model of Munich.

To forestall such an outcome, the American government first tries to pacify the natives by offering them a carrot. But such efforts almost inevitably fail. For in the absence of genuine democracy, the United States will support the very elements within the revolutionary society that exploit and oppress the now turbulent masses. American civilian "advisers" are unable, with the best will in the world, to persuade ruling elites to relinquish their exploitative power. And those elites find ready allies among American military "advisers." Conor Cruise O'Brien elegantly analyzes the problem that confronts the United States in any such situation:

> In the poor world, . . . the oppressed are not minorities but the masses, and they are confronted by ruling classes that cling avidly to their traditional large share of scarce resources. The interests of the ruling classes are simply not consistent with any social change in the interests of the people as a whole. The landowners, usurers, sweat-shop owners, corrupt political bosses, and parasitic bureaucrats who now control in varying combinations most governments of the third world are precisely those people who must be deprived of their *raison d'être* if there is to be a social revolution. Why should these people allow themselves to be peacefully ousted as long as they have the money to pay others to defend their interests? Such defense need not always be as obvious as the employment of white mercenaries by the government of the Congo. Rulers of most poor countries, by reason of that very poverty, can recruit mercenaries from among their own people. This method is less conspicuous than the Congolese method, but it is also less reliable because the danger of defection and mutiny is inescapable when national forces are used in a revolutionary situation. . . . If this line of reasoning is correct, and recent history seems to support it, then it is not likely that social revolution will occur without political revolution; political revolu-

tion will be opposed by force, and cannot prevail without greater force.[10]

But, for the reasons O'Brien cites, the indigenous ruling class is not likely to be able to muster the force necessary to repulse the revolutionaries without outside aid. At the same time, the United States, given its desire to stabilize the situation and its further tendency to view the threat of Communism as absolutely inimical to the growth of freedom and democracy, is quite responsive to a request that it buttress pacification efforts with military assistance. So the ruling elite turns to the United States, and that powerful nation responds by providing her suppliants with a stick. If the ruling elites do not request aid, the United States is likely to act anyway—as we did in Iran and Guatemala, and as we tried to do in Cuba. One way or another, American policy reinforces counterrevolutionary efforts to maintain existing injustice—all in the name of stability, freedom, and democracy.

The United States has neither the power nor the competence to promote freedom and democracy in societies in which prerequisite institutions have not sufficiently matured. But the American counterrevolutionary posture in the world is a greater evil, and reflects a deeper domestic disorder, than failure to acknowledge our limitations. For the American populace is well insulated from the human agony that exists in underdeveloped lands—agony that, as Conor Cruise O'Brien points out, is unlikely to be eliminated without bloody revolution. And once having intervened, Americans are further protected from grasping the full extent of the additional suffering caused by their armies.

It is not simply that we are a bourgeois society—with all the defenses bourgeois societies have for making human suffering invisible. We are a society that has used its technology to erect a gigantic screen through which filter only those images from around the world that will not unduly discomfort our people. We have automated and computerized bourgeois misperception—we have created great technological engines for preserving our complacency. We are the first people in human history

[10] "The Counterrevolutionary Reflex," (*The Columbia University Forum,* Spring 1966, p. 21).

to have produced a technology for creating institutional indifference, and then to have made of that institutional indifference an essential ingredient of our conception of the good and virtuous life. Other malevolent societies may have been wicked; we are the first society in human history to have achieved automated amorality.

The extent, nature, and remediability of chronic suffering in underdeveloped nations creates a presumption in favor of revolution. The idea that, given the alternatives normally available to these societies, gradualism is typically preferable to revolution is morally fraudulent. The facts of misery, exploitative power, and greed in the Third World argue against such a comforting illusion. Few nations in history have achieved a humanly tolerable stability based on industrial and cultural development without bloody revolution; certainly not the United States, which underwent two revolutions; nor Britain, France, or Russia. And, despite the undoubted advantages of peaceful, self-determined industrial development within tolerably democratic societies, no nation has developed its economic potentialities without enormous human suffering. Putting to the side other long-term benefits, it is not at all clear that the cost in human misery of British or American industrial development exceeded that imposed on the Russian people by its Stalinist masters. This is not the whole moral story; but it is a part of it that needs to be reiterated and emphasized if false righteousness is to be avoided.

I have offered a *general* analysis. A presumption in favor of revolutionary movements has been defended; no more than that. Revolutions may be cruelly wrong. The proper course for even a poor nation may be evolutionary rather than revolutionary. And this will tend to be so to the extent that the prerequisites and traditions of an authentically free society have been established. Within the framework of the analysis there are all sorts of distinctions to be drawn; all sorts of qualifications to be made. But those refinements are the business of another essay. Here it is my intention only to develop the broad lines of an analysis that, in a number of important respects, runs counter to the conventional American wisdom about revolutionary movements.

Suppose a given society is better advised to take the evolutionary rather than the revolutionary path. Suppose also it embarks on the revolutionary course all the same. And suppose, finally, the revolutionary movement is Communist-dominated. Does it automatically follow that U.S. intervention is justified? From the fact that a given Communist-dominated revolution is unjustified, it does not follow that unilateral American intervention—military or politico-economic—is right. In general, revolutions are the product of human misery sufficiently intense for men to put their lives and the lives of those they love in jeopardy. Intervention typically compounds the mischief the revolution may itself be doing. Few who oppose the American intervention in Vietnam have many illusions about the quality of political life that would result if the National Liberation Front comes to power in South Vietnam. But one does not have to romanticize the rebel cause to oppose an American military onslaught that enlarges and intensifies the suffering of the Vietnamese people, diminishes rather than enhances their prospects for a good life, despoils their land, and threatens us all with nuclear extinction. Even from the legitimate claim that a given revolution is morally wrong, it does not follow that preventive intervention is morally right. For intervention of even a nonmilitary sort is likely to lead to military intervention, and it surely cannot be obvious that bloodshed in putting down a Communist revolt is invariably better than the blood spilled in making the revolution. Nor is it obvious that the sins committed by rebellious forces justify greater sins by counterrevolutionary armies.

The thrust of these remarks is that there is a presumption in favor of bloody revolution in lands in which massive exploitation and tyranny transparently occur. This is so *even if the revolution is dominated by Communists*. For it has become increasingly clear that "wicked" Communists are no better able to forecast and shape the future than are "benevolent" freedom-lovers. Both are amply endowed with arrogance, ignorance, and stupidity. Both are, in any event, limited in their power to control the future.

During the past fifteen years the two major triumphs of Chinese policy have been in Korea and Vietnam. In Korea, by hurling American forces back to the 38th parallel, China proved to the world that it was a power to be reckoned with. In Vietnam it watches the Americans bleed, the Vietnamese grow increasingly disaffected, and the Asian masses grow more anti-American, without having to expend much of its material resources or any military manpower. Wherever else China has tried to play a controlling role—in Indonesia, Africa, and Latin America—it has suffered rebuff and humiliation. And while American statesmen like to think that these diplomatic defeats are primarily a result of their cunning policies, the facts are typically otherwise. Everywhere the gap between arrogant Chinese pretensions and China's power to affect events has been the principal cause of failure. Communist China would probably have failed had the United States disappeared from the face of the earth.

The Soviet Union, through its armies, achieved great successes in the postwar period. Yet, since 1948, Eastern Europe has been the theater of unanticipated centripetal change, the emergence of a polycentric system. Again, this development has been due less to American policy than to reassertion of nationalist priorities combined with a maturation of the Soviet system that owes little to external pressure, much to the dynamics of a growing industrial order. In fact, changes similar to those that have occurred in the Soviet Union are happening in every Communist state. For in each a liberalizing dialectical process, rooted in a common commitment to industrialization, is taking place.

Though new forms of tyranny inevitably result during each Communist society's post-revolutionary period, there is a difference. For bread is provided, and industrial development is promoted. It is not Maoism to recognize that freedom and democracy mean little to people who remember too vividly their recent misery.

But memories die, and tyranny produces new discontents, new forms of personal insecurity and a generation that has known less misery. The demand for institutions that mitigate oppression, promote human dignity and personal development, is reasserted. The prerequisites and consequences of a growing industrial order—principally education and economic sufficiency—will ensure that this happens. The scientific and technological communities will be the first to hold an oppressive regime to ransom—and the ransom they will demand will be not only affluence, but relief from arbitrary power. Rule of law and personal autonomy will be established; at first in limited spheres and only precariously. But over time new seeds of discontent will be sown; the demand for freedom will grow. For the exercise of freedom is contagious unless those who have it are insulated by feudal walls from those who do not. Only ruthless oppression can block these liberalizing tendencies; and such ruthlessness would prove industrially self-defeating.

Liberal progress may, therefore, receive many setbacks. A "cultural revolution," a purge or reign of terror will occur. But as soon as repressive measures begin to prove industrially harmful, counterrepressive social processes will develop. The dialectical movement in the direction of greater personal liberty will recommence.

There is nothing inevitable about such developments. The world's history tells of many madmen who have frustrated rational calculations that justify belief in the *probability* that certain things will happen. But statesmen should base the main lines of policy on reasoned probabilities, not outside chances.

Failure to act on the basis of probabilities rather than possibilities lies at the heart of the Vietnam catastrophe. The Munich analogy, which Rusk and Humphrey are so fond of invoking to defend American actions, rests on nothing more substantial than the fact that Hitler and Mao have both used an aggressive rhetoric. Beyond that the similarities end. Germany was a highly developed military and industrial power. *Its* armies moved across frontiers without provocation. Germany moved against societies that had mature parliamentary institutions. At every critical juncture Hitler backed his bellicose language with steel. There was little prospect that internal change would de-fuse the German bomb before a German move to blow up the world.

By contrast, China is weak industrially, weak in terms of military technology. China is only tenuously connected to either North Vietnam or the National Liberation Front, has not moved its armies across the contested frontiers without provocation, and is not subverting or seriously threatening established parliamentary democracies. At every critical junc-

ture China has acted with prudent restraint—a fact that every
student of that country admits. Finally, there is every reason
to believe that, given China's deep commitment to industrialization, its energies will be harnessed for internal tasks rather
than outward mischief if some of the tremendous military
and political pressure America exerts is relieved. This also is
the sober judgment of almost every China expert outside the
U.S. government. Should this highly probable judgment be
true, it would give the liberal dialectic a greater chance to
function. When a bitterly disaffected Chinese technician was
recently asked by an equally disillusioned diplomat friend who
had decided to defect whether he too would leave China if he
had the chance, the technician replied:

> Despite my supposedly unacceptable background and despite
> the fact that my immediate superiors know fairly well what
> my sentiments are, they will do nothing against me.
>
> Our leaders have established a simple, old-fashioned war-
> lord autocracy using witch-doctor mumbo-jumbo. To compete
> with the modern industrial nations, huge numbers of tech-
> nicians are needed. Anyone trained to the necessary degree
> of technology, however, can see through their mumbo-jumbo.
> So the people needed most by the regime are the most dis-
> affected.
>
> In my case, there are a growing number of politicians who
> take my ideas as their own. I don't care. I have ideas that
> they don't. My security is based on the number of people
> whose status comes from taking credit for what I create.

When the diplomat told his friend that these views made him
want to stay too, the technician replied,

> Please don't. When I'm on the Central Committee I'll invite
> you back for a big celebration. Meanwhile get as far away
> from here as you can.[11]

I would take issue with the technician only in what he says
about Mao's China being simply another war-lord regime. It
is a war-lord regime *committed to industrialization,* and that
makes all the difference.

The conclusion that emerges is that among available alternatives the United States may best serve both its interests and

[11] Tung Chi-ping, "Growing Up in Mao's China," the London *Observer,* March 5, 1967, p. 11.

liberal values by supporting, or at least not opposing, revolutionary movements dominated by Communists. In South Vietnam, if the only realistic choice were between a government dominated by Marshall Ky and his ilk or Premier Ho and his ilk, it is fairly clear that the differences would be, from a moral point of view, not sufficiently consequential to justify jeopardizing a single American life. This does not imply that a regime subservient to the Communists of the North would be the best of all possible governments. Nor am I suggesting that the posited alternatives exhaust America's present options. I simply want to stress that from an authentically liberal point of view, given a narrow range of real alternatives, Communism would normally be preferable to supporting landlord regimes through force of arms. To say that military intervention, in a revolutionary situation, would normally be required, to accept this implication, is in effect to admit that Cold War perspectives are morally irrelevant to problems of the Third World—a position which, incidentally, Pope Paul had the wisdom to acknowledge in his recent encyclical dealing with problems of underdeveloped nations.[12]

Stability or Order

The recognition that stability as the focal aim of American policy has counterrevolutionary consequences, and that promotion of these consequences is presumptively immoral, does not justify abandoning the Moderate Cold Warrior's point of view. For if, in the long run, the peace of the world and the security of the United States depend on the maintenance of international stability, then frustration of revolutionary movements in underdeveloped countries might be a moral price worth paying. The tribe that lives on the margin between famine and survival may feel justified in killing a certain percentage of newborn infants; but there is no morality in it.

In fact, stability and the balance of power theory that underlies its adoption as the most important goal of foreign policy are irrational because they are self-defeating. The stability achieved in the short run promotes international chaos and

[12] "On the Development of Peoples," the *New York Times*, March 29, 1967.

imperils the survival of mankind in the long run. A stability orientation is not a requirement of an intelligent, properly realistic foreign policy. To the contrary, stability is regarded as the *summum bonum* by men who have forsaken the serious pursuit of an order that transcends the international system. For we live in a jungle—a Hobbesian *state of nature*.

The central claim made by more sophisticated defenders of America's Vietnam policy is that international stability required the intervention. They argue: had we not acted in firm, though limited, ways in Southeast Asia, the precarious balance of Cold War power would have been disrupted; the world would be on the brink of nuclear holocaust. This claim lies at the core of the Administration's insistence that it really seeks peace. And there is no reason to doubt its sincerity.

But the 1967 Middle East crisis makes it abundantly clear that even the short-term consequences of our adventurous effort to stabilize Asia have been chaos and disorder. For it is highly unlikely that the Israeli-Arab War would have erupted had it not been for America's unilateral intervention in Vietnam. Russia is unlikely to have encouraged Nasser, Nasser is unlikely to have taken the risks he took, U Thant is unlikely to have acted so precipitously in withdrawing U.N. forces from the Sinai border, Israel would have been as unlikely to doubt the credibility of quite definite U.S. commitments—had they not all thought that unilateral U.S. involvement in Southeast Asia would embarrass the United States and make doubtful serious U.S. efforts to solve the crisis in the Middle East. The net result of the episode is that the credibility of American commitments has diminished as an indirect result of our engagement in an Asian war that is supposed to make more credible our willingness to fulfill our commitments.[13]

But the mare's-nests in Southeast Asia and the Middle East only reveal the jungle environment in which nations live. Underlying such episodes are two factors that intensify developments promoting a state in which, in Hobbes's words, "the

[13] I wrote this passage before General de Gaulle analyzed the large meaning of the Mideast crisis in similar terms. Were it not for the fact that de Gaulle, like Hobbes, fails to look beyond international anarchy to civil society, I would be proud to regard myself as Gaullist in these respects.

life of man [is] solitary, poore, nasty, brutish, and short"—
increasing disparities in the wealth of nations and nuclear
proliferation.

The growing gap between the affluent, industrialized nations
of the world and the have-not states will be a source of inevitable future conflicts, which are more likely to occur because material wealth correlates so closely to color of skin.
The United States has about 6 per cent of the world's population and more than a third of the world's productive resources.[14] In justice *and in prudence* she therefore bears the
heaviest responsibility for reversing world-wide economic
trends. If Americans think they can avoid the worst during
their own lifetime, they should consider the prospects of those
yet unborn.

But even if America did acquire the political will to meet
this historic responsibility, which she presently lacks, she would
be in a bind. For unilateral economic commitments create interests, demands, and conflicts that too often result in military
commitments. Such involvements generally undermine the
growth of the institutional prerequisites of healthy self-rule.
Hence, some alternative way of meeting her obligations must
be sought by the United States. And what holds for the United
States in this instance holds in lesser degree for all the other
developed nations of the world.

The conclusion that forces itself on the industrialized nations is that they must work to close the affluence gap through
supranational agencies where possible, and through multilateral agencies where necessary. They must begin to channel
resources in ways that *replace stability with legal order*. The
need to reinforce this tendency within the international sphere
is made even more evident when we consider the problem of
nuclear proliferation.

It will soon be technologically possible for small nations to
produce nuclear devices that can be carried into the Moscow
subway by a Paraguayan agent or fired into Boston from an
Algerian submarine. Thus the national origin of the attack
can be well concealed. In these circumstances neither Russia

[14] Computed on the basis of statistics available in the *United Nations
Statistical Year Book, 1965,* by Dr. Daniel B. Suits, University of
Michigan.

nor the United States would be likely to deliver a nuclear reply to Paraguay or Algeria.

A nonproliferation treaty is a useful, but tiny, step toward inhibiting such dangers. For the task of policing such a treaty would be enormous, and not every nation will sign. Hobbes insisted that men could not abolish the state of nature's "war of all against all," or establish "peace," without creating civil society. His prophetic insight has never been more poignantly relevant to international affairs.

The creation of a world state is no longer the Utopian aspiration of idealistic politicians, but the urgent, practical, realistic requirement of statesmanship in a Hobbesian world. What the gnawing fact of the relative impoverishment of nations suggests, the threat of nuclear proliferation confirms.

But a world state is not going to emerge, like Venus, from the sea of present discontent. Rather we shall have to take short steps in its direction—one following another, patiently but insistently. Every opportunity to rely on multilateral rather than bilateral relations ought to be pursued. Every effort to create and utilize supranational agencies ought to be made. This obligation falls most heavily on those nations that are currently most powerful; for they have the defensive power that makes them less liable to suffer vital injury through pursuit of this realistic goal. This is why the decision of the United States to bypass the United Nations in Vietnam is perhaps the greatest of the many tragedies of that pointless war.

In other words, the United States ought to become "neo-isolationist" if by that phrase is meant the progressive reduction of unilateral commitments in favor of multilateral action where that is the best alternative open to us—support of supranational efforts whenever possible. But "neo-isolationism" is in this sense perfectly compatible with the demand that the United States apply its vast power and resources to the solution of grave international problems. Its niggardly allocation of national resources to the problem of world poverty must be multiplied many times over. The full weight of its massive power must be placed behind the effort to induce the nations of the earth to pass from the state of nature to civil society. And in this respect few aims are more important than mutual tension reduction and disarmament. To do any of these things is far from being isolationist in spirit or substance; it is just the reverse. For such "neo-isolationism" constitutes even greater involvement with other nations—but "involvement with," not "intervention in."

Yet we must live in the world as it is. There will be an interim—prolonged by political realities—during which the United States will have to meet existing threats and crises. How should it do so, given the analysis of the Cold War this essay has developed?

1. The American military force need not be dismantled. Nor should it be precipitously removed from various strategically important areas of the world. The U.S. government cannot escape the duty, imposed by the very fact that we do live in a Hobbesian jungle, to maintain its power in order to defend its vital interests. But this in no way requires us to maintain the incredible concentration of power, the capacity to "kill" all nations of the world many times over, that we have built up.

2. We should redefine our vital interest so that it embraces first security, and second the defense of reasonably stable, mature, equitable parliamentary democracies. We have no obligation to defend parliamentary democracies like those of South Africa and Rhodesia. For democratic practice in both those countries is restricted by law and by custom to small, white, fantastically exploitative minorities. On the other hand, the hopeful parliamentary systems of India, Ceylon, and Israel, among others, deserve our support and, *when all else fails,* our unilateral protection against genuinely foreign aggression.

3. Our power should be deployed loosely. The noose of steel we have constructed around China is, whatever may be our intentions, objectively provocative and aggressive. In correspondence to the loosening of our military hold on certain areas, we should attempt to educate the American public to think more flexibly about the nature and threat of Communism. Our main enemies in the world are not Communists— they are any forces that perpetuate poverty, racism, and those virulent aspects of nationalism (within and outside our country) which promote disorder and undermine efforts to build a world community.

4. We should make clear to the peoples of the world that

there is not a single American economic interest abroad which is so vital that it justifies military intervention in the affairs of another sovereign state. We should recognize that our market power is a much more effective and desirable means of protecting legitimate American interests than is our military power. No nation in the world can afford to ignore for very long the American power to consume and to produce—as the history of the Arab oil boycott after the recent war in the Middle East makes abundantly clear.

5. We should often support and almost never oppose revolutionary movements. Even bad revolutions are typically better than the results of the unilateral American intervention intended to forestall them. It is almost inconceivable that any revolutionary movement can succeed unless underlying discontents are so intense, forms of exploitation and oppression so severe, that popular sentiment has reached a boiling point.

In brief, we should abandon the Cold War, substituting for it reasonable national prudence combined with determination to help the world move toward social justice and a supranational order. When liberals like Vice President Humphrey say, "I want to be tolerant, but I can't see the difference between containment of communism in Europe and Asia,"[15] we who believe otherwise should be equally tolerant, even while we relentlessly work to remove from office those who are so unreflectively, recklessly ignorant.

[15] In the Atlanta *Journal* and *Constitution*, interview with Saul Pett, April 10, 1966.

A Case Against Interventionism

WILLIAM PFAFF is co-author of three recent books on international affairs and contemporary history: *Power and Impotence: The Failure of America's Foreign Policy; The Politics of Hysteria;* and *The New Politics.* He has been an editor and foreign correspondent, an executive of a political warfare organization, and a member of Hudson Institute, a policy research group. He writes a foreign affairs column for *Commonweal* and regularly contributes to other magazines.

The intervention of nations into the affairs of others is one of history's inevitabilities. Interests collide and interlock; states want to change the conduct of others. What is interesting—and perilously relevant—is why they do it, what means they use, and how far they are prepared to go.

In American policy today, the great controversy arises not so much from the fact that we are intervening abroad as from the scale and character of our interventions. In Vietnam, in Latin America, in Western Europe, an American political intervention was well established, supported by an American public consensus, and tolerated (or even welcomed) by the greater part of the international community, long before the present policy crisis. What seems to have gone wrong is that the United States has crossed a threshold of acceptable means. The objection is to the use of war as an instrument of intervention in Vietnam, large-scale military intervention in a Caribbean political crisis, the *kind* of pressures we have employed to attempt to isolate France and to affect West German policy. The judgment in these cases is that our methods are disproportionate to what reasonably can be expected to be achieved.

The objection is to excess—to a failure of political judgment and discrimination. It makes a sound argument, one of practicality rather than principle, and it probably is more persuasive for the omission. But there are two issues of principle involved in the present situation which are worth some attention for the light they throw on what may be expected from the future of this American world involvement.

The first concerns the morality of our means. Without attempting a scholastic determination of when it may be licit to kill in a political cause and when not, it ought to be a counsel of mere prudence—given the record of violence in recent history—to err on the side of restraint. Totalitarianism, political purges, and genocide, to say nothing of the mass slaughter of civilians by Allied airpower during World War II, ought to have given us a lively sense of the fragility of civilized standards. Behind much of the outcry against the American course in Vietnam is an instinctive (or historically conditioned) reaction against a casualness about violence, against an advertised "tough-mindedness" about the established conventions of war and international law, which are literally demoralizing to international society.

The second issue of principle has to do with the rationale for American interventionism. The evolution of our foreign policy since the 1940s has not been wholly deliberate, and the commitment this country made to international "leadership" after 1945 was accompanied by much domestic controversy. The policies we adopted in Europe and the Near East, and subsequently extended in Asia (and even later, in Africa) were a series of improvisations in the face of what were understood as major crises. (The revisionist arguments that find the source of Cold War in Truman Administration aggressiveness seem to be unconvincing—as well as reflecting, often enough, a willful sentimentalization of the Roosevelt era.) None of that series of major commitments made in the early years after 1945—the Truman Doctrine, the rearmament of Germany and establishment of NATO, the commitment to a permanent program of foreign aid, the intervention in Korea —was accepted with enthusiasm by the American public. Each was undertaken in a public mood of soberness and even of apprehension. The Truman and Eisenhower administrations had to fight for these programs in Congress; and together the individual programs amounted to a reversal of a one-hundred-fifty-year-old American policy of isolationism.

The roots of isolationist policy lay very deep in the American consciousness—in the experience of physical isolation, of ocean barriers, but much more important, in the peculiar American historical experience of repudiation of Europe. The founding of this country was an act of self-separation from the tradition of Europe, making a new "compact" among men which superseded the old forms of political society. The great immigrations of the 19th and early 20th centuries were almost entirely made up of people who rejected Europe and wanted to cut themselves off from the past. In these conditions a foreign policy of isolation gratified deep and complex impulses within American society. More could be said about this, but for the purpose of illuminating the interventionism of American policy today it is enough to say that the American historical experience conduced us to a view of the United States as a society morally different from and superior to the rest of the world, and to a view of other nations as politically unredeemed, waiting—as Woodrow Wilson put it—to "turn to America for those moral inspirations which lie at the basis of all freedom . . . [For America's] flag is the flag not only of America, but of humanity."

This strain of messianism in American political attitudes found gratification, but also a practical check, in a foreign policy of isolationism. But when the events of the last two decades forced an American policy reversal, that messianism inevitably sought expression in the new policy. And indeed the appeal to messianism was one instrument by which the change was effected: the public was constantly told that ours was a "unique" challenge, a responsibility to create, in Secretary of State Dean Rusk's formulation, "A world free of aggression; a world which moves toward the rule of law . . . a world of better life for all mankind."

If such is the meaning and goal of American foreign policy, what compromises are plausible? And the practical obstacle to gaining this imposing objective is no mere nation or nations, but an ideology—a force which itself purports to be universal in relevance and morally inspired. The messianism of Lenin, looking beyond the borders of Russia to a world-wide class struggle, and of Mao Tse-tung, preaching the revolutionary unity of the "rural" peoples, today confronts the liberal messianism of America.

The Vietnamese intervention is hardly intelligible outside this intellectual framework which makes the political fate of a weak and remote society crucial to our own affairs. A justification may be argued in domino theories or indefensible analogies with Europe in the 1930s, or warnings that if we don't fight here we soon will have to fight (the miraculously amphibious Chinese? native revolutionaries?) in Hawaii or California. Or it may be given a *Realpolitik* but question-begging statement which limits itself to arguments of past commitment or national prestige—we are there because we are there. Yet underlying all of this is a kind of universalism: we are threatened by world Communism, able to challenge "freedom" anywhere if it is not "taught a lesson"; or by Asian Communism, potentially the vehicle of all "rural" Afro-Asian discontent; or (as Mr. Rostow now puts it) by "romantic revolutionism" derived from 1789 and about to be given a final blow in Vietnam; or by multiple factors of poverty, racism, and human discontent which manifest themselves in Vietnamese Communism at this moment but will break out in some other violence elsewhere unless they are contained here and ultimately disarmed by energetic world-wide programs of social reform and political development.

The left, often enough, is contemptuous of the former arguments but inclined to accept the last one. Much of the controversy in the United States over Vietnam is really an argument over method, not over assumptions or objectives. Liberals, after all, supported our early intervention on behalf of Ngo Dinh Diem. They backed his programs of national unification and social reform in the 1950s. The disillusionment with Diem led the Kennedy Administration—intellectually representative, surely, of contemporary liberalism—to signal his overthrow but simultaneously to enlarge our intervention and restate its objectives in exceedingly ambitious terms. That many of these same people now object to Mr. Johnson's militarization of the intervention does not change the fact that they wanted, got, and presumably still support, a vast American intervention, as such, into the affairs of Southeast Asia. They simply want it to be carried out through aid missions, political counsel, and the Peace Corps, rather than with combat troops. They want the same objectives Mr. Johnson wants, and share the same essential assumptions about America's responsibilities and role in Southeast Asia, but they want to do it all with clean hands. The government officials, the American diplomats and agents in Vietnam, the troops, who have felt themselves compelled to bloody their hands in the service of this American enterprise, may be forgiven for rewarding this kind of criticism with anger or indifference.

Contemporary interventionism—"globalism"—then is a democratic society's rejoinder to the transnational ideological challenge of communism. It flourishes on both left and right of the political spectrum because the old American sense of moral separateness and superiority disposes virtually all in this country to an interpretation of international politics as essentially a struggle of values—and to the historicism implicit in such a notion of universal struggle (a struggle which both we and the enemy assume to be to determine the character of "the next and higher stage of history"). The principal controversy is simply over the particular form which intervention should take —economic, social, educational, military?—and in fact American foreign policy in the last two decades has used all of these instrumentalities. For the CIA simultaneously to support leftist trade unionism abroad and sponsor rightist military cliques should not be surprising, for these merely are aspects of a general American effort, supported by nearly all the elements in our society, to bring about a world-wide "conversion" to the values we embrace.

I began with the remark that some measure of intervention is inevitable in the relations of nations. The problem of interventionism as we today practice it is that we have made our objective in foreign policy a fundamental moral change in the condition of men in history. We have adopted a sentimentalized reversal of our opponents' ideology, a kind of counterfeit Marxism equally committed to universal struggle for historicist goals. In practice we have proven less aware of the practical limits of intervention than the Soviets, whose original challenge in 1945–1952 drove us into this game. Their interventions in Eastern and Western Europe during the early Cold War were unsentimental, backed by plausible military threats and, in Eastern Europe, by rigid police controls. Moreover, the Soviet leadership was prepared to be entirely ruthless in cutting losses, exploiting its allies and sympathizers, and dealing expediently with the enemy; the overriding Russian national interest was never lost sight of. This much of the lesson the United States did not learn—perhaps to our credit, though not to our advantage.

The Vietnamese war should then be understood as the end-point of a policy of sentimentality and intellectual complacency, rather than as an example of neocolonialism. Vietnam is the fulfillment of a kind of vulgar liberalism which assumes that the political experience and aspirations of all men everywhere are essentially identical with our own, and that the desire for peace, democratic government, and material welfare are the dominant ambitions of men everywhere. Corollary to this belief has been the conviction that when the conduct of peoples abroad contradicts these ambitions—which are our own, and should thus produce alignment with us—it must be the result of intimidation or evil, which must be fought, or deprivation, ignorance, or misunderstanding, which can and should be removed.

In Vietnam an American preoccupation with the freedom and well-being of other men, morally inspired but sentimental in its analysis of real possibilities, has converged with an American fear of Communism which naively exaggerates the unity, power and threat of the Communist movement. A serious foreign policy of containing Soviet power, and a decent national concern for the condition of our fellow men, have over two decades been allowed to degenerate into a program that is messianic, intolerant, and intellectually unserious. The worst of America has proved stronger than the best, and the result is a war whose solution is not easily foreseen, conducted by a distracted and divided nation whose serious internal problems are ominously exacerbated by this war. The outcome of it all seems to me to include more disturbing possibilities than are ordinarily understood. And the prospect for a reform of policy, for a constructive or progressive remedy, seems to me rather bleak.

Let me deal first with what the outcome of present trends might be. The concern commonly expressed is that the war in Vietnam will grow bigger, that China or the Soviet Union might be provoked into counterintervention, and that major war or even nuclear war could result. That the war will get bigger before it can be ended seems a virtual certainty. That it will produce a nuclear confrontation with Russia seems much less likely—because of the spirit of withdrawal, of isolationism, evident among the present Soviet leadership, and because the intellectual weight of the Pentagon today is almost wholly on the side of nuclear prudence. However extravagant the American faith in military power to achieve political solutions, a vast system of intellectual and institutional inhibitions have been built up in Washington against risking direct challenge to the Soviet Union.

More plausible is an enlargement of the war which simply deepens our commitment and increases American frustration and domestic controversy, producing a further hardening of government policy at the same time that it produces a further erosion of the government's confidence and assurance. Bad policy will be reinvested in and reinforced out of the unadmitted need to vindicate the human and moral investments already made.

The outcome, then, would undoubtedly be an eventual compromise—possibly under a Republican Administration—which amounted to a disguised capitulation, not to the NLF so much as to the intractable realities of Vietnamese society. But while officially there would be neither victory nor defeat, it would be a self-defeat for the United States. The domestic reaction could, I think, be very bitter self-laceration accompanied by vengeful public controversy and a repudiation of the individuals, the party, the foreign policy advisers responsible for creating the conditions for this debacle.

I hardly think that in these circumstances public opinion would turn left. I do not think it necessarily would turn right, either, or at least toward the right now politically recognizable as such, although a hardening of American attitudes, a deepening intolerance toward the world abroad, is plausible enough. There might, as one French critic has suggested, have to be an American "Algeria" in some such place as Brazil, before interventionism can die.

But the more likely turn in American attitudes is inward. Isolationism remains very close below the surface of both left and right in this country today. The interventionism of the Republican right is simply a caricature of liberal interventionism, addicted to the language of military solutions and near-Manichean in its political simplifications. The instinct of the right remains conservative—resistant to ground wars on foreign soil, hoarding the peculiar treasure of Americanism. And the more benign interventionism of the rest, committed to a belief in the power of social and economic reform to dissolve conflict, expresses an American moral isolation—our innocence of that experience of civil devastation, betrayal, popular aggression, and mass political hysteria which has dominated the history of much of the world these last fifty years. That prosperity and popular government are inconsistent with war is, of course, sheer myth. And one source of the crisis within Vietnam is the very impact of the alien political and social forces which mass government and industrialization represent. The "development" of the new nations is a matter which proceeds through the destruction and discrediting of established systems and cultural assumptions, the dislocation of human lives and beliefs on a scale comparable only to the early industrial and nationalist revolutions in the 18th- and 19th-century West.

What I suggest, then, can happen as a result of the Vietnamese war is a profound American disillusionment, not with interventionism so much as with the possibilities of national action itself. Vietnam represents the fullest expression of the interventionist spirit; but our policies toward Europe and Latin America are also obsolete today, resisted by the most dynamic elements on both continents, and we show little interest in any policy changes except those which would reinforce the old ambitions and defend the old assumptions. A general collapse of American policy is not out of the question. The ensuing retreat could be an American popular retreat from internationalism, from liberalism as well, and a renewal of an intolerant American messianism that becomes wholly exclusivist, directed inward to national self-reassurance. There is precedent for this in other societies which have had an external mission repudiated by those whom they intended to save. For 16th-century Spain, frustration abroad resulted in an internal hypocrisy and decline which was undramatic in its progress but decisive in effect, a failure of confidence that eventually rendered Spain irrelevant to modern Europe. Nothing so dark need be predicted for the United States for the weight of the precedent to be felt.

There is another possible outcome. Interventionism could be continued and reasserted in collaboration with a Soviet Union whose own political messianism is today badly shaken. Russia clearly is in a period of political disorientation—or reorientation—today, an aftermath both of the excesses of Stalin and the failures of Stalin's successors. For a nation which defined itself as marking a new stage in man's social organization, the present condition of the Soviet Union and of its international bloc must prove deeply demoralizing—however well disguised the political truth may be by goulash and ballet. Proposals for Soviet-American collaboration to settle the war in Vietnam over the heads of the Vietnamese, to contain China, to contain nuclear proliferation and check the arms race, imply the possibility of collaboration to "contain" a good many other forces in the contemporary world whose collective effect is to reduce both Russia and the United States to the place of mere nations among nations. This, it seems to me, is a more plausible course for "convergence" between Soviet and American societies than any convergence in social democracy. But collaboration to protect one another's super-power status, however well rationalized it might be as preserving the peace or controlling arms, would amount to a neo-imperialism which genuinely deserves that epithet.

These are two outcomes which are plausible within the present course of American foreign policy. There are less bleak possibilities, the best probably being a series of half-failures of American policy—including a Vietnamese settlement on bad terms—which we refuse to acknowledge as failures. In this case the trend would be an enforced retreat from commitment but without the harsh decisions and sharp reactions of the first of the possibilities I have discussed. Yet even here the result is likely to be a creeping sense of American failure which obstructs domestic reform, a growing social stagnation.

But is this deep a pessimism warranted? In the immediate perspective I think that it is. The fact that our present foreign policy is under attack from as many different positions as it is today is a good sign. Yet beyond agreeing that we should get out of Vietnam, the New Left, the civil rights movement, the disestablished liberals, the literary left, the neo-isolationists, the academic "realists," and the late Robert Kennedy's supporters have little enough in common, and in some of these cases it is not at all clear that they understand what they should expect, or want, of a foreign policy. Yet clearly the more creative elements in American society reject what existing policy has come in practice to mean. Elements in American life which are indispensible to serious government, to a serious national political consensus, have gone into opposition, even if it is a largely incoherent opposition.

Their opposition is not, alone, enough to bring down the Johnson Administration. The public—which today clearly is highly volatile in opinion—can be expected to support the President's general position so long as no convincing alternative to present policy is stated at the level of national politics and national candidates. A dramatic failure of interventionism could bring down the Johnson Administration, but this is politics by provisional catastrophe and, moreover, the successor administration could be worse—intellectually. The way would still be open to national stagnation, self-laceration, and retreat. It is important, then, that the alternative put forward in 1968—or even in 1972—be a serious, an intellectually responsible alternative.

For too many elements in the opposition are against Mr. Johnson's Vietnamese policy yet are committed to the same assumptions of universal crisis and universal goals which underlie that policy. They are no less ambitious in what they believe can and should be accomplished by an American foreign policy. Against them are the "neo-isolationists," presumably including all of those who believe that an increas-

ingly intense and intolerant mission to the world has come
to serve for America as an evasion of domestic realities and
domestic accomplishment. But by definition this is an ill
assorted group, drawn from the left, center, and right of
national politics, and an effective alliance is not easy to
imagine. Yet if there is to be a turn away from interventionism the national political leadership will have to come
from here.

Intellectual leadership remains the immediate problem
because a new policy which does not deal with the established
reality of American power and our inevitable involvement
in the affairs of others would be fantasy; isolation is no
longer an American policy option, even for neo-isolationists.
Yet the existing community of foreign policy specialists
and professionals is precisely that group most responsible
for our present situation. The public has faithfully supported the foreign policies of the last three administrations
as it accepts Mr. Johnson's leadership today, and the foreign
policies of all these administrations have fairly faithfully
reflected the counsel of the foreign policy establishment—
in the universities, the foreign affairs institutes and policy
centers, the government departments concerned with international relations. If sentimentality, messianism, an egregious lack of realism, have increasingly marked American
conduct and resulted in the present crisis, this must ultimately be accounted the failure of an intellectual class.
And this failure is a sobering one—for our world power and
world involvement cannot be repealed.

It may be that the American historical experience all but
precludes a sustained foreign policy of limited objectives
and assumptions. That such a policy, once established in the
early Cold War years, should have been undermined and
then transformed by the enduring forces of American optimism and isolation, is a cautionary sign. Yet the effort must
be renewed.

Such a policy is intrinsically defensive. Foreign policy is
fundamentally a means by which the American nation is protected, and it is not an appropriate vehicle for the reform or
revolution of foreign societies. The objection to the latter
definition is, first of all, prudential—such is the course of

ideological politics, unlimited in ambition and expedient in method. But it is also a practical argument. The fact is that nations and societies work out their own fates, and while outside powers can help them or crush them, true national successes (like national failures) result from the character of the society itself. Our power to help others in the matters that really count, in establishing decent and representative government, practicing humane social policies, achieving "development," is not very great. It necessarily is auxiliary to their own efforts and decisions, is warped by our own preoccupations, and is distorted by the very great problems of comprehending the character and rhythms of other cultures. (The last is a matter in which the United States is notoriously weak.)

The values of American society are relevant to the world beyond America: to call for a limited foreign policy is not to discount the importance of the constitutional and social achievements of this country. It is, rather, to argue that these will not be promulgated by means of propaganda, military action, or—except minimally—by foreign aid and diplomacy. It is conventional today to warn about the limits of power, yet the warning seems hardly comprehended even by the government officials who issue it.

A new American policy could not abandon a commitment to values and to moral influence in world affairs, but it would be skeptical in its expectations and would understand that its primary obligation is to defend the international conditions which secure a civilized domestic society—for the United States, and by indirection for others. This means limiting conflicts, not enlarging them in the name of an ultimate banishment of conflict from the world. It means containing and isolating the disorders of international affairs, not inflating them and intervening in them on ideological—and ultimately historicist—arguments. It means strengthening the established institutions and conventions of international arbitration and legality, not breaking them. It means dealing with the ideological attacks of others in terms of what those states actually do and can do to harm us, rather than adding our own voice to the clamor of rhetoric and hysteria which embitters international relations.

Described as a policy of limit, this is perhaps better understood as an existential policy that deals with international
realities as they exist and with nations as they act—not as they
conform to purported historical imperatives. Thus we must
take seriously those who can hurt us or our friends—as we
have been hard and prudent toward Russia since 1945. We
would take seriously the unstable situations today which
involve the commitments of powerful states; as in Europe
where a settlement which can get Soviet troops out of Eastern
Europe, will open up further the European Communist
states to the creative political forces of contemporary Western Europe, and redefine Germany's status on terms the
Germans and their neighbors can live with. This is a problem whose growing urgency threatens to burst the obsolescent
political structure established twenty years ago.

In Asia (and Africa and Latin America) a new policy
would isolate and neutralize conflicts and the inevitable
disorders of a part of the world now going through a
profound upheaval which nonetheless—so long as the great
powers keep, or are kept, out—is of intrinsically limited
consequence. A mobilization of any major part of the bitterly
nationalist and reactive Third World under a single aggressive leadership is as much of a chimera as the Third World's
unification under liberals. Real threats from this area can
come when such states as China (or Brazil, or India)
achieve the national power Japan already possesses—if they
succeed in doing so. But unless we are prepared to try to
"solve" this problem by repression or destruction there is no
alternative to restraint, and to prudent containment or deterrence of such threats as actually emerge—when they
emerge. Tolerance and patience are banal counsels—yet time
steadily recasts the situations and ambitions of nations, and
while this may be a matter for pessimism, it is also the
ultimate argument for existential judgments. No doubt this
makes up an unsatisfying prescription for America in its
hour of world preeminence; and that is precisely our problem.

Yet history simply is not susceptible to solutions, any
more than the essential anxieties and frustrations of individual life can be "solved." The personal analogy can be pursued. The nations that count in history are those which

civilized themselves, establishing a standard of justice, and of social, intellectual, and artistic accomplishment. Here is permanent achievement, where the United States thus far has done not badly, but not so well as to earn that world leadership which our foreign policy so insistently asserts. And the discrepancy between claim and achievement has grown disquietingly large, with danger in this to others, but primarily to ourselves.

HENRY M. PACHTER

Collective Security, Interventionism, and the Left

HENRY M. PACHTER (HENRI RABASSEIRE), a co-editor of *Dissent*, teaches European history at the New School for Social Research in New York City and contributes to a number of European magazines. His books include: *Wirtschaft unterm Rutenbündel; Nazi-Deutsch; Magic into Science; Collision Course; España Crisol Politico;* and *Terms of Coexistence.*

> *A great deal of politics in America, both thought and action, consists of little more than an opposition to power—a deep reluctance to think in terms of the concept at all, and thereafter, when an element or issue of power has been identified, a strong impulse simply to consider it an evil and to "oppose" it.*
>
> DAVID BAZELON

Our thinking about collective security suffers from an inner contradiction: we wish to restrain the powers, yet to do that we have to resort to them as powers. We expect states to conduct their affairs responsibly, yet we have given them no yardstick, term of reference, or guidance as to whom or to which principle they should be responsible. We vaguely hope for some kind of community spirit to emerge among them, but whenever we have an opportunity to strengthen the institutions of collective action, we fail to enforce what little law there is in the world of nations. We do not insist on, we do not rush to support, we do not fight for wider recognition of an international order. Yet we ought to sacrifice all for the collective security of the world.

"We" means people generally identified as "the left" and, for the purpose of this essay, characterized by the common view that peace is more important than greatness, that an international order is more vital than the interest of any particular nation, and that mankind has more claim on our allegiance than race, tribe, religion, or nationality. My definition excludes those who have such particularistic allegiances and therefore are less interested in peace than in the promotion of their sectional advantage. Arbitrarily, I address those who care about peace and collective security, and it will be of little benefit to pseudo-radicals who promote "wars of liberation," national revolutionaries who have shown nothing but contempt for collective security, pseudo-pacifists who are more concerned to save their private souls than to safeguard the peace, the fascists of the left who have failed the international institutions whenever the cause of peace called for their strengthening. However, since many of these people count themselves (and are counted by others) among the left, I shall have to criticize their attitudes—a critique which seems to me the more necessary while the entire left is vulnerable to ideological terrorism.

I shall begin with an example of this susceptibility of the left to influence by sectional interests. To finance the action against Tshombe's mercenaries, the United Nations General Assembly had voted assessments. When the Russians and others refused to pay up, Ambassador Stevenson tried to rally the small states to the defense of the international police. It was his last fight for collective responsibility. One would think that the small nations must uphold the principle that members have to abide by the decision of a duly constituted majority. But, strangely enough, the majority of small states demurred; they were either cowed by threats or bribed by promises, and now the United Nations has established another principle—that no member (or at least none of the big members) need obey a resolution it does not approve. Stevenson's successor gleefully pointed out to the Assembly that henceforth the United States might not be bound by anything the United Nations might resolve collectively.

Surprisingly, the left deserted Stevenson on this vital issue. On other occasions, people on the left insist that the United Nations must be more than an exchange for political commodities and propaganda. They think of the United Nations as a judicial authority which dispenses justice, and in every international crisis they have pleaded with the powers to submit their disputes to its arbitration. This left, which is deeply committed to the dismantling of the great defense establishments, aimlessly tolerated the dismantling of the international police force, and failed to protest when willful men like Khrushchev, Nkrumah, and de Gaulle established the principle that they alone can judge their obligation to collective security. The reasons for this intellectual collapse of the left, I think, are threefold: first, there is a confusion about those to whom the left owes allegiance. This derives from their error of including among their friends those nationalist demagogues from whom my definition tries to separate the left. Second, most of the American (and international) left now are more concerned with faulting the U.S. government than with building up the United Nations; hence, in a conflict they automatically take sides with the "neutral" or "third" world. Third, few people have thought about collective security; most, in fact, assume that the term means the arrangements which have been provided to keep the other side from doing mischief, or else, exhausted by this kind of hypocritical or self-righteous reasoning, many people on the left have concluded that "collective security" is but another Cold War slogan.

It is my contention that "collective security" not only is meaningful, but vital. How shall we define it? Much of the shallowness of thought on the American left is due to its tendency to abstractly define its ideals, ideals which then are found wanting and hence are declared to be so much eyewash. In real life and even more so in politics, of course, we always find a tension between the ideal and the performance, and unless we keep our definition of terms sufficiently loose we shall never bridge the gap between theory and praxis. Ideally, collective security is an undertaking by a significant number of governments, open to all governments, mutually to guarantee the sovereignty, independence and integrity of all territories, not to initiate or join acts of unilateral war, but to support decisions to deter or to punish an aggressor. But one has only to attempt further definition, and the loopholes of such definition are seen in their gaping ugliness: What is an act of war? are we to protect every malodorous government against a change in the status quo? may aggressors participate in the vote to censure aggression? etc., etc. Moreover, how much is a guarantee of collective security worth unless all, including would-be aggressors, adhere to it? Have we not seen that in practice either there has not been anything remotely approaching our definition, or else the term has been used cynically in order to cover some international crime?

Chastened by experience, let us try to conceive collective security not in terms of an institution, such as the United Nations or the League of Nations, but in terms of policies: an attempt to assure collective security by maintaining the system of states in such a balance that it will not pay an aggressor to try upsetting it. Under the first definition, an aggression is an aggression, whether it occurs in the rice paddies of Vietnam or in the desert of Sinai. Hence the new left was consistent with its general style of thinking when it applauded the Soviet-Arab motion to condemn Israel and to order its retreat from all conquered positions. Under the second definition, the Sinai conflict of 1967 made it incumbent on the great powers to restore the equilibrium in the Near East, to prevent arbitrary changes, to keep the conflict from escalating, and above all, to refrain from getting involved themselves.

Unfortunately for the simple-minded, the maneuvering of the U.S.S.R. and the United States on that occasion disclosed a dialectical relationship between the two and between their aims and means: in order to restrain themselves they had to restrain each other, and in order to stay out of the conflict, they had to be involved plausibly enough to talk turkey to their respective clients. In other words, the merest attempt to ascertain a certain measure of imperfect security requires the display of power, and the word "power" certainly belongs in any definition of collective security; I had left it out only to make sure that the reader would not dismiss me from the outset as a "Cold Warrior." To ease such readers' minds, I hasten to mention that I am not any more "for" power than I am "for" tramways. The mere admission that something exists and must be used does not imply a moral or a value judgment.

Most leftists will admit the use of force "only defensively." But, to allude to a recent example: what is "defensive" in asserting American shipping rights in the Strait of Tiran? Yet in May 1967 some left writers asked President Johnson to secure these rights. Moreover, in the interest of collective security one must be prepared to intervene in behalf of peace, or of a rightful principle, or on the side of any victim of aggression, at the request of the community of nations and, if necessary, with all one's power. Unless all nations are prepared to use their power to intervene in behalf of peace, the purpose will not be fulfilled. But we have seen that nations do not act unselfishly; they use power not on behalf of their neighbors, but for their own purposes; in the Security Council they make deals instead of rendering judgments of right and wrong. (To cite again the example of the Near East conflict: India and Pakistan will never find any merit in Israel's brief because each of them needs the fourteen Arab votes in their quarrel over Kashmir. Whose bloody hand also was raised to condemn Israel's aggression? Franco received payment three months later, when the Arabs and their friends in the decolonization committee voted to prevent a plebiscite in Gibraltar.)

One must also admit that small nations, those which should be the most interested in preserving and enlarging the judicial character of the United Nations, are the worst offenders against its ideal spirit, having contributed most to its transformation into a logrolling brokerage. This transformation now has gone rather far, and if the United Nations ever had a will, it now has none. But the sad truth is that the United Nations never was supposed to have a will or to represent what might be called the community spirit of nations. It was able to sanction the U.S. intervention in Korea only because the Soviet delegation failed to participate in the decisive meeting where it might have cast its veto;

the Russians have always protested that the Korea resolution and the Congo operation were "illegal," and these
are the two instances which are always quoted as examples of a duly authorized intervention. On the other hand, the
United Nations failed to act in the Nigerian conflict, though
in point of law there is no difference between the secession of
Katanga from the Congo and the secession of Biafra from
Nigeria, and in both cases the danger of foreign involvement on at least one side was patent. In the Congo the
United States supported the central government by means
of a U.N. expeditionary corps; in Nigeria the U.S.S.R.
is supporting the central government without benefit of
the U.N. flag. In intermediate cases, unilateral intervention
may be covered by use of the OAU or OAS, which are
authorized by the U. N. Charter as well as by explicit Assembly votes.

There is then no formal criterion which differentiates
between authorized and unauthorized interventions. The powers intervene much as they see fit or as they suppose is
tolerable within the system of states. This last qualification
is very important as a last remnant of collective security:
under the threat of nuclear extinction the powers do not
go to war lightly. Their intervention is restricted by their
rival's ability to retaliate and to escalate; in fact, stalemate
is reached not by design or convention but by playing the
power game according to rules which both sides tacitly
observe. The nuclear threat mitigates the intervention but
also calls for constant counterintervention; otherwise there is
no mitigation.

This development poses a serious problem for the left,
particularly for its ideologists: in a happier age a radical
was able to stand by with crossed arms when the powers
were at war; he was confident that the outcome would be
the mutual destruction of the imperialists, and the New
Men would be their heirs. There will be no new men after
the first minute of the next world war, and they will have
nothing to inherit. The old attitude is a luxury we can no
longer afford. We cannot cynically wait for war and keep
our own hands clean, nor can we be satisfied with exhorta-
tions and righteous declamations while the powers are to-

bogganing into war. The ritualistic admonition to the powers: "Submit your quarrel to the U.N." serves no purpose, except to provide an excuse for having no policy. He who wishes to submit a question to the United Nations must know what kind of decision he expects the United Nations to make in this matter, and he must be prepared not only to lobby for it in the corridors but to tell them how many soldiers he is willing to put behind this resolution.

In the pre-atomic age radical policies could consist in opposing an ideal but altogether imaginary United Nations to the selfish power play of the governments, and the exercise was mainly hortatory; in the nuclear age radicals must have the courage to face the real United Nations and to deal with the power situation as it exists between nations. We cannot afford any longer the luxury of abstract policies dealing in ideal images. We cannot reject all interventions wholesale but must recognize those which may maintain the peace.

That it has come to this is altogether deplorable, nay disastrous; to admit it means to admit a severe defeat of radical policies. One must not have illusions about this medicine; it is bitter and promises no cure. In the old days one could be a pacifist because it did not matter when, i.e., after how many wars, peace would come for good. Today it does matter that there is no war now, and therefore what once was the noblest political attitude, that of complete defiance, has become an irresponsible, private satisfaction but not a solution for any community of men or of nations. To rebuild such a community one must start from scratch, and that means first to recognize for a fact that we are almost back where Hobbes left us: nations, regarding each other, are in a state of nature and keep the peace only because they fear each other. We must look for better and more solid building stones to support collective security.

As mechanisms of restraint, the diplomatic community has at its disposal a number of tools or institutions. In former times the most useful method was the conference or the so-called "concert of powers." Incidents were disposed of by a meeting of ambassadors or ministers or even monarchs, and the power that had taken too much territory was forced to retreat enough to restore the balance. This happened to Russia after the Balkan War, to Japan after her wars with China and Russia, to England and France after Suez. The United Nations also might have become something like a permanent conference, and it recognized the concept of a "concert of powers" by giving the Big Five a veto. But it was based on the assumption that the big powers were able to agree and willing to dictate to the small ones. Both conditions are not present today. Security is not collective but mutually exclusive—each in his sphere of reference—and the big powers woo the small ones by demagogic promises.

The smaller, backward, and (mostly) southern colored nations have used their numbers to obtain relief of their legitimate grievances but also to gamble with collective security beyond their own ability to control the situation which they created. Thus, while desirable change has been generally guided smoothly and peaceably by the United Nations, in a few cases the majority has crassly abused its liberty of action. Whenever the risk became too great, the big powers simply had to ignore the will of the majority, and in such cases the rule has been that the mass of small powers indeed was unable to impose its decision. As a result, we have anarchy mitigated by big-power dictation—the worse of two evils.

This raises the grave question, indeed the crucial one: how responsibly have the big powers behaved in the past and how responsibly can they be expected to act in the future? And further: who shall restrain the restrainers? who is responsible for keeping the big powers responsible? The answer to the first question obviously depends on the answer to the second. If no external or internal force controls the governments of the super-powers, there will be "arrogance of power" and intervention for intervention's sake; for power thirsts after power. Plebiscitarian dictatorships and secret organizations are more likely to follow the path of power without inhibition than governments which are at least partially controlled by public opinion and by the requirements of open accounting. But it is far from true that only dictatorships are expansionist and warlike. On the contrary: Khrushchev was able to yield in the Cuban missile crisis because he controlled public opinion and no one outside the initiated could accuse him of having betrayed patriotism. A democratic government is not only restrained by the doves but also urged on by the hawks, and it cannot easily make secret deals. On the whole, however, the manifold demands made on a democratic government are themselves a restraining factor on its foreign policy, and the opposition has the opportunity not only to disagree with a particular policy but to inhibit its execution. The U. S. Senate forbade the Johnson Administration to intervene in the Congo (with as little as the loan of three transport planes to the legitimate government), and the French Chambre made it impossible for Léon Blum in 1936 to help the Spanish Republic, for fear of committing the country to a course that might end in war with Hitler. Likewise, the isolationist senators extracted from Roosevelt neutrality laws at a time when he knew that the opposite was required. The neo-isolationists wish to prevent Johnson from undertaking any commitment which might "entangle" the United States in war or intervention on a larger scale.

This brings up a very important question: how responsible is an opposition expected to be? Does it have the right, beyond verbal disagreement and free expression of disapproval, to impede a major effort which a duly elected government with the consent of a majority of the Congress has decided to pursue? Turning the question around: when does a government have the right and an opposition the duty to declare the debate closed? This is the problem of the draft resister and pacifist but also the problem of "liberation armies." Fairness requires us to demand equal rights for doves and hawks: if the CIA or a semi-private organization such as Radio Free Europe has the power to commit the United States to intervene somewhere, whoever disagrees with this particular intervention must have the right to opt out, or perhaps must have the duty to render the government impotent to carry out its intervention. Such a situation, where the U.S. government apparently is no longer master of its own decisions, may even lead to large-scale disobedience and revolution. But apart from revolutionary situations, we must admit that the equation may be read both ways: what ought to be forbidden to the CIA or the United

Fruit Company must also be illegitimate for an individual; he may neither commit the U.S. government nor prevent it from honoring its commitments, except by persuasion. Most emphatically, this must be true in particular if the commitment is to preserve the peace by means of collective action.

We now must decide who or what makes such commitments, how they are to be justified or invalidated. It is a problem generally recognized not only by the left but by all students of modern government, that the complexities of international affairs have outstripped the safeguards of the U. S. Constitution and even the slogans of good faith. The formula "open covenants openly arrived at" means nothing in an age where foreign policy is no longer a matter of treaty obligations alone. Long before any relationship is codified the foreign offices and other agencies of government must assume commitments which engage the power of the country in ventures deemed necessary not only for its own security but for the security of the world. It is a mistake to think that only power-hungry, vicious, depraved minds or schemers under evil influence think of such commitments. The promise of aid to a small country which wishes to defend its independence, the loan of equipment to a legitimate government besieged by rebellious generals or by foreign mercenaries, the vow of assistance to any government that might be attacked by any other (the essence of collective security as embodied in the U. N. Charter and in the regional agreements authorized by it), the granting of development aid or its refusal—all these are legitimate tools of foreign policy which may be used for legitimate purposes of preserving the peace, but may also be perverted into tools of political and economic infiltration and even into pretexts for arbitrary intervention. They are the daily bread of diplomacy today. It is impossible to judge abstractly in advance which commitment may and which may not lead to complications or abuse. There is no formula which permits us to recognize the dangerous commitment in advance, and there is no such commitment which does not imply the possible use of power and indeed, to say the word, of force.

The left has long been addicted to a fascination with the word "neutral." If we cannot have collective security, so runs this argument, then let as many nations as possible be neutral. Neutral between what? Only with respect to the Soviet-American conflict! But Tito, the foremost "neutralist," has not been neutral either on the question of Kashmir, or between Israel and the Arabs, or on the repression of the Hungarian revolution; nor has India's neutrality protected her from China's aggression or prevented her from occupying territory which desires self-determination, or cautioned her against opposing the non-proliferation treaty. Nor are any of the African countries "neutral" in the affairs of their neighbors. It is a sad, though deliberately ignored, fact that usually the big powers are not pressing their services on the small ones, but factions in the underdeveloped countries call on big-power support against their rivals and invite intervention rather than abhor it. Under the cover of "neutrality" the old game of power politics is being played with a few new twists. Austria's "neutrality"—embodied in solemn treaties and in her constitution—means that the Soviet government can cruelly veto her desire to join her natural market. Finland is a poor dependency which, again under the "neutrality" provision, is not allowed to choose her own government. In Laos—whose "neutralization" usually is held up as the great act of Kennedy's statesmanship—Communist rightist and "neutralist" armies are fighting each other, not to speak of the operation of the North Vietnamese in that country. But to many people who think of themselves as "left," peace is assured by painting an area on the map gray and declaring it "neutral." This is due either to lazy thinking or to prejudgment. Besides, one is never neutral; in taking no sides, one actually is siding with the wrong side.

The idea of neutrality appeals to the imagination because it seems to imply some measure of disarmament; this conception has received further encouragement by the suggestion of Adam Rapacki, Polish foreign minister, to keep atomic weapons out of certain areas of Europe. Those who favor this plan usually don't care to admit that it presupposes the existence of those very "blocs" which it is supposed to overcome. Only if the United States remains preponderant in Western Europe and the U.S.S.R. in Eastern

Europe and they guarantee its frontiers, only then could they enforce limitations on the armaments of their respective allies. The desertion of de Gaulle from NATO has increased the atomic anarchy and I fear the day when Germany will declare her "neutrality" and start manufacturing atomic weapons. Frankly, it is incomprehensible to me that de Gaulle could ever become a hero of the left (except to those whose instinctive reaction is to be anti-American and who, therefore, will applaud any international marauder whom the State Department does not like). The old free-for-all is a poor conception of security. A more realistic approach would be to form a "third bloc" capable of mediating between the Soviet and the American camps; but so far the neutrals are neither powerful enough all together nor united enough in their purpose to be reckoned with as a meaningful "third force." Some neutrals have merely been passively neutralized, while others simply find it to their advantage to pump both sides, and a third group is ardently revisionist and aggressive. To weld them together into a larger unit, however, might have the advantage that bigness brings diplomatic responsibility. Small nations usually have one overriding national aim which they pursue with relentless lack of consideration for the rest of the world. Larger units with worldwide interests are aware of the disparateness of the problems and they usually are able to compose frontier disputes precisely because they don't exaggerate their importance. (The obvious rejoinder, the Vietnam War, has characteristics which make it the exception proving the rule.)

In light of these observations and of recent experience, we must conclude that regional and other pacts often are a better guarantee of peace than an amorphous, completely unorganized congeries of states. It is customary on the left to rejoice at the dissolution of empires and blocs. I am not sure whether the crises of the last five years have been preferable to those of the so-called Cold War. Then, as the name implies, the conflict was in a deep freeze, its external manifestations strictly controlled. Even in the Korean War and the first war at Suez, our sense of extreme danger was not as acute as in the Cuban missile crisis, the Vietnam War, and the second Suez War. The gleefulness with which some writers on the left have greeted the "end of alliances" may at least be said to be premature; while the sharpening of international crises may not be a direct consequence of the dissolution of Dulles' pacts, it certainly is untrue to say that a weakening of the alliances is tantamount to a relaxation of tensions. To avoid misunderstanding, however, I should like to add two caveats. Alliances in themselves do not ensure the tight control which is necessary for a guarantee of mutual security. This is assured only in a *system* of alliances which embodies an equilibrium, and only so long as each of the empires has its attention focused on problems or areas away from the others' spheres of influence. Second, the peace which is assured by the hegemony of an imperial power may be burdensome to its allies—the heavy hand of Athens lay on Melos, the United States presumes to tell the Caribbean republics "to elect good men," and the Germans are forbidden to unite in order to allay their neighbors' fears.

The main difficulty with "peace through empire," however, is the instability of empires. We have seen them falling apart before our eyes, and the lesson of the Cold War is precisely that one cannot keep any problem in deepfreeze over the long run. The essence of history is change; but unfortunately for the left, the same observation also applies to its nostrum, "neutrality." Just as it is not possible to keep the client states in two hostile camps, neither can one simply declare a country "neutral" and thereby close its book of history. It will not cease to have a foreign policy or to be the object of other nations' foreign policy, especially if the country has valuable resources or a strategic location. Unless the country can defend its neutrality, "neutralization" will add to the insecurity of the system of powers; but to defend its neutrality the country must join the power game. We are where we started, having described a full circle around the inescapable, ineluctable fact of power. Can we ever get away from it?

Experience has shown that power relations cannot be *wished* away; they are the essence of relations between states. Visiting lecturers and ballerinas, a model constitution and excellent race relations, decent examples in dealing with other nations, even renunciation of ideology—all these may at best *aid* a well-conceived policy, they cannot replace it. Unfortunately, most thinking on the left is centered around the idea that nice behavior not only substitutes for a concept of foreign policy, but also really *is* good foreign policy. The examples which Senator Fulbright has given in his book and in two *New York Times Magazine* articles are taken from the nursery (and they would not be more convincing if their author were not a filibusterer). Fulbright approaches foreign policy as he approaches race relations in Arkansas: if we were all to behave, he says, then there would be no need to use power either at home or abroad. Dale Carnegie, Emily Post, and Horatio Alger combined could not make as nice a Secretary of State as Senator Fulbright. He would conclude no entangling alliances and—if he were to follow the resolution he has submitted to the Senate—make no promises or commitments of money or other aid which might lead to further entanglements or be interpreted as interference in other nations' business; in fact, he could have no foreign policy and would refrain from using power as other nations do. As long-time chairman of the Foreign Affairs Committee, Senator Fulbright knows, of course, that initial small commitments are the daily bread of diplomats in the conduct of negotiations, and that to deny a Secretary of State this tool is tantamount to abolishing foreign policy altogether.

This is indeed the secret desire and the common denominator of all thinking on the left. Moreover, it carries a long and honored tradition in American life. Not only George Washington, in his famous farewell address, but before him the thousands who emigrated to this Arcadia, conceived their purpose to be to create a country where there would be no need to use power, either domestically or abroad. Government was evil and foreign policy a trumped-up justification of expansion. Only the greedy, the corrupt, the enemies of the people and of freedom could wish war and engage in overseas enterprises— a notion which touchingly united the Populists and the Progressives before World War I, which was nurtured by Senator Nye's investigation of war profits in the twenties, and which still lingered in the left wing of America first. It still is found in C. Wright Mills's *Power Elite*. Nor is it mere accident that today's neo-isolationists are from the same general region as

Borah, Nye, Wheeler, La Follette and William Jennings Bryan.

If such attitudes were heroic in 1917, they had become anachronistic by the time of the Spanish Civil War and outright foolish in the Second World War. Yet I have met even Jews whose "radicalism" forbade them to fight against Hitler while he also fought "the imperialists"! Later I shall suggest that it is necessary to remove ideology from foreign affairs, but first let us take ideology out of anti-war attitudes. The most doctrinaire of all ideologies is the American notion that power is necessarily evil and always leads to "arrogance." Ironically, the same might be said of pacifism—has not Lord Russell been compelled, by the inexorable logic of his pacifism, eventually to "lean to one side," as the Chinese say? This should not surprise radicals; they have always maintained that necessary change will not come by itself but must be gained in bitter fight, by class war, race rebellion, independence struggle, etc. From a radical point of view, the fashionable pseudo-science of "conflict resolution" is at best a pious illusion and at worst a bourgeois fraud. This same radical left also inclines toward existentialist thinking, which, at its best, stresses the need for commitment. But strangely enough, the moment they are required to shift their attention from domestic and personal to international affairs, these same radicals expect a society of angels, or at least they measure the activities of their own government by a yardstick of saintliness which applies to no one else.

This rejection of the use of power or the abhorrence of its very notion, so typical of American radicalism, may be due to the angle of vision under which foreign policy appears to the public. One usually does not see the business end of foreign policy, the daily dealings; one only sees the results, which usually are ugly, when they can be seen. The newspapers don't report the useful and successful applications of power, for it is in the nature of such successes that they are not "events" and cannot be dramatized in a picture or a story. Those who are enamored of power think of it in terms of silvery aircraft streaming over foreign skies or mighty battleships plowing the oceans; those who are afraid of power see it in photos of people being killed and maimed. Neither group sees it as the daily relationship of states, and radicals in particular refuse to see it as an interplay of pressures, economic, social, military and cultural, in the context of power. Just as the most expert public relations counsel cannot improve the image of a corporation unless its products are acceptable, so foreign policy cannot be conducted as a public relations job without reference to the power behind the image.

To say that foreign policy should be conducted without reference to power amounts to saying that foreign policy cannot be conducted decently at all and that the system of states should be abolished—a time-honored revolutionary position. From such a point of view the criticism of foreign policy is not advanced with a view to improving it, but in order to show up its futility, to expose, subvert, and overthrow the existing order. From this point of view it also makes sense to deny the government all means of conducting its foreign policy, to denounce all alliances and other arrangements, to brand as "interventionism" all uses of influence for whatever purpose.

Disregarding the partisans of the Viet Cong who are not really pacifists, and placing the best possible interpretation on the attitude of genuine pacifists, the protest against power politics should be seen as the human outcry against an inhuman system; precisely by opposing to the state the morality of the individual, the protester seeks to say that this society cannot behave decently and to assert his right to resign from it. Precisely by formulating his demand in this utopian way, the pacifist explodes the benevolent, hypocritical slogans and ideologies.

While he is doing all this, and salvaging the cleanliness of his hands and shirt too, the pacifist does not answer the one question we have been asking: how to assure peace in a world of power. He expresses his innocence of spirit; he recoils from becoming involved and implicated. But he leaves the game of power in the hands of those who enjoy it and are sure to abuse its potentialities. By opting out he does not act as an opposition should, i.e., to show alternative policies. For obviously, such policies would have to be spelled out in terms of legitimate uses of power, and at least emotionally, though not always in theoretical awareness, American radicals deny that power can be used legitimately. It is a bad Hegelian term. The attitude which rejects power altogether is justified where the system can be abolished by revolution alone (as in August Bebel's slogan: Not a cent and not a man for this system); but normally the alternative policies of an opposition do not call for the complete abandonment of every project. Here, as in so many other things, the Vietnam War is exceptional: the alternative to escalation may be total abandonment of the project, and by adopting a strictly pacifist, absolutely anti-interventionist attitude, the opposition may indeed have forced the Administration to see the solution in these terms of either-or.

But as in so many other respects, the Vietnamese War has confused the issue of intervention, too. On the one hand, it has produced the bizarre partisans of a Viet Cong victory; on the other, it has created the optical illusion that doctrinaire opposition to all interventions is the only honorable and politically realistic course. There are a number of good and poor reasons why a man might think that this particular war is bad business or morally wrong, but might reserve judgment on other seemingly similar situations, such as the Korean War or the Laos pact (after all, Kennedy's much admired "neutralization" of the country was achieved by sending a division of paratroopers to Thailand). An opposition should be the government's conscience; but it need not negate in order to negate only. It may oppose any particular intervention, but it should know which kind of intervention it will criticize and which it will condone. An opposition may have to speak its conscience in quite a different setting—let us remember the Spanish Civil War—where it must criticize not the government's lust for war and arrogance of power, but its indolence, its mood of appeasement. We now know that World War I might not have occurred if England had let the Kaiser know, in good time, that it would be in it; that the German generals were ready to depose Hitler if the Western powers had opposed his occupation of the Rhineland; that even on the day of Munich it still was possible to avert the Second World War. But in those days Chamberlain was able to taunt Labor: you cannot ask me to contain Hitler and refuse to vote for the defense budget.

The case of Hitler is extreme, and many who oppose intervention in general may make an exception in this case; and they may hasten to add: but Ho Chi Minh, or even Nasser, is not Hitler! Correct, I do not intend to compare any living leader to Hitler, and I am going to argue that it does not matter what kind of a man goes to war and what philosophy he professes. I am writing precisely against *all* ideological wars, anti-Communist, anti-fascist and anti-anything. I agree that even at the time of Munich the correct argument for defense measures against Hitler was not that he was a Nazi or that he was going to kill 6 million Jews (he had not yet started); the correct argument was then, as it is now, that the Munich surrender would not appease him or end his demands, that eventually there would be a domino which refused to fall and war would more probably come by appeasement by containment. Though some might debate this point, containment has worked in the Stalin and Khrushchev era—worked not in the sense of containing Communism but in the sense of halting the expansionist drive of a great military power, thereby avoiding general war. To repeat: no physical, intellectual, or political resemblance between Hitler and Stalin is implied; I am comparing not two political systems but two political situations. (I was as happy when I learned in school that Themistocles had stopped the Persians at Salamis.) Finally, to show that ideology and political system are quite irrelevant to my argument, I remind those friends who were for the capitulation of Munich that at the time their reasoning was exactly, word for word, the reasoning that now appears in Senator Fulbright's book; that the domino theory is ridiculous; that a democracy cannot defend itself by imitating the methods of its enemies; that we are in danger of becoming totalitarian ourselves; that we must have faith in the democratic sense of the peoples.

Yet, as I have remarked, the pacifist-isolationist tradition is not the only tradition of the left. There also is the Jacobin tradition of the good war, in particular the revolutionary war. This tradition is much more alive in Europe than in the United States; it goes back to the Catholic doctrine of the "just war" and the "legitimate revolution." But the conditions which St. Augustine, St. Thomas, Father Suárez, S.J., and (later) the unknown author of *Franco-Gallia* and Baruch Spinoza laid down cannot give us any guidance today. They are all based on three assumptions: that a duly constituted political body has exhausted all peaceful means of getting redress of grievances; that the cause for taking up arms is a clearly recognized injustice; and that the aggrieved party can take up arms. As the case of Israel in the recent Sinai conflict has shown, the U.N. procedure is likely to put the aggrieved party in the wrong or the majority may procrastinate until the aggressor has assembled all his forces for a surprise attack. As to the second assumption, justice and injustice no longer are recognized as absolutes, but what appears to be just to one party is injustice to the other, and once we open this floodgate, we are sure to encounter the ideologies which may justify any war. I shall come back to the subject of ideological wars in a moment; but first I have to comment upon the saints' third assumption: when we are speaking of collective security, we may occasionally have to contemplate intervention in a conflict where one side already has taken up arms on its own behalf. But normally we mean situations where the international community or some states feel a responsibility to intervene before the aggrieved party resorts to self-help. Collective security means precisely this: that we must intervene on behalf of others.

Since clearly this can be done only in the name of some ideology, this brings us back to the question of ideological wars. It may be possible to distinguish in time of peace between (a) the sober reasons of collective security which persuade a coalition of governments to arrange a common defense, and (b) the propaganda which persuades their peoples that this is a good and just cause. When actual fighting does break out, however, one cannot avoid identifying his cause with a great idea; for it is humanly impossible to fight unless one sees the conflict as one between light and darkness. But the policy-makers' job is precisely to avoid this contingency; they must know that white and black are pretty evenly distributed among them, and they must shun ideological wars, and even commitments for the sole sake of supporting their religion, philosophy, or system abroad. Crusades may be a good thing, but we have had enough of them and we can't afford any more. I would agree with those who said that even a Hitler does not justify a crusade, and if I were to think of the closest approximation to Hitler, I am reluctant to follow the U.N. majority in demanding a war against the South African and Rhodesian governments. It may be frustrating that we have to wait for a provocation which clearly marks these governments as a danger to peace; but until an insurgent government can be recognized, there are many things a private citizen can do for Africans which the U. S. Government cannot do and which the opposition cannot ask it to do.

The only ideology one can possibly invoke—and which has always been invoked by thinkers who have studied the question—is security itself. The powers must intervene to stop intervention. Unfortunately, here again modern technology creates a difficulty. It is no longer possible to wait until aggression has occurred and is a *fait accompli*. Counterintervention begins with a judicious arms policy, with commitments to small countries, with alliances and guarantees. Readiness to use military force is only the threat of last resort, a deterrent; but it must be credible and therefore cannot be forsworn. A second difficulty derives directly from the first. It may not always be possible to persuade a majority of the United Nations, in good time, that the danger of aggression exists or that their long-range interest is in stopping it rather than in going along with it (as Poland's jackals took a piece of Czechoslovakia at Munich). The conclusion which may have to be drawn in such a situation may not go down well with some readers, but I think it inescapable: those governments which feel a responsibility for collective security must act so as to enunciate norms or to anticipate situations in which intervention may be permissible, but it would be wrong to exclude in advance any such necessity. The contingency is calamitous and therefore it may be doubly important to watch out for self-serving deceptions which may seem to justify arbitrary interventions. One source of such deceptions is ideologies, and the more we succeed in banning ideology from foreign policy, the safer we may be from unjust wars. This means, brutally speaking, that we must trust power to be self-regulating within a given system of powers. History offers enough examples to assure us that this is not utopian, but assurance is no certainty, and there is no absolute security under such a system. The system is fluid and the delineation of borderlines is futile. Nevertheless, if one rule may be suggested as more generally applicable than most others, it is the one embodied in the constitution of the Security Council: that the big powers have a joint responsibility to maintain the equilibrium. Coexistence here becomes antagonistic co-operation, where the powers compete with each other within a framework of well-understood controls and limitations, and may tacitly co-operate in keeping some Cold War burning low.

Our criterion for commitment and intervention is not the justice of the cause or the morality of the execution. The criterion of legitimate intervention is whether it serves to stabilize the peace or increases the likelihood of war. It seems to me that no effective argument can be made against continued intervention in Vietnam as long as one confines oneself to the question whether the war is moral or justified or anti-Communist or based on the domino theory. The strongest argument, it seems to me, is that this war is getting out of hand and no longer can be confined to the local conflict situation. The war could be justified for some time on the ground that it was marginal and prevented other dominos from falling, or that it was intended to lead toward a negotiated peace. But it no longer does either of these things. On the contrary, the war moves further from negotiations and, at the time of writing, offers no prospect of being closer to an end at the time of publication.

By contrast, Kennedy's intervention in Laos and Thailand, which stood on no better moral ground than the Vietnam War, did lead to a stabilization of the peace, though not to a liquidation of local wars in the area. Despite the unfortunate state of affairs in these countries, it was justified *ex post facto* by its apparent, though perhaps temporary, success. It is possible to name a considerable number of interventions, on the part of the United States as well as of other countries, which must be considered sound from the viewpoint of maintaining security. These have all been unilateral or bilateral, without the sanction of a moral or judicial authority. This is regrettable, most of all because it introduces an element of uncertainty and arbitrariness, or, as Senator Fulbright says, "arrogance," into the conduct of foreign affairs. It is precisely here that the opposition must fulfill its function. It may warn of overcommitment or complain of undercommitment. In the recent Near East crisis at least some members of the American left felt that the Arab provocations which led to war might have been avoided if the United States had quickly committed itself to the defense of maritime rights. This is only one example of a genuinely pacifist opposition, even while it advocates caution in one area, advocating boldness in another.

The greatest mistake which the American left could make in the wake of the unfortunate Vietnam situation would be a relapse into nineteenth-century isolationism. The resolutions which Senator Fulbright has presented to the Senate are an outgrowth of the fear of overcommitment. They show awareness of the fact that small initial investments might lead to large-scale rescue operations, but they show no remembrance of the fact that no Secretary of State can conduct foreign policy without daily making small commitments. To forgo the ability to commit this nation to the defense of collective interests means to lose the flexibility which any great power needs in handling foreign affairs as well as domestic problems. To renounce the use of power and to fear "interventionism" means to abandon the search for peace. Even if the United Nations were a better-functioning organism than it now is, the United States would not be released from its duty as a great power to design a policy for itself and to argue its point of view.

PHILIP   GREEN

Necessity and Choice in American Foreign Policy

PHILIP GREEN is assistant professor of government at Smith College. He is the author of *Deadly Logic: The Theory of Nuclear Deterrence* and, forthcoming, *The Political Imagination in Literature* (with Michael Walzer). He is a contributor to *World Politics, Bulletin of the Atomic Scientists, Dissent, The New Republic,* and *Commentary.*

. . . [A] great power does not have the range of freedom of action—derived from the freedom of in-action—that a small power possesses. It is entangled in a web of responsibilities from which there is no hope of escape; and its policy-makers are doomed to a strenuous and unquiet life, with no prospect of ultimate resolution, no hope for unproblematic exist-ence, no promise of final contentment.

. . . [T]here is no way the United States, as the world's mightiest power, can avoid . . . an imperial role . . .

Though there is much fancy rhetoric, pro and con, about "the purpose of American foreign policy," there is really nothing esoteric about this purpose. The United States wishes to establish and sustain a world order that (a) ensures its national security as against the other great powers, (b) encourages other nations, especially the smaller ones, to mold their own social, political and economic institutions along lines that are at least not repugnant to (if not actu-ally congruent with) American values, and (c) mini-mizes the possibility of naked, armed conflict. This is, of course, also the purpose of the foreign policies

*of such other great powers as Soviet Russia and Mao-
ist China. Nor could it be otherwise . . .*

*The experience of World War II, the revolution
in military technology symbolized by the heavy
bomber of that war and then by the atomic bomb,
drove home the unmistakable fact that the security
and well-being of the United States, even its very
survival as a free nation, was dependent upon the
utilization and application of its power to shape the
international environment in a manner compatible
with American interests and security . . . It is not
surprising that the United States—thrust into the role
of great power and world leader in a time of historic
change—has had to feel its way, to experiment, and
to improvise.*

*Policy-making has consisted in a progression of
reactions to major crises. Having failed to define, to
anticipate, and to deal with forces loose in the world,
having tried merely to keep the great machine of
government ticking over from day to day in the face
of issues even operators could not ignore, at last the
problems either never recognized or swept under the
rug came ticking in over the incoming cables. Then,
at last, the reality of the matter was recognized, but
at a time when the options were narrowed.*

*The responsibility that rests upon the United States
to lead, inspire, and aid free men and free nations to
draw ever closer together, and together to build ever
stronger the conditions of freedom, is heavier than
any that has ever rested upon any nation. It is also
the greatest challenge and opportunity ever offered
to any nation to save its own life and its own soul.*[1]

[1] The first quotation is from Irving Kristol, "American Intellectuals
and Foreign Policy," *Foreign Affairs*, XLV (July 1967), pp. 602, 605,
609. The next two quotations will be found in Andrew M. Scott and
Raymond H. Dawson, eds., *Readings in the Making of American For-*

Taken together, the above quotations, all from sources noted for their responsible and authoritative treatment of American foreign policy, represent a perspective on that subject which is intellectually dominant in America today. That perspective consists primarily of a theory of choice which we may call the theory of "challenge and response" (the title of several well-known discussions of American foreign policy, including a famous statement by John Foster Dulles); it implies, additionally, a motivational theory which is usually known as the idea of "national interest," or, more often nowadays, "national security."

According to this widely accepted view, our foreign policy is made as follows. Someone, or some sequence of events, "challenges" us: threatens our interests or other interests that may ultimately impinge on ours, such as those of the "free world" community, or even of "world peace." Having been so "challenged," we "respond": we *react* to the threat by taking countermeasures, or issuing a counterthreat. If our reactions are farsighted, planned (to take account of potential counterresponses and future challenges),[2] and appropriate, then we will have a successful foreign policy; if they are shortsighted, haphazard and inappropriate, our policy-making processes (or personnel) need improvement. If, further, other nations would only stop challenging us, or provoking us, or attacking our interests, then and only then could we lead the relatively peaceful existence our forefathers planned for us when we were not yet an "imperial power." Of course the theory would apply as well to small powers; the difference is that they are not *continually* challenged, as is an "imperial

---

eign Policy (Macmillan, 1967), pp. 17 and 315; they are by Walt W. Rostow and Paul Nitze, respectively. The last quotation is from Joseph Marion Jones, *The Fifteen Weeks* (Viking, 1955), p. 266.

[2] Even Rostow, who in the third quotation seems to be *complaining* about the treatment of foreign policy as a series of responses to challenges, actually treats the United States as a reactive agency in the world, one *forced* to deal with problems; he simply wants our reactions to be farsighted and anticipatory.

power" with "responsibilities" for maintaining world order. As it is, our position of world dominance is one which we have not chosen voluntarily but have been forced into by the necessity to defend our interests, which by a fortunate coincidence happen to be the interests of "free men and free nations" everywhere. Reluctantly—even, as an important member of the foreign policy establishment has recently put it, "agonizingly," we but do what we must.[3]

In general, this picture of Uncle Sam calls to mind no one so much as Hamlet, the reluctant dragon-killer. If, like Hamlet, we at times provoke carnage by our actions, only our hesitation in making the hard decision to use power, or our inability to use it properly, have been to blame. The necessity for that use—for a kind of worldwide American guardianship —and the misguided wishful thinking of those who decry it, are equally beyond question. John Donne is often invoked to make this point.

These comments are admittedly oversimple, especially as applied to commentators who, after all, are of widely varying opinions about specific policy choices. Still, it is a commonplace observation that people who are divided by profound disagreements may also be united on other points by equally fundamental agreements. What is important about the challenge-and-response, national interest approach is that at least two of the assumptions on which it is based, and which *are* shared by most of our influential theorists, go to the heart of any foreign policy discussion: and they are decisively misleading assumptions.

The first of these assumptions is that national decision-makers act always in "good faith": the motives they offer publicly for their decisions are in fact their real motives. The second assumption is that what they define as "the national interest" or "national security" really deserve those names in the eyes of reasonable men. That is to say, our leaders may be slow, they may be thickheaded, they may lack important talents, but they are genuinely trying to do what they must. The conclusion that obviously follows from all this has been often spelled out: "responsible critics" may question the judgment

[3] Roger Hilsman, *To Move a Nation* (Doubleday, 1967), ch. 32.

or wisdom, but never the motives or goals, of our decision-makers.[4] This conclusion, shared by both apologists and critics within the mainstream of American politics, is clearly hostile not only to muckraking, but to any radical political critique of leaders or policies. It badly needs rebuttal.[5]

It is indeed possible to argue that all choice consists of necessary responses—molded by environment, expectations, institutions, etc.—to challenges, just as the behaviorist argues that all choice consists of responses to stimuli. Carried to its logical conclusion in the field of international politics, this theory depicts a situation in which nation A responds to nation B's challenge to its interests, which challenge itself has been necessitated as a response to some other nation's challenge—perhaps one posed by nation A. Immediately we see that we are dealing with a determinist approach to history; with history seen as a continuous unfolding of causation in which one can never pin down the beginning or end of a particular cause-and-effect sequence. As a theory of decision-making, such a determinist view must lead to our seeing tragedy, or at least fatality, everywhere. We are all trapped in a web of circumstance; neither moral judgment nor therapeutic criticism is possible: only merciful understanding and, sadly, necessary action.

For obvious reasons, few theorists have been Olympian enough consistently to see international conflict in this light: why study a subject if one is completely detached from judgments about it? (In fact, many of those who refer glibly to "tragic" choices turn out to mean only *our* choices. Somehow Hitler, Mao, Stalin, Franco, and Batista rarely earn considera-

[4] Kristol's article cited above is a gold mine of insults and veiled invective directed at critical intellectuals. On responsible and irresponsible criticism, see Noam Chomsky, "The Responsibility of Intellectuals," *The New York Review of Books,* February 23, 1967, pp. 16–26.

[5] Under the impact of the Vietnam War and similar recent incidents in American foreign policy, some of those anonymously—but recognizably—identified here as exponents of the view I am attacking can no longer really be counted among its exponents, having moved from restrained to radical criticism: my apologies to them.

tion as victims in a historical tragedy: they really make history, and always for the worse.)[6] Most academic commentators, rather, attempt to use the challenge-and-response approach as an explanation of certain events only—usually the most important ones. This modification, however, still does not go far enough. For though all policy-making is in a sense reactive, the reaction is always, at least in part, not to the deeds of *others*, but to one's own world view. Except in instances where gross physical survival against conquest or destruction is at stake (and perhaps not always even then), the "national interest" or "national security" makes no *particular* demands; it does not exist "out there," it exists in us. What must be understood, therefore, is not merely the web of history in which we have been wrapped, but also the web of ideology in which we have wrapped ourselves.

Thus Khrushchev, for example, posed a challenge to Kennedy by establishing a missile base in Cuba. But on the one hand, this was in large measure true because of previous actions which Kennedy (and Eisenhower) had taken out of their own definition of the Cuban situation, and perhaps of the arms race itself.[7] And on the other hand, Kennedy posed an even greater challenge to himself by interpreting that act as a

[6] Kristol is an apparent exception to these parenthetical remarks. I do not, however, recall ever having seen from his pen sympathetic treatments of Stalin, Khrushchev, Mao, or Hitler as policy-makers "doomed to a strenuous and unquiet life." The same holds true for Roger Hilsman, I think.

An example of this kind of "tragic" view, from a respectable academic source, is the statement and additional remarks by Sidney Hook, in "Western Values and Total War: A Round-Table Discussion," *Commentary*, XXXII (October 1961).

[7] Christopher Lasch has written of an earlier "crisis": "When Wilson threatened reprisals after the sinking of the *Sussex* (May, 1916), and thereby forced the German government to give up its submarine attacks on Allied shipping, he appeared to have scored a diplomatic triumph; but by committing the country to war if the attacks were renewed, he had in truth handed over to Germany the decision for war or peace—a decision that a more realistic statesmanship would have reserved to itself. As so often happened, the 'tough-minded' liberals had mistaken the rhetoric of realism for its substance" (Christopher Lasch, *The New Radicalism in America 1889–1963*, Knopf, 1965, p. 213).

decisive threat which must instantly be countered to protect
"the national security"—as though Soviet security had not survived exactly such a threat for fifteen years. To understand
what Kennedy did, then, is to understand not merely the objective situation of tension and change we were in, but also
the *subjective* situation of danger we perceived ourselves to be
in. Always among the possible ways of understanding our own
perceptions, surely, are the two which the accepted viewpoint
rules out of court: 1) that our leaders have hidden motives
not genuinely represented by their expressed statements;[8] 2)
that their definition of the "national interest" or "national security" is in some way, as it has consistently been in the Cuban
case, unreasonable. (On the reasonableness of the Cold War
in general, see below.)

With regard to this notion, that the very definition of national "interest" and "security" may be unreasonable, an analogy may be of help. Recently some philosophers and anthropologists interested in reviving naturalist ethics have argued
that though differing ethical precepts are operative in different cultures, *all* cultures engage in essentially the same kind of
utilitarian ethical—or metaethical—reasoning. For example, we
are asked to consider the Aztecs, who engaged in human sacrifice, as metaethical utilitarians. They believed, goes the argument, that the cosmos was ruled by an angry god who
demanded human hearts as the price of withholding his vengeance; and in paying that price they were actually doing their
best to assure, in our terms, the general good. But though
superficially reasonable, this argument is in the end defective.
For what the naturalists have neglected to do is to ask themselves two necessary questions: what kind of people could
possibly have conceived of a cosmos ruled by such a bloody-
minded god? Is it helpful to think of them as ethically reasoning people, as engaging *on any level* in the same kind of ethical enterprise as, say, the Quakers?

The implication of the above questions, of course, is that
the ability and willingness to engage in mere instrumental reasoning is not as important a fact about people as the reason-

[8] See footnote 20 below.

ableness of their goals and perceptions. That view of the Aztecs, in other words, lacks a *psychological* dimension; and so
does the view which accepts "the national interest" or "national security" as a kind of metapolitical standard to which
all statesmen ordinarily repair. National *interests* as opposed
to parochial interests may be easy to define; but what *the* national interest is or requires is a matter for argument; and when
we decide, we have made in part a willful and subjective
choice which reveals the kind of persons we are. Such choices,
further, far from being necessarily "agonizing," may often be
made out of misplaced zest, bravado, egoism, *hubris,* political
malice, or the other defects of character and social position
that decision-makers possess just as much as natural men. On
the whole we should restrain rather than encourage our feel-
ings of sympathy for such persons. If, though educated, intelligent, powerful—capable, in other words, of acting with reason
—they still act badly, then their deeds should be judged in such
a light. Any other standpoint, indeed, is intellectually and morally false.

Rather than being irresponsible, then, a critical view that is
skeptical about the motives of policy-makers and their claims
to act from necessity and compulsion is absolutely essential.
Otherwise we may become unending and unwitting victims of
the way they arbitrarily and unreasonably define the requirements of national interest and security. In the remainder of
this essay, therefore, I shall sketch an alternative approach to
the understanding of foreign policy-making: an approach
which makes possible a radical critique of policy.

What the "real" motives "behind" a foreign policy are
must remain ambiguous, obscure to all but psychoanalytic interpretations in depth—and perhaps even to those. However, it
is usually realistic—at least in politics—to believe that motives
reveal themselves in expressed attitudes; and the latter are ob-
servable. To understand foreign policy decisions, then, we need
to understand the attitudes of those who make them, and those
who set the context within which they are made. By and large,
this means that we must understand elites—those who hold
formal decision-making posts, key positions in the mass com-

munications media and the educational system, and other positions of public prestige, influence, and power.[9]

My basic assumption is that we may understand the relevant attitudes of policy-makers and influential elites in, among others, the three dimensions diagrammed below. These are meant to reveal, respectively, attitudes about the nature of one's responsibility in and to the world community; dispositions toward other nations when they interact with one's own; and modes of identifying one's own interests as opposed to the interests of others.

1)   ATTITUDES

	Non-interventionist	Interventionist
Nationalist (unilateralism)		
Supranationalist (multilateralism)		

2)   DISPOSITIONS

	Defensiveness	Aggressiveness
Egoism		
Altruism		

3)   SOURCES OF INTEREST IDENTIFICATION

Personal	Group or Party	National	Supranational

The above diagrams do not, of course, give an exhaustive account of the types of attitudes that can be relevant in foreign policy; nor would the terms used be necessarily relevant

[9] Examples of elite studies are Robert C. Angell, Vera S. Dunham, and J. David Singer, "Social Values and Foreign Policy Attitudes of Soviet and American Elites," *Journal of Conflict Resolution,* VIII (December 1964); Karl Deutsch et al., *France, Germany, and the Western Alliance: a study of elite attitudes on European integration and world politics* (Scribner, 1967); and Harold D. Lasswell, Daniel Lerner, and C. E. Rothwell, *The Comparative Study of Elites* (Stanford, 1952).

in describing such policy in all places and at all times. Rather, I have deliberately chosen those terms, and depicted those attitudes, which are the common coin of current arguments about American foreign policy. Keeping this in mind, we are able to cast some light on several of those arguments.

The most noteworthy point that emerges from such a typology, I think, is the falsity inherent in the use of "isolationism," and especially "neo-isolationism," as a term of abuse in American political discourse: a usage accepted and indulged in by even the soberest and most tolerant foreign policy experts.

On diagram 1) above, the intersection between "nationalist" and "non-interventionist" clearly locates what was meant by "isolationist" in 1940.[10] Undoubtedly there were ideologues of that persuasion, above and beyond those persons who were simply masking their ethnic (or other) pro-Germanism, etc. But even then there was another strain in the isolationist position; and it is the strain which is today predominant in the so-called "neo-isolationist" camp. The hallmark of the position to which I refer is the absence in it of *nationalist* thinking, its emphasis on *multilateralism,* and in some cases on *supra*nationalist ethical principles which, it is held, should be the determinative factor in one's assessment of proposed foreign policies. Especially among those who have been led by the disasters of our Caribbean and Asian policies to offer a concerted defense of non-interventionism,[11] a primary consideration is the association of interventionism with aggressive American nationalism. Thus Senators Morse and Fulbright attack the foreign aid program, but because of its connotations and the impulse behind it, not because of an unwillingness to spend money on "foreigners." Indeed, one can hazard that Senator Fulbright at least would support a much *greater* foreign aid program than the currently programmed one—if that program were

[10] This and all succeeding remarks attributing dispositions and attitudes to specific persons should be read in terms of "more or less," rather than as absolute identifications. It is impossible to indicate degrees of gradation in a two by two matrix; that is the only reason they are missing.

[11] See the remarks of John Schrecker and Michael Walzer, "American Intervention and the Cold War," in Irving Howe, ed., *The Radical Papers* (Doubleday, 1966).

multilateral. And even those who (like Kennan and Galbraith) occasionally adopt a "put our own house in order first" approach to the world have done so out of a perception that our ideologically aggressive behavior abroad springs from our aggressive and outdated individualism at home.

Thus the abusive treatment of "neo-isolationists"—a party which encompasses many, such as Senators Clark, McGovern and Church, who would once have been recognized as genuine liberal internationalists—cannot honestly be justified by appealing to one's own superior appreciation of how "small" the world has become, etc. Rather, abuse is nowadays more often justified through the specious notion of necessity, which in this context gives color to the accusation that critics have not offered a practical alternative to the official policy.[12] Indeed, since the official policy is "necessary," *no* real alternative to it could be "practical." Kristol's comment that the United States—"nor could it be otherwise" —desires to establish a world order that "encourages other nations . . . to mold their own . . . institutions along lines that are at least not repugnant to . . . American values" is a perfect example of this kind of intellectual bullying. A perfect example, especially, in that as soon as one asks "Why?" the proposition collapses in its own emptiness. There simply is no logical connection between being a great power and wanting other nations to share one's own values: the sense of necessity, as almost always, is spurious. The greatness of "great nations," in fact, might as reasonably be said to consist in being properly detached from a domineering concern with how other peoples live.

Worse yet in this kind of thinking, perhaps, is the casual assumption that there is a single version of American (or Russian, Chinese, German) values—an assumption which

[12] Certain theorists of "the national interest"—but *not* those who believe in America's international mission—sometimes claim that belief in one's own nation as the ground of all ethical commitments is "natural" and therefore the only "practical" attitude in international politics; supranationalism is said to be utopian. However, this reasoning is based on a fallacy in ethical logic that goes back to Aristotle's criticism of Plato: the notion that "mine" and "thine" are mutually exclusive terms. On the contrary, "my" interest can be *your* well-being, or that of the community as a whole.

seems inherent in the very concept of "national interest."
(How else speak of interest in the singular, and of "national"
rather than class or ethnic interest?) On this assumption
apologists can criticize such groups as neo-isolationists not
only for being opposed to the "necessary," but for being
out of touch with that *Zeitgeist* or consensus which must
undergird all national action. Contrary to the spirit of
that assumption, in all societies there are *conflicting* definitions of value. Which of these dominates is a matter not
merely of "consensus" but also, in part—depending on which
nation we speak about—of the distribution of power. Invoca-
tions of "national interest" are therefore invariably also defenses of or attacks on (less frequently) the existing power
arrangements, and as such are political acts as well as intellectual statements. As soon as one troubles to inspect the actual
content of foreign policy positions such as (military) non-
interventionism,[13] rather than rest content with tendentious
accounts of them based on the challenge and response approach, one sees this quite clearly. The real "necessity"
behind most policies is simply that someone's power and
prestige depends on their continuance; and a hidden but
real objection to dissenting viewpoints is that they question
that power and prestige.

The rejection of neo-isolationist non-interventionism as a
foreign policy, then, can be upheld by appeal neither to
historical necessity nor to national values. That is not to say,
of course, that such a rejection must be groundless. There
is a case for the official stance of American foreign policy,
and that case should be looked at in its own right.

In state documents and often even in the academic literature, including the specimens quoted earlier, American
foreign policy, though clearly and self-proclaimedly interventionist, is presented to the public and the world as defensive, internationalist whenever that is at all possible, and
essentially altruistic. There is, of course, a gross discrepancy between this description of American policy and a

---

[13] A great deal of unnecessary debate about the supposed unrealism
of the non-interventionist position could be avoided if that phrase were
always prefaced by the word "military." Wherever it appears in this
essay, that phrase should be so understood.

critical description of it. In part this discrepancy is due to the sometimes incredible self-righteousness of certain American statesmen and politicians (a self-righteousness reflected in at least two of the above quotations). However, to say that is not to say enough. Self-righteousness only flowers where there is fertile soil for it; that is, where the attribution of virtue to oneself is at least plausible. In the case of America's relationship to the rest of the world—to the ideas of collective security and international cooperation—that attribution is literally plausible: believable, but only at first glance.

The ideas of imperialism, be they those of Roman peace, Christian salvation, English civilization, or Communist classlessness, are always couched so as to brook no contradiction; to be the *sine qua non* of all expressions of human well-being; the order to end, finally, all disorder; the conquest to end all conquests: that, after all, is what makes them truly imperial. In all this, the American urge to save the world for freedom and democracy—"to build ever stronger the conditions of freedom"—is no exception. At the same time, however, all imperial ideas must pass the empirical test of events if they are to remain credible. If, a reasonable length of time having passed, they do not accomplish what has been promised, anyone who doubts the self-evident rightness of their mission must begin to see them as self-serving and exploitative. For the ancient (not recent) notion of American beneficence to have survived so many wounds that should have been fatal—the Mexican War, the Indian wars, the Spanish-American War, the nature of the armed intervention in World War I, the Siberian intervention, a pathological Far Eastern policy throughout this century, the attempt to dominate Latin America from the Monroe Doctrine to the Bay of Pigs and the Dominican affair, etc.—testifies to the strength of our missionary idea: but also to a certain gullibility on the part of those who continue to believe in it.

To be sure, the overt motive of American interventionism and expansionism is, like the overt motive of Aztec sacrifice, "good," or altruistic; and also "necessary," given, so the argument goes, our great power to do good or ill even when we abstain from doing anything. But if one inspects American policy not merely in terms of its overt motives but also in light of the schema I have suggested, a clearly different picture emerges.[14] In Asia and Latin America especially, but also even in Europe, the "defense" of "freedom" reveals itself in many cases (though certainly not all) to be merely the unsolicited expansion of American influence; to be, all too often, a series of essentially aggressive acts. American altruism in many of its manifestations is but a thinly veiled form of egoism;[15] American internationalism but a matter of convenience to be decided upon by ourselves, and forgone when the occasion is seen to demand national self-assertion: ". . . the security and well-being of the United States, even its very survival as a free nation, was dependent upon the utilization and application of its power to shape the international environment in a manner compatible with American interests and security." That is indeed a fearful kind of altruism for other nations to be confronted with: as fearful as ever was the Christian messianism with which Crusaders and missionaries warred upon the heathen.

In recent years, it is true, the American posture of reluctant virtue has been reinvigorated by the rise of expansive totalitarianisms. It is claimed that we seek not a democratic world but, more reasonably, only a non-totalitarian one; specifically—since Nazism comes more and more to seem a unique interlude—a non-Communist one. And the policy of containment of Communism is, certainly, the clearest case in American history (outside of the belated confrontation with Hitler) of a policy that may be said to have been adopted in a genuinely reactive manner.

Even here, though, the challenge and response approach

[14] The critical literature on American foreign policy is much too extensive to be cited here; a good beginning is the other essays in this collection.

[15] In 1917 Woodrow Wilson, rejecting the idea of being "honest broker" between England and Germany, admitted that the English had different ideas than we did of what the peace should be like, but noted that when the war was over "we could force them to our way of thinking, because by that time they will, among other things, be financially in our hands . . ." (Quoted in Lasch, op. cit., p. 240.)

falsifies history in the end. For however one views the question of Soviet responsibility for the Cold War, one cannot reasonably make of the Soviet threat everything that American policy made of it. If American physical survival has ever been at stake since 1945—the only case to which the challenge and response theory would be self-evidently appropriate—that has been due to the existence of nuclear weapons; and the Soviets can hardly be blamed for that situation. Perhaps one can also argue that a nation may have obligations to other nations which go so deep that a threat to others "must" be viewed as a threat to oneself. The only conceivable such nation—from our point of view—threatened with a Communist takeover after the war was France (having lived peaceably with a Fascist Italy for eighteen years, we must have difficulty arguing that the prospect of a Communist Italy was too unbearable to be borne). To that threat, if one accepts it as having been a burning threat, the Marshall Plan *was* a "response" that can easily be defended; it was also, I think, a creative policy that would have been every bit as justified if the Soviet Union did not exist. As for the rest of the threats and counterthreats that make up the origin of the Cold War, however, they bear the imprint of American as well as Soviet self-assertion. For example, one does not have to go beyond the data offered by D. F. Fleming and Gar Alperovitz (ignoring their interpretations) to see that ultimate responsibility for the German situation cannot be fixed on the U.S.S.R. alone. For the Soviet definition of *their* interests in Eastern Europe was at least as reasonable as our definition of *our* interests. Our refusal to see any justice in their definition is explained not by any kind of "necessity" but by a long-standing American anti-Communist ideology.[16]

[16] American fear of the Communist menace goes so deep that it has not only existed in periods of no worldwide Communist threat, but even existed in its present form before there was a Bolshevik Revolution. The career of Senator Vandenberg—the great hero of those who believe in America's response to the postwar "challenge"—is instructive in this regard. Vandenberg was an isolationist only by historical and ethnic accident; and his dramatic "conversion" was due not to any change of heart or philosophy, but to the fact that the only enemy his Lockean being had ever really cared about was now at the center of the stage. (One

Similarly, one need not defend the stifling of free elections in Eastern Europe to point out that a unilateral response to that event—which we have always taken to justify a heightening of Cold War feeling on our side—could never be necessitated by the requirements of American "national interest," but only by the requirements of American ideological imperialism. The same thing is true with regard to the so-called threats to Greece and Turkey and thus the origins of the Truman Doctrine—which much more than the Marshall Plan has defined the basic American postwar posture. Even George Kennan protested against military aid to Turkey and against all but the most minimal military aid to Greece.[17] And in any event, even if one were to argue that anything constructive which would not have come about otherwise has in the end come out of this adventure, one would still have separately to defend the use of this minor problem to justify the declaration of a global anti-Communist crusade "to support free peoples . . ." Just so, we might add, one can also defend the Korean response as one to which there were few viable alternatives, and yet see our overall response to the Chinese revolution—which in large part defined the actual course of the Korean War—as being, in its horrific version of a gigantic conspiratorial Communist monolith, paranoid, unhistorical, and intellectually irresponsible in the worst way.

All this is merely to say that though situations do arise in which *some* response is necessary, the rise of expansive Communism being one such situation, the exact nature of the response is generally, and was in this instance, much

of the most interesting discussions of the roots of this tendency in American foreign policy is Roger D. Masters, "The Lockean Tradition in American Foreign Policy," *Journal of International Affairs*, XXI [1967], pp. 253–77.)

[17] The account of Kennan's views on the Truman Doctrine is contained in Denna F. Fleming, *The Cold War and Its Origins, 1917–1960* (Doubleday, 1961), vol. I, pp. 433–60. Fleming's work and the writings of Gar Alperovitz are the major contributions to the literature of Cold War revisionism, as it is called. See Gar Alperovitz, *Atomic Diplomacy: Hiroshima and Potsdam* (Simon and Schuster, 1965); and "The Double Dealer" and "How the Cold War Began," *The New York Review of Books*, Sept. 8, 1966 and March 23, 1967, respectively.

more open to freedom of choice than statesmen and pub-
licists in their retrospective accounts like to pretend. The
United States, to be precise, defined the threat of Communism in such a way that in almost every case our policies
inflated the threat, and the need to counter it, beyond any
realistic bounds. In short, by switching the terms of their
argument from Manifest Destiny to The Free World vs.
Totalitarianism, American spokesmen have but traded off
liberal messianism for a dangerous and potentially destructive Manicheanism.

It is true that instead of forcing everyone to be Good in
our way, we wish only to keep them from being Bad—but
almost without exception Badness consists of succumbing to
the threat of Left Wing, never Right Wing, dictatorships. Is
this, we should ask, a reasonable definition of the world's
political problems? Again the test of events must be taken
by a supposedly beneficent imperialism—and again that test
is failed.

Thus it is argued, for example, that there is *no* escape from
the totalitarian pit; and yet, on all the available evidence
that is neither harder nor easier to climb out of than the
more traditional sinkholes of tyranny. (Does anyone really
expect oppression in Communist Cuba to last as long or as
dreadfully as it has in non-Communist Paraguay and Haiti?)
It is argued too that if people cannot live democratically they
at least deserve indigenous tyranny rather than manipulation
by outside conspiracy. But on all the available evidence
again, outside of the areas where World War II is still being
settled, Communism as a purely external force is negligible,
and always has been, with or without the exertion of American
pressure against it.

To be sure, there are real issues of economic development
and political independence in the world, and the choices
that are made will be affected by the strength or weakness
of pressure from the various Communist nations. For development, the Soviet Union, China, and Cuba offer a guide that
is probably of dubious value; for independence, there are
several nations that will probably be less free than they would
otherwise be if Communist domination of them goes un-
checked. But it is a far cry from these cautious statements

to the assertion that America must unilaterally check the spread of Communism if no one else will do the job. That on balance American influence and protection have produced or will produce more good results than bad, is something that will probably never be known; and agnosticism—surely the only position that can be defended with both conviction and reason—is not enough to justify arguments for the necessity of an American imperium.[18] Nor are more long-range and speculative fears for our own survival; for most of the Communist actions by which we have so immediately and directly felt threatened have seemed so threatening largely because we chose to see them as part of a non-existent plot to take over the world.

Thus the outrages of Guatemala, Iran, the Congo, Lebanon, the Dominican Republic, Cuba, Vietnam, and Greece are not unfortunate detours made necessary by Communist provocations on the road to a freer, more peaceful world. They are merely outrages, involving the use of our armed might to force other nations to accept *our* definition of *their* self-interest—a definition which almost invariably justifies our support for those among the conflicting elements in a society, no matter how corrupt or tyrannical, who promise to be subservient to us in interpreting those interests.[19] The important point is that the results of such adventures are inevitably outrageous, not because they involve willfully malevolent actions by American statesmen, but because the Manichean view of the world, once adopted, is *ipso facto* a mortal enemy of tolerance, restraint, and reason. Those who live by it *always* feel "challenged": not because their enemies take actions that undermine their interests, but merely because those "enemies" exist. It is because this perception of the world's otherness as a threat

[18] Nor can erroneous equations of Communism and Nazism, nor bad analogies to Munich and the 1930s. There *was* a purely destructive, purely malevolent impulse at work in Nazism, and a lack of attention to the obvious limits of continuous self-aggrandizement. Communism has manifested neither of these characteristics—not even Chinese Communism.

[19] See the comment by Nathan Miller, "The Latin Americans Teach the Greeks," *The New Republic*, July 22, 1967, p. 17.

is essentially hysterical that the challenge-and-response approach is inadequate to describe the meaning of so many
of our actions in the international arena. A nation that
rings with its armed power every other nation in the world,
great and small, pleads today for appreciation on the grounds
that it is in a state of siege. Surely what is needed to understand its policies are not so much analyses of the Communist threat, as analyses of the American imagination; not
Dean Rusk or Dean Acheson, but Louis Hartz.

Of course, in discarding the notion of objective challenges
and necessary responses we do not want to render ourselves
incapable of making any distinctions. What I implicitly propose, rather, is that for the idea of objective constraints we
substitute the idea of *reasonableness* in defining challenges to
our interests, as the concept around which fundamental
judgments in foreign policy should be constructed. Decision-
makers, after all, often genuinely think that they are con-
strained. Therefore, at the same time that we reject this
notion in principle, we must be prepared imaginatively to
put ourselves in their positions, to understand their reasons
for so interpreting events, and to estimate the degree to
which we think they were justified. We must ask, that is,
whether *any* intelligent man, regardless of personal and
class interests, moral limitations, political and ideological
commitments, etc., would have pursued the same policies.

To sum up the questions of Cold War responsibility and
American interventionism in this perspective, then, I have
suggested that no decision-making moment since the end of
World War II necessitated the actions we took quite as
compellingly as is suggested by the authors of our intro-
ductory quotations. The United States undoubtedly has obligations—Kristol is certainly correct in his distinction between the responsibilities of great and small powers—but,
to repeat, where the way we have chosen to define those
obligations has been dictated by ideology, they have to all
intents and purposes been self-assumed, fashioned out of an
impulse to self-aggrandizement. At the same time, however,
some of our actions were more comprehensible in a perspective of constraint and "responsibility" than others were:
the Marshall Plan more than the formation of NATO (could

any reasonable man have. expected battered Russia to start another major war?) or the Truman Doctrine (even then it was unreasonable to see Communism's threat in the same light as that posed by Nazism); the Berlin airlift (a necessity partially created by our own policies) more than the phony Berlin crisis of 1961 or the Cuban blockade; the Korean War more than the Vietnam War.

In this catalogue, furthermore, one notices a fairly steady degeneration of the justifications offered for Cold War policies since 1947. This degeneration, I think, is not surprising. For out of motives on our part that were much more than merely responsive, the Cold War began (to us) in an atmosphere of frenzied necessity that was unjustified (though this is admittedly hindsight). Because of this tainted beginning it has since decayed into a lazy-minded excuse for policies that lack not only necessity but any semblance of wisdom; and for policies that comport with the primary national impulse to messianism and Manicheanism. Eliot is fanatical in advising us that the worst treason is to do the right thing for the wrong reason, but the general idea is certainly valid when applied here: imperialist statesmanship becomes, in the end, simple imperialism. And this should perhaps suggest to us an important general rule: the more a course of action is justified by saying that it permits of no alternatives, the more likely we are to be mindlessly trapped in its original suppositions long after they have lost any relevance to our condition.

I have referred above to the influence of decision-makers' interests and commitments on their judgments. So far we have said nothing about the third of the diagrams above. In extremely oversimplified fashion I have there attempted to depict the most important set of distinctions for understanding the manner in which decision-makers actually go about identifying "the national interest."

Interests are not, after all, plucked out of thin air. Since "the national interest" and "national security" are, as we have seen, phrases that denote a subjective version of reality, we should expect that arguments about the proper content of those phrases will be resolved in the same fashion as are other social conflicts involving differing versions of reality. That is, those arguments will be settled through the political processes of conflict and adjustment and particularly, in the United States, through the operations of the accepted system of pressure and influence. The diagram, then, suggests that one way to understand a given definition of what "the national interest" supposedly requires is to specify the political, social, and economic pressures that most successfully impinge on decision-makers as they fashion that definition.

Such pressure may come from the international community, from a national consensus (or the assumption that one exists), from sub-national groups, or, ultimately, from the individual psyche. I have already commented on the distinction between the first two of these sources of decision-maker identification of interests, and the implications for policy of those differing perspectives of nationalism and internationalism. As for the last-named source of identification, little need be said about the psychoanalytic approach. Parlor analysis is not often persuasive; in a policy context it is likely to be helpful, if at all, only when it relates individual drives to some convincing version of "national character" or class behavior.[20]

About sub-national pressures, however, something more should be said, for they are often crucial and identifiable determinants of policy. Liberal expansionism, or militant "welfare imperialism"[21] is hardly the whole story of Amer-

[20] George Kateb's article on the sources of Kennedy's world view, Hartz's description of American liberalism's effects on foreign policy perspectives, and Christopher Lasch's account of American liberal intellectuals during World War I are examples of what I have in mind. Lasch's speculation that the willingness of intellectuals to do violence abroad may be related to their exclusion from the seats of real power at home might be of some use in explaining the current liberal fantasy in which college professors like Rostow, Roche, and Hilsman bring democracy to Vietnam. However, one must always be somewhat dissatisfied with such speculations, even when we lack any other explanation of events, precisely because they are so completely speculative. (George Kateb, "Kennedy as Statesman," *Commentary*, XLI [June 1966], pp. 54–60; Louis Hartz, *The Liberal Tradition in America* [Harcourt. Brace, 1955], ch. 16; and Christopher Lasch, op. cit., ch. 6.)

[21] An exceptionally good example of parlor analysis is George Kateb's "Kennedy as Statesman," *Commentary*, XLI (June 1966), pp. 54–

ica's pursuit of national security. On occasion, as I have already noted, that policy appears, more sublimely, to spring from the genuinely internationalist motives ascribed to it in the quotations above. On other occasions, conversely, the interests that inspire the decision-making process seem to be more crass than those described above, representing attempts to define and satisfy not the "needs" of the nation as a whole, but the needs of particular groups and classes. Often those interests are no less crass for hiding their true nature behind the mask of America's anti-Communist world mission.

To begin with, any theory of foreign policy that neglects the influence of domestic partisan politics in decision-making will be a useless theory. And though this is true for all nations, it is especially true with regard to the United States, for an American government cannot count on its being allowed to govern effectively. The combination of fragmented government, shared powers, built-in institutional jealousies, non-ideological parties, and deference to mass public opinion ensures that the political advantage of those temporarily in positions of power must always be a paramount factor in policy-making. At times, decisions simply cannot be made, or are effectively sabotaged. At other times, what appear to be foreign policy decisions, justified as such to the attentive public, may actually be the outcomes of a bargaining process in which questions of *national* interest have long since—sometimes even cynically—been lost. Recent manipulations of the Food for Peace program by the Johnson Administration are but the latest in a long line of episodes—the Spanish-American War, the escalation of war aims for propaganda purposes in 1917, and Republican exploitation of East European ethnic politics during the Cold War are among the most notorious—in which the grounds for determining the "goodness" of or necessity for a policy were essentially derived from such a process, rather than from an attempt to transcend particular interests and discover "national" ones.[22] Even seemingly

---

60. See also Harold D. Lasswell, *World Politics and Personal Insecurity* (McGraw-Hill, 1935).

[22] By "national" interests—note the plural—I mean those which are so defined that "the people" are only considered, for the moment, as an intermingled unity, to be set against the inhabitants of all other nations.

technical questions, such as the number of American soldiers needed to prosecute the Vietnamese war more successfully, may be answered within such a framework.[23] Furthermore, not only do domestic politics influence the course of foreign policy, but, similarly, diplomacy itself is often used "as a weapon of domestic politics."[24] To understand foreign policy choices in a society is to understand the society itself, the direction in which it is moving, and especially its allocation of power and influence in the political process.

When the question of power and influence is raised, moreover, our attention should immediately be directed to the influence of economic elites in the policy process, and thus in the definition of national interest and security.

To be sure, the orthodox Marxist theory of foreign policy-making has fallen into disfavor nowadays—and rightly so. One reason for this is that even if we imagine that theory to have produced correct predictions in many instances, we still cannot *demonstrate* its over-all correctness. We can surround a President with businessmen and their considerable influence, but we cannot *know* that he has listened to the former, or felt the latter. That much acknowledged, however, we would obviously be absurd to leap to the opposite conclusion, and assume that old-fashioned economic imperialism is somehow absent from the calculations of policy in the United States (or any other nation, including Communist ones).

Thus whenever we observe that the personnel closely involved in dealing with a policy problem have pronounced and special economic interests, we should assume until further notice that this condition has a significant impact on policy choices. It may be, no doubt, that the President, who formally makes all ultimate decisions, ignores the advice of

[23] See John McDermott, "Welfare Imperialism in Vietnam," *The Nation*, July 25, 1966. As far as I know, the phrase is original with McDermott.

[24] Among the best treatments of foreign policy-making as a political process are Samuel Huntington, *The Common Defense: Strategic Programs in National Politics* (Columbia, 1961); and Bernard C. Cohen, "Military Policy Analysis and the Art of the Possible," *Journal of Conflict Resolution*, VI (June 1962).

such persons and countermands their actions; it may also be the merest coincidence when the results of a policy choice are recognizably beneficial to those who participated in the choice process. But *those* cases should be treated as the unlikely ones, rather than the reverse. Certainly there are many instances, particularly regarding the Mideast and Latin America, for which the documentation of economic influence is fairly overwhelming. In other words, a little muckraking, whether old-fashioned or more sophisticated, is definitely in order.[25]

In addition, it is always of equal importance to know exactly what persons tangibly represent our economic interests and carry out our economic activities in foreign nations. For to the extent that our leaders feel their crisis actions to be "compelled" by the nature of our prior commitments and involvement, those who have made the commitments and been active in the involvement are helping to define our "necessary" interests and thus our policy.[26] As Michael Walzer has commented in discussing the interplay between American business penetration and political intervention in Greece:

> An expansive economy, like the American, is always represented abroad by particular people, never in its entirety, and these particular people and their self-defense and aggrandizement play an important part in determining policy. Today, many American businessmen abroad are involved in catering to local upper classes and a kind of mutual identification tends to grow up that expresses itself both socially and ideologically, affecting the whole tenor of the American presence and reinforcing its rightward bent.[27]

[25] See, for example, Robert Engler, *The Politics of Oil* (Macmillan, 1961), especially chs. 4, 8, and 9; Charles L. Robertson, *The Emergency Oil Lift to Europe in the Suez Crisis*, Inter-University Case Program, #86 (Bobbs-Merrill, 1965); Daniel Friedenberg's recent essay on Latin America in *Dissent*; and the data, though not always the interpretations, contained in Carl Oglesby and Richard Schaull, *Containment and Change* (Macmillan, 1967).

[26] George B. Young and John A. S. Grenville, *Politics, Strategy, and American Diplomacy* (Yale, 1966), p. xiii.

[27] Michael Walzer, "The Condition of Greece," *Dissent*, XIV (July–August 1967), p. 431.

Regarding both these points, it is impossible to avoid asking whether our Presidents and other official policy-makers consistently follow the advice of certain types of economic elites, and if our interests abroad are consistently represented by those same types of elites. For if investigation bears out that suspicion—and I think it often would—we must then deal directly with the subject of social class and political power: we must point out that not all of us have equal power to define the national interest, and that membership in an economic elite has a good deal to do with the possession of that power, and with the way it is used.[28] This is but another way of saying, once again, that we understand a nation's foreign policy by understanding the nation. And if we wish to change a nation's policies, it may be that we must begin by changing the nation. This crucial step cannot be taken, either in thought or action, until we finally realize that policy consists of choices, not necessities.

To summarize: foreign policy decisions, and the definition of the situation that precedes them, rarely have an immaculate conception in historical necessity. They are made by men who almost always have a little leeway, and they have that leeway—which the rest of us do not—because they have effective political power; other men wielding the same power might make different decisions. Policy, then, must be defended on some other grounds than that there are no available alternatives. Even within the American

[28] It may be objected here that given the attitudes of organized American workers, equalization of influence on the policy process would mean more of the same, only worse. On the whole this might be true, even though Labor is hardly the only group excluded from an equal voice in policy-making (and even though one wonders what foreign policies workers would propose if they had the *initiative* in proposing them). However, such defenses of elitism, which emphasize the irrational and even pathological chauvinism of the masses, always miss the point. The last century has surely demonstrated that in an inequalitarian mass society such as that of the United States, nationalism even more than religion serves an essentially narcotic function. In the long run, I think, policy will be made to serve more rational ends, not by preserving stratification arrangements that help alienate large numbers of citizens, but by democratizing and humanizing society in all its choice-making processes.

consensus, skeptical and cautious conservatives who decry aggressive interventionism (Fulbright and Kennan come to mind), as well as consistent liberal internationalists such as Clark, McGovern and Church, have steadily criticized American policy from perspectives which can be cavalierly dismissed by the Rusks and Kristols only because they have never been tried. No doubt, the advocate of the official view may reply that although we have admittedly made wrong choices *in the past* (always in the past!), we committed ourselves so deeply by making them that no one could act differently from those who presently wield responsible power.

To surrender to the supposed dictates of history—which are often but the dictates of political, economic, or ideological interest—without making a concerted effort to escape them is itself a voluntary choice. We need only reply to such self-serving determinism—which ought to be the resort of petty bureaucrats and political opportunists rather than of intellectuals or leaders—that a mode of reasoning capable of producing impassable policy morasses for the most physically secure nation in the world is exactly the kind of reasoning that must be repudiated at the earliest opportunity. If Gordian knots have been tied too well to be untied, they must be cut. And in politics the way to cut them is by being *radical:* by going to the roots of what is wrong with decisions, rather than by "understanding" decision-makers too quickly and too sympathetically.

Such critics as I have mentioned here are now accused (in some cases incorrectly) of never having endured the "agonies of decision." The accusation reminds one of the old phrase about college professors never having met a payroll. The Great Depression laid that bit of folklore to rest, as it became evident how little meeting a payroll had to do with making reasonable economic decisions. The debacle in Vietnam, it hardly needs saying, urges that it is time for a similarly fundamental reassessment of the way self-styled professionals make our foreign policy decisions; and of the interests those decisions are designed to serve.

RONALD STEEL

Beyond the Power Blocs

RONALD STEEL, who has served in the Foreign Service, is the author of two books on foreign policy: *The End of Alliance,* a study of European-American relations, and, more recently, *Pax Americana,* an inquiry into America's global role.

The Cold War has been a demoralizing force in American life, forcing us to concentrate on such questions as security and prestige. It inspired the hysteria of the McCarthy period and the anxiety that has marked our relations with the rest of the world. But the Cold War has also been an exhilarating time in American history. It has pushed our frontiers beyond the Western hemisphere to the mainland of Asia and the jungles of Africa. It has made the United States, for the first time in its history, a global power.

Because of the contest with Russia over power and ideology, the United States became involved in countries very remote from traditional American interests and pledged itself to a struggle that knew no territorial limitations. The Cold War both caused and justified the creation of a benevolent American empire. Although it made us afraid, the struggle with Communism also excited us with the knowledge that we were one of the world's arbiters. Beginning as a struggle for power in a war-shattered Europe, the Cold War soon became an ideological contest embracing all the continents. Soviet messianism—sweeping in its presumptions, although usually tailored in its actions to serve the interests of the Russian state —was matched by an equally fervent American messianism in the form of anti-Communism.

The Cold War was real and it was deadly. Yet each time they have been drawing to the brink, the superpowers have pulled back, fearful of a conflict whose destruction would nullify whatever issue was at stake. Provocations—such as Berlin, Korea, Hungary, Cuba—which in an earlier time would almost certainly have led to open war, were smothered and ultimately resolved by compromise. This is not because superpowers today are more reasonable than those of the past, but because the atomic bomb has made full-scale warfare suicidal between major powers. The obscene guardian of an uneasy peace, the Bomb has forced America and Russia to find ways of resolving, or of learning to live with, their differences. To invert Clausewitz's famous dictum, it has forced them to resort to diplomacy as a continuation of warfare by other means.

As the balance of terror has become more stable, so the struggle between America and Russia has been muted. Ideological differences remain, but they are no longer proclaimed with the old fervor, nor are they allowed to stand in the way of political agreements. Even the political differences have now been accepted with resignation and a certain mutual respect. Neither Washington nor Moscow has any intention of attacking the other, and each is willing to let his rival reign within his sphere of influence. The Cold War between Russia and the West is no longer a contest for world supremacy so much as a kind of military gymnastics with vague moral overtones. Europe—once the major area of contention between America and Russia—has now become a haven of stability. Today it is virtually unthinkable that either side would launch a war over Europe, or that they would allow any situation to arise in Europe that could threaten to ignite such a war.

The superpowers have kept a firm hand on their allies and are in unspoken agreement that territorial changes in Europe will not be settled by force. If this means that they will not be settled at all during the foreseeable future, then so much the better as far as the interests of Moscow and Washington are concerned. The reunification of Germany has been put into the deep freeze along with the multilateral nuclear force (MLF). Europe today is no longer the cockpit of the world, but a rather tiresome sideshow whose inconveniences the superpowers are willing to tolerate so long as it does not get out of hand. It has now become clear that the focus of American diplomacy is shifting away from Europe, where the Soviet

Union has long since been contained, to the impoverished and unstable states of the Third World.

With the achievement of both an ideological and a power balance between America and Russia, the blocs they lead have been subject to severe strain and even the threat of disintegration. The Atlantic Alliance is foundering under the impact of a new European nationalism, and the East European states are no longer behaving as though they were satellites of Moscow. With the lessening of the danger of a European war, the Cold War alliances have lost their cohesion, and even much of their reason for being. There is a new fluidity and even a new independence in European politics as nations on both sides of the Iron Curtain explore new ways of resolving the differences that have kept them separated for more than 20 years.

Outside the system of rival alliances, the Cold War neutrals have found that their allegiance to one camp or another is no longer so ardently desired by Moscow or Washington, and that it is not impossible to maintain the middle course they have proclaimed as their goal. But as neutralism becomes easier, so the rewards of commitment are less enticing. Now that the superpowers are less interested in the formal loyalty of the neutrals, they are also willing to pay less for it in the form of military assistance and foreign-aid bribes. Removed from the Cold War arsenal, economic assistance to the poorer countries is coming to seem more of a chore than an opportunity to America and Russia. Neutralism has lost its "immorality"; it has also lost some of its economic rewards.

The world of the Cold War period—a world rigidly divided into two rival blocs—has now passed into history. The ideological struggle has shifted from Europe to Asia and the revolution-prone states of the Third World. The atomic monopoly, so long enjoyed by Moscow and Washington, has now been broken by China. Even if the Cold War between America and Russia were resurrected, it could never again take its old form. This can be seen in at least four crucial areas:

1. First, there is the disintegration of the Soviet-ruled bloc and the open rebellion of Peking. Soviet control over Eastern

Europe has been sharply diminished, and such states as Hungary and Rumania have shown a willingness to pursue their own national policies even in the face of Russian objections. The recent decision by Bucharest to extend formal diplomatic recognition to the West German government in Bonn, over vehement protests from Moscow and Pankow, is simply a case in point. The East European nations, which are satellites no more, are free to pursue their own internal policies, and even their own foreign policies so long as they do not endanger the security of the Soviet Union. "Communism has come to embrace so wide a spectrum of requirements and compulsions on the part of the respective parties and regimes," as George Kennan has written, "that any determined attempt to reimpose unity on the movement would merely cause it to break violently apart at one point or another."

Communism has failed as an economic system in Eastern Europe; it has failed even more dramatically in its effort to provide a more potent ideology than nationalism. Everywhere in the Soviet bloc Communism has been forced to take a back seat to nationalism, as each nation seeks its own road to prosperity—sometimes at the expense of its neighbors. Allegiance to a common ideology did not prevent the Yugoslavs from defying Moscow, nor has it prevented the Rumanians from expanding their Western links over Russia's objections. The revival of nationalism is even expressed in territorial disputes once again coming out into the open in the factious Balkans. Eastern Europe may be nominally Communist, but it is burdened with a heavy history of xenophobia and suspicion that two decades of Communist rule have not overcome. In Eastern Europe today there is no "bloc"; there is simply a group of states proclaiming formal allegiance to the same ideology, and dependent upon Soviet power for external protection.

Instead of a single Communist Church centered in Moscow, there are a variety of churches, each with its own Pope. One can no longer be sure what constitutes Communist orthodoxy because there is no single orthodoxy. With considerable reluctance, but with virtually no choice, Moscow has had to accept the equality of its erstwhile dependents in matters of ideology. Thus Communist authorities throughout the world are evolving their own solutions for local problems: the Rumanians are inviting Western investors, the Yugoslavs are creating a mixed capitalist-socialist system, the Czechs are imposing a market economy and dumping an old-line administration, and even the Russians themselves are following the lead of their protectorates and experimenting in economics.

In foreign affairs the disintegration of Communist unity has, of course, been even more dramatic. This is not yet pronounced in Eastern Europe, where such states as Poland and East Germany feel themselves dependent upon Moscow for protection against possible West German "revanchism," and where the other Communist states recognize that they must remain formal members of the Warsaw Pact so long as Russia insists upon it. But it is the basic fact of life in Asia, where there has been an open rupture between Russia and China. The rise of an independent, and now defiant, Communist government in Peking has shattered whatever hopes Moscow entertained for controlling the world Communist movement. This is no doubt why Stalin persisted for so long in backing Chiang Kai-shek against Mao Tse-tung, for he must have realized that a Communist China could be a powerful rival to Russia within the Communist system. Once again masters of their own country, caught up in the flush of their revolution, seething with resentment against the foreigners who dominated them for so long, determined to gain a place in the world commensurate with their immense potential, the Chinese are today challenging the Russians not only over the interpretation of Marxist scripture, but over the disputed territories they claim were seized from them by the Czars during the nineteenth century.

A common ideology has not glossed over the sharp differences separating two giants—one pursuing affluence and "peaceful coexistence," the other mired in poverty and preaching world revolution. Their mutual dedication to Marxism has apparently only sharpened their differences, for it has added the problem of heresy to the normal conflict of national interest. This break between Moscow and Peking has removed the old fear that world Communism could be put at the service of the Soviet state, a fear that for so long haunted American diplomacy. Further, it has given the smaller Communist nations a remarkable freedom of action to pursue their individual paths—a freedom which has been evidenced in Albania's defiance of Russia, and by North Korea's remarkable warning against Chinese interference.

The breakup of the Communist bloc has made it clear that Communism is no more capable of providing a cement for power alliances than is capitalism or Catholicism. The Communist victory in Yugoslavia did not augment Russian power, any more than a Communist North Korea or a Communist North Vietnam has increased Chinese power. Thus we can no longer assume that a Communist revolution in one country will necessarily benefit an existing Communist regime in any other country. It may, in fact, weaken it—as a Communist China weakened Russia's hold over other Communist states. This is a phenomenon which we admit in Europe, although we deny it in Asia and are today engaged in demonstrating our denial by the most violent means in Vietnam. Diplomacy has yet to catch up with history.

2. A parallel development is decay of the Atlantic Alliance. As the Russian military threat has diminished and as the solidity of the Communist bloc has cracked, so the united front in the West has seemed less important. And in turn this has been reinforced by the extraordinary recovery of Western Europe. Not merely is Russia less a threat and the Communist bloc less a reality; but Western Europe is no longer so weak and prey to Communist pressures. Indeed, the reality is quite the reverse. Today it is the Communist states of the East that are subject to grave internal stresses, while it is the nations of Western Europe that are strong, prosperous and relatively stable.

Europe's resurgence from defeat and demoralization to prosperity and self-confidence is one of the most extraordinary success stories of modern history. Only 20 years ago the West Europeans seemed prey to revolution from within and aggression from without. Incapable of protecting themselves, they sought American protection on virtually any terms. Today the Europeans are chafing under what they term American "hegemony" and face with equanimity the day when American soldiers will have departed from the continent. Economic stagnation has been confined to the history books, along with the worst nightmares of the Nazi period, and the feeling of political impotence is now being replaced by a new European quest for identity.

The division and occupation of Europe by foreign powers—a division that has now lasted for nearly a quarter century—has come to seem as unnatural as it is undesirable to Europeans on both sides of the Iron Curtain. The American occupation, benevolent though it may have been, is becoming an anachronism to a Europe in quest of reconciliation. As this desire to reconcile the two parts of a divided continent becomes increasingly important to Europeans, the ties of the Atlantic Alliance seem unduly restrictive. To many Europeans it now seems that the rival alliances can be maintained only at the cost of keeping Europe divided, and if the Iron Curtain is to be demolished, it can be done only by dismantling the rival blocs directed from Moscow and Washington.

The resistance of the European allies to American direction can be seen not only in the withdrawal of France from NATO —a withdrawal which is supported by virtually all shades of French opinion—but even in the reluctance of West Germany to accept Washington's lead in such matters as defense costs and nuclear non-proliferation. Long the fulcrum of NATO, and indeed the basic reason for its existence, West Germany is now seeking to play a freer role between East and West. While dependent upon Washington for protection, the new government in Bonn refuses to antagonize Gaullist France and is showing a surprising initiative in launching its own "opening to the East."

Insofar as the containment of Russia is concerned, the European allies are willing to support American strategy—even though they are often reluctant to contribute to it. But outside of Europe they have shown an indifference to American diplomacy that frequently borders on disdain. Not a single European ally has come to our aid in Vietnam, and virtually all of them disapprove of what we are doing there—France publicly, the others mostly privately. They are not gravely concerned by the expansion of Communism in Asia and share none of our apprehension about China. Indeed, they look with favor on the growth of Chinese power, for they see it as a means of balancing Russian power in the East. As far as the containment of Russia is concerned, China is Europe's natural ally, and the Europeans are setting the stage for this alliance by aiding China's attempts at industrialization.

Even in economics the identity of interests between Europe and America—always more apparent than real—has begun to break down. The tortuous negotiations of the "Kennedy round" for mutual tariff reductions and the refusal of the Europeans to lower their tariffs without American concessions have shown that the Europeans have gained a great deal of leverage through the Common Market. This refusal to accept American leadership is also shown in the negotiations over the treaty on the non-proliferation of nuclear weapons. Not only have the Germans declared that they will not sign a treaty which discriminates against them, but so have the Italians—while the French, of course, refuse to sign altogether.

Perhaps these differences over economics, politics, and even military strategy would be less important if there were a common consensus on the basic problems that affect the Atlantic allies. But it is precisely this consensus which now seems to be lacking. There is no common accord between America and her allies on the crucial issues now facing American diplomacy: the war in Vietnam, the containment of China, the non-proliferation of nuclear weapons, the defense of Europe, or the struggle against Communism in the Third World. Even the disintegration of NATO itself is being accepted by most Europeans, who look upon the transfer of its headquarters to Belgium as the final acknowledgement of its descent into bureaucratic irrelevance.

France has shown that the alliance will endure even though NATO is dismantled, and that even if American soldiers were withdrawn from Europe the American guarantee would still remain valid. This is not because of Washington's noble heart, but because America's own interests require that Western Europe be defended from a Russian attack. Now that this elementary fact has begun to be grasped by most European governments, the old loyalty toward NATO has given way to skepticism and even open indifference. Yet while the military organization decays, the alliance will endure so long as it seems to the mutual advantage of America and Europe. But the

Atlantic bloc is no more, and America is now faced with allies with a mind, and policies, of their own.

3. The decay of the two rival blocs has been accompanied by the sudden rise of the underdeveloped states to global prominence. Only a decade ago much of Africa and even parts of Asia were ruled directly from Europe, or had just begun to emerge from such rule. Today the European colonial empires have virtually disappeared, except for the Portuguese territories in Africa and a few curiosities such as Rio Muni and Timoz. Throughout Africa and Asia scores of new nations have been carved from the remnants of the European empires, and are now demanding their rights to political equality and economic development. With a few fortunate exceptions, these nations are mostly poor and ill-equipped for the ordeals of independence. But what they lack in riches and technical skills, they more than compensate for in a fierce nationalism that is Europe's most troublesome legacy to the Third World.

The passage of the colonial world to formal independence is one of the great revolutions of our time—greater in impact than even the Russian Revolution. Through their challenge to the nations of the West, and by the extraordinary human and material potential they possess, these nations have re-framed the world power structure. Less concerned with the differences between Communism and anti-Communism than with the struggle for equality and economic development, they have put the Russo-American Cold War into a new focus. These new nations are concerned with political ideology only insofar as it can be used to achieve the goals they want—above all, the development of their economies. Rephrasing diplomacy in terms of economic development, the emerging nations have helped take the ideological sting out of the Cold War. They have shown that the real struggle for most of mankind is not between Communists and anti-Communists, or between Americans and Russians, but between the rich and the poor, between the developed nations and the economically-backward ones. Yet in trying to raise themselves from economic primitiveness and exploitation, they have had nowhere to turn for help but to the rich nations—and above all, to the superpowers. In so doing, they have forced America and Russia to realize that as wealthy, stable, and prosperous societies, they have more in common with one another than with the aspiring poor in the Third World.

4. A fourth factor contributing to the passing of the Cold War world has been the declining importance of nuclear weapons as a diplomatic tool. Experience has demonstrated that the atomic bomb has not permitted its possessor to impose its will upon any rival. The Bomb serves as a means by which one nuclear power can deter another. This is vitally important, for without the Bomb it is quite likely that America and Russia long ago would have been at war over one of their many areas of disagreement. The Bomb has helped to keep the peace, and in this sense its development may be less of a misfortune than we now realize. But the Bomb has not given its possessors the means to settle their political grievances, nor even to assert their will over non-nuclear powers. For the nuclear powers it has frozen the status quo—as in central Europe. Where the non-nuclear powers are concerned, it has been basically irrelevant. Possession of a Bomb did not help the British avoid costly colonial wars in Malaya and Cyprus; it did not aid the French during the long agony of the Algerian War; and it has not been of any use to the United States during either the Korean or the Vietnam War.

It is a paradox, but an unavoidable one, that the Bomb has kept the peace between the superpowers, while permitting lesser grievances to be fought in its shadow. Further, it has now become apparent that both Russia and America have had their effective power diminished by the development of the atomic bomb. Without the Bomb they are the two greatest powers on earth, incomparably superior to any current rival. But the development of the Bomb and its gradual dispersal to a host of relatively minor powers has deprived Russia and America of some of their advantages of size and power. It has not made the small equal to the great, but like the pistol it has helped bridge some of the disparities of power.

The present détente, and the joint effort to forge a treaty banning the proliferation of nuclear weapons, comes as a result of their realization of this fact. To retain their preeminence, the superpowers must prevent other nations, whether allies or foes, from upsetting the nuclear balance or forcing them into a nuclear confrontation. Thus, they have tried to close the atomic club to new members, an act whose self-serving cynicism is not diminished by the fact of its probable desirability. Wealthy giants in a world of restless allies, resentful pygmies, and hostile challengers, America and Russia find themselves drawn together in a search for common solutions to common problems. The implacability of the Cold War remains only in the ideological rhetoric of which neither side has been fully able to unburden itself. Behind that rhetoric, however, lie the elements of an accord dictated by common interests.

The rise of new powers and the shattering of the old alliances have threatened the dominance the two nuclear giants have enjoyed. Their ability to control or speak for others is steadily diminishing, and the days of their hegemony appear to be numbered. A world which revolved around the twin poles of Moscow and Washington has been split into scores of minor and major poles. Instead of a "Communist world" and a "free world," there are a confusing series of shifting relationships between great and small powers. Confronted by the insubordination of their allies and the defiance of the neutrals, America and Russia are in the declining days of their condominium. Keeping restless allies in check, trying to maintain a nuclear balance, resentfully financing the development of the emerging nations, and trying to prevent the instability of the new states from drawing them into an open confrontation with one another, Moscow and Washington are moving toward an unacknowledged, but nonetheless real, cooperation. They are learning to carry on their competition in terms of a traditional power rivalry. Each remains committed to its ideology, but the détente and the nuclear balance take precedence over ideological proselytizing.

A tacit cooperation between the superpowers has been in effect for some time, even though both would be reluctant to admit it officially. This has been evident not only in the nuclear test-ban treaty of 1963 and the proposed non-proliferation treaty, but also in the current war in Vietnam. This pattern of self-restraint dates back to the worst days of the Cold War, and has now been reinforced by the dictates of "peaceful co-

existence." As the United States refused to support the rebellious East Berliners in 1953 or the Hungarians in 1956, and
accepted the Berlin Wall in 1961, so the Russians tolerated the
Berlin airlift, have respected the security of West Berlin,
and have not challenged our devastation of Communist North
Vietnam. Rather than agitate trouble in such places as Laos
and Kashmir, the superpowers have tried to smother grievances, and after the dissatisfying experience of the Congo
they have sought to keep the Cold War out of Africa. Russia
has been quiescent in Latin America since the Cuban missile
crisis, and the United States has been reluctant to exploit the
revived nationalism now sweeping Eastern Europe. They are
now engaged in an attempt to stabilize the arms race by an
agreement on anti-missile systems, are sharing the burden of
building up India as a rival to China, and are apparently
agreed that Castro should be kept isolated. This tacit cooperation between Washington and Moscow has gone so far that
the United States was embarrassed by the request of Stalin's
daughter for asylum, and persuaded her to go to Switzerland
instead. Even the propaganda war has come to be considered
bad taste in both rival capitals.

Aware of their common interests, determined not to be
drawn into a nuclear war against their will by actions of nations such as China or Germany, the superpowers are now
forced to reconsider the value of their alliances. Their primary value now seems to be that of keeping recalcitrant allies
in line and maintaining an essentially bipolar balance of
power. This, of course, is what de Gaulle has warned of all
along, what the Chinese mean when they talk about Soviet
cooperation with the "imperialists," and what West German
Chancellor Kiesinger meant when he accused Russia and
America of "a form of atomic complicity" in the non-
proliferation treaty. In a sense, all of these complaints are
right. There is a kind of collusion taking place between the
superpowers: a collusion to keep Europe divided into rival
alliances, to restrain China, to keep the lid on the Third World,
to prevent new members from joining the atomic club. That
this may be true, however, does not necessarily make it undesirable. One might argue that it would be a wholesome development insofar as world peace is concerned. Far better,

after all, to have the world controlled by two satiated super-powers acting in cooperation than to have it contested by two implacably hostile nations bent on world dominion. The more serious problem is whether it is still possible.

Roosevelt's vision of a great power directorship over the world is theoretically feasible. But may it not be too late? Can Washington today decree a German settlement without the accord of Bonn? Can Moscow do so without the agreement of Pankow? The disintegration of the Cold War alliances has diminished the usable power of the nuclear giants. It has sharply restricted the agreements they can impose upon other nations. Having been incapable of decreeing a European peace treaty or reaching an accord on nuclear weapons during a time when they could enforce it upon weaker nations, they now find that the agreements they reach may be binding upon no one but themselves. The alliances they maintain are usable only for defense against one another. They are no longer viable instruments by which the superpowers can assert their will upon weaker nations. Gaullist France may have been the first to realize that American military protection need not entail American political domination, but it is Germany and China—two nations with real grievances—that pose the real danger to the unspoken accord of the superpowers.

The break-up of the power blocs directed from Washington and Moscow has brought a new fluidity, and a new instability, to world affairs. The decay of NATO and the Dulles complex of alliances, the disintegration of the Communist bloc, the spread of nuclear weapons, and the diminution of the Bomb as a means of superpower control, the revolutionary rise of the ex-colonial peoples—all this has radically changed the world power structure from what it was during the Cold War period. The past is now prologue to the post-Cold War world that we are living in.

Relief with the passing of the Cold War struggle between America and Russia is natural, particularly among liberals who all along have decried both the goals and the methods of the Cold War. But that relief could well be tempered by even a cursory glance at the new power struggle emerging on the horizon. The coming struggle is not going to be one between Communists and anti-Communists—despite the inflated rhetoric of the war in Vietnam—but rather between rising states and established ones, between those who seek and those who already possess. Although remnants of the Cold War remain, particularly in the official language of the State Department, the main dispute between nations is not so much over ideology as it is over power and influence. Gradually, we seem to be returning to an older kind of struggle, the kind Metternich tried to deal with after the Napoleonic wars and the appeasement of ideological fervor in republican France. The language of the French Revolution had spread throughout Europe, even after France herself returned to conservatism and monarchy. But what was important was that this ideology expressed itself in nationalistic fervor and the struggle for political equality by peoples who were, or believed themselves to be, suppressed.

Perhaps the Austro-Hungarian empire was not such a bad thing. It helped to spare Europe a major war for nearly a century, and it tolerated a certain degree of diversity for the states it encompassed. Perhaps historians will decree that the American empire, too, has not been such a bad thing: that it has been maintained with a minimum of overt coercion, that it has helped keep the peace, and that it has been relatively benevolent for most of the peoples who live within its confines. Such a judgment may have a good deal to recommend it, but it is not really to the point, for the real test of an empire is not whether it is beneficent but whether it is viable. On that count the benevolent American empire cannot expect to maintain its cohesion without the use of methods which may be repugnant to the American people. The war in Vietnam can be justified to public opinion in terms of the Cold War rhetoric of Communism v. anti-Communism. But even there that justification no longer carries its old conviction, and much of the uneasiness over the war among people who are neither liberals nor radicals stems from the fact that Communism per se is not considered to be the menace it once was. This is why the Administration has struggled so hard to bring the specter of China into the Vietnam equation, even though this has involved a considerable twisting of logic and evidence.

It may be that, beneath the fury of an outdated rhetoric, Vietnam is not so much a war of ideology as a war for power and influence: a war to demonstrate to China that the United States is, as the President has said, a Pacific power, and even an Asian power. In this sense it may be not so much a hangover from the Cold War (although to some degree it is, insofar as our assessment of Ho Chi Minh is concerned), as an attempt to stake out the boundaries of America's global power. It would be a tragic irony if the passing of the bipolar Cold War confrontation should be succeeded by the attempt to assert an American suzerainty over the areas lying along the fringes of the Communist giants. This is, however, precisely what we have maintained in Europe, the Middle East, and Japan along the fringes of the Soviet Union, and what we have achieved along the fringes of China everywhere but in Vietnam. Perhaps this is why the Administration considers the Vietnam War such a "test case," for it fears that if the war is lost to the Viet Cong guerrillas, China will establish a sphere of influence in Southeast Asia, and America will no longer be an "Asian power."

At the very least, the war in Vietnam has demonstrated that the break-up of the Cold War power blocs has not brought about the tranquility that many liberals and radicals unrealistically imagined. Even if the United States were to pursue a more restrained concept of where her national interest lay; even if Washington and Moscow were to cooperate overtly in such areas of mutual concern as Central Europe, there is little reason to assume a decline in international tensions. On the contrary, the subsiding of the Cold War between the giants has permitted smaller powers to give vent to their grievances against one another, and violence to take place on a local level without necessarily threatening the nuclear balance and the Russo-America détente. When faced with the turmoil of the Third World and with the rise of new powers, such as China, to challenge American pre-eminence, there is the temptation among many to have the United States play the role of a global policeman. But this is not a desirable role for America, and it has now become apparent in Vietnam that it is not even a feasible one.

What lies beyond the Cold War and the break-up of the

rival power blocs is a world where even such great powers as America and Russia cannot hope to assert their will in areas outside their own vital interests. The best they can do is to seek to smother conflict where it affects them directly, and cooperate, insofar as possible, to isolate the violence in the emerging countries so that they are not dragged into these disorders. Cooperation, accord, even collusion between Washington and Moscow is possible, and in many respects desirable. But above all what is necessary in the post-Cold War world is a clear recognition of where our real interests lie and what are the limitations our actions must be guided by. We cannot contain all the violence in the world, and perhaps the best we can do is to make sure that it does not involve us over causes that are not our own and whose reasons we do not understand. The passing of the Cold War world has not solved our problems; it has only changed them, for, as Churchill said as long ago as 1945, "when the war of the giants is over, the war of the pygmies will begin."

—————◆—————

PART II

WALTER LAQUEUR

Reflections on the Third World

WALTER LAQUEUR is director of the Institute of Contemporary History (the Wiener Library) in London and holds professorships at Brandeis (History of Ideas) and at Reading University. His most recent books are *Russia and Germany, The Fate of the Revolution,* and *The Road to War.*

Cassandra, daughter of King Priam of Troy, (we are told) had her ears licked by a serpent while asleep and so got her prophetic gift: forever after she was fated to foretell the evil results of successive events. All civilizations have had their Cassandras, but probably none more than twentieth-century Europe. A symposium in *Le Figaro* in 1898 ("What's wrong with France?") reads uncannily like a *Partisan Review* symposium seventy years later. Visions of doom have been fashionable for a long time, and their prophets sometimes address large audiences. Brahmaism taught that the world was in decline, Horace and Livius are full of dire predictions following the general relaxation of Roman discipline, and every self-respecting writer in the tenth century began his chronology: "While the world is approaching its end. . . ." Henry and Brooks Adams wrote long ago about the decline of Western man and Baudelaire hated Paris (*"centre et rayonnement de bêtise universelle"*) as much as do Sartre and Simone de Beauvoir. Between the two world wars fascism proclaimed the impending demise of the senescent West—and the rise of the young nations.

Since World War II prophecies of doom have come from many quarters and on the basis of different political convictions. Usually, these are frightening visions. Arnold Toynbee regards Western civilization as an apostasy of Christian civilization, the fatal plunge from faith into the barren grounds of secularism. Western civilization, he says, exhibits authentic symptoms of breakdown and disintegration, and the only thing that can save it is a fresh religious revolution.

Such reasoning is not shared by many. Toynbee has been chided by (among others) Geoffrey Barraclough, a British historian now a resident of California; Barraclough criticized the "breath-taking oblivion to the enormous genocide involved," as well as the lack of accuracy and consistency in Toynbee's historical judgment, the wishful thinking and dubious speculations in his reflections on the prospects of Western civilization.

Yet Barraclough himself is the author of a recent introduction to contemporary history which could, with equal justice, be entitled "New Light on the Decline of the West." In one of his essays he wrote that in 1943, when Stalingrad was relieved by the Russians, he suddenly awoke to the fact that he had mis-spent his life dealing with such recondite subjects as the machinery of papal chancelleries in the thirteenth and fourteenth centuries. Such an awakening to the winds of change by people educated in an Eurocentric tradition should only be welcomed.

That Europe is no longer the center of the world is hardly in dispute any more. The realization of this fact, however, came too abruptly for some who were led to believe that Europe was finished altogether. What did Hitler and even Stalin matter in a world whose history was only to begin? For how could one be blind to the wave of the future personified by Mao and Sukarno, by Nasser, Nkrumah and Ben Bella? Politically and economically the European age was over, and with it the predominance of European values. Culturally too Europe had had its day; new peoples were arising, new energies seeking expression, a definite view of life set in conscious counterpoint to the weary disillusion of Europe. These, at any rate, were Professor Barraclough's conclusions, and he was not alone in holding them.

Toynbee rejects Western civilization on the basis of religious-mystic convictions. Barraclough, on the other hand, is a radical, a left-wing liberal. The politics of Frantz Fanon are different again; his rejection of Europe is total.[1] *The Wretched of the Earth* ends with a passionate appeal to all the downtrodden in the ex-colonial world to leave this Europe where they are never done talking of man yet murder men everywhere they find them:

> The European game has finally ended. . . . We, today, can do everything so long as we do not imitate Europe, so long as we are not obsessed by the desire to catch up with Europe. . . . Europe now lives at such a mad, reckless pace that she has shaken off all guidance and all reason and she is running headlong into the abyss. . . . When I search for Man in the technique and the style of Europe, I see only a succession of negations of man and an avalanche of murders. . . . What we want to do is to go forward all the time, night and day in the company of all men.

The Third World is here assigned the task of starting a new History of Man. The number of these prophets of doom is legion, and they have all seen the writing on the wall: Europe is a spent force, America incurably ill. But despondency is a mood, not a way of life. If the old idols have been shattered, men need new ideals and new gods. For two previous generations Soviet Communism was the great beacon illuminating the darkness, showing the road to a better future. But Russia's attraction in the West as the standard-bearer of progress has diminished in the same measure as its economy has advanced. Some former admirers now believe that the price that has been paid for this progress was too high; others find the Soviet preoccupation with production and things material uncongenial, the emergence of a new autocracy and all-powerful bureauc-

---

[1] "Europe" for Fanon includes the United States: "Two centuries ago a former European colony decided to catch up with Europe. It succeeded so well that the United States of America became a monster, in which the taints, the sickness, the inhumanity of Europe have grown to appalling dimensions." Professor Toynbee would disapprove of the language but likewise regards the United States as an extension of Europe. Barraclough, on the other hand, seems to consider America a case of *sui generis*: the positive European heritage (he wrote) has become embedded in both the Russian and American civilizations.

racy distasteful. Others yet, while not denying the "progressive" character of the Soviet regime if seen against the background of Russian history, doubt the validity of the Russian lesson for the rest of mankind.

During the last decade more and more of the sympathetic attention formerly devoted to Russia has been transferred to China and Indonesia, to Ghana and Guinea, to Algeria and Egypt, and to some other countries attempting against heavy odds to carry out national revolutions on the basis of Marxist-Leninist concepts differently interpreted and applied. It is now believed that only in these countries (to quote Frantz Fanon) is there the opportunity "to do everything," to advance a step further beyond Europe, to learn from the mistakes committed elsewhere, "to bring the problem of mankind to an infinitely higher plane." These regimes have been in existence only for a comparatively brief period, but long enough to draw an interim and tentative balance. It is not too early to ask whether their progress has been encouraging, and to what extent others could benefit from the example set by them.

A Balance Sheet on Maoist China

What lesson can the outside world draw from recent events in China? China has become strongly isolationist, almost entirely preoccupied with internal affairs; it has virtually cut itself off from the outside world. As these lines are written the cultural revolution is still in progress. There is little doubt that some of the antics of this extraordinary movement will be revoked in coming months and years: this is the dialectic of history. But it has happened, it cannot be explained away. It took place, not at the beginning of the Communist era, not during a civil war, but eighteen years after the establishment of Communist China. It came as a surprise not only to the friends of Communist China, it surpassed the expectations of its worst enemies. No Sinologist expected such outbursts; area experts, however critical of their subject of study, are motivated by a certain ambivalence. In this case they clearly exaggerated not merely the depth of Mao Tse-tung's thought but the general intellectual level of Communist China. They overrated (it now appears) the element of rationality in Communist China—and they underrated the impact of such elements as obscurantism, nationalist passions, the struggle for power between various factions; they were aware that China was economically backward, but they underrated the extent of *cultural* backwardness in twentieth-century China. They read into official pronouncements and speeches hidden meanings and a sophistication that never existed.

Inasmuch as this second Maoist revolution has a rational purpose (and it may be wise not to overrate this aspect), it aims at the perpetuation of the revolutionary fervor of both the Chinese elite and the masses. This aim can only be achieved by frequent changes in the leadership on all levels, by combating specialization and "bureaucratization," and by preventing the emergence of a "new class," the technical intelligentsia. There is a certain logic in these aspirations. Equality, after all, is one of the basic socialist aims even though historically the most neglected. But the inner contradictions of Maoism are glaring, and, in all probability, self-defeating. From a Marxist point of view it is a major heresy; there are, of course, Marxist elements in Maoism, but the "utopian" element, not to mention the nationalist motivation, seems to be stronger. The idea that Chinese man (equipped with Mao's thought) can overcome all obstacles, achieve all aims is an attractive one, but what has it in common with a political system concerned with the study of the laws governing historical and social change?

Mao's second revolution is a romantic-idealist movement, a primitive reaction against the trends inherent in a modern industrial society that make it more and more difficult to stick to the way of life established in the caves of Yenan during the 1930s. It is interesting that such a movement finds support, temporarily at any rate, among the very young in China. But it conflicts with another basic aim of the Chinese revolution— to modernize the country, to increase industrial and agricultural production, to raise the standard of living. Constant change is the one way to defeat the danger of revisionism in China, whereas the opposite—stability—is the prerequisite for the economic development of the country. Such a movement is unlikely to be more successful than the Luddites; it either adjusts itself to historical forces stronger than itself or it is swept away. There are no precedents for Mao's second revolution, but it can be said on the basis of much historical experience in other parts of the world that movements with a fervent belief in the omnipotence of a great leader and that "everything is possible" often end by pursuing policies very different from, sometimes diametrically opposed to, those they originally set out to accomplish.

The cultural revolution may be a temporary aberration, a setback, from which the country will eventually recover. What has been the balance sheet if we ignore the upheaval and the confusion of 1966–67? On the credit side there is the fact that China is united, that the country received a great national uplift after 1949, that there are few unemployed, that China has produced the bomb. In foreign affairs China has been less successful—perhaps it does not bother; why should a country of 700 million be unduly worried about the opinions and susceptibilities of others? Its foreign policy has been clumsy and arrogant. It has lost ground in the battle for influence in the Communist camp. It has antagonized most of its well-wishers in Asia and Africa, despite the great sympathy for China that originally existed and the "objectively revolutionary situations" in many sections of the Third World. China's promises to give aid and its subsequent default have antagonized even such a well-disposed regime as Castro's. The antics of the "cultural revolutionaries" have made China the butt of ridicule almost everywhere outside Tirana.

What is the internal balance sheet? During the 50s there was very considerable progress. The great leap forward ended in a fiasco; about seven years were needed to recover. Broadly speaking, Chinese industry and agriculture are only slightly ahead of where they were eight or nine years ago. These estimates do not take into account the effects of the "cultural revolution," the extent of which cannot be assessed for some time to come. Since the population continues to grow at a rapid rate, the standard of living is now no higher than it was ten years ago. Real earnings in industry and agriculture may have slightly declined since 1958. Chinese industry can only expand on the basis of "primitive accumulation." But agriculture during the next five years will hardly increase at a faster rate than the population. Where will the industrial investment come from? Mao's little red book may be a source of spiritual comfort to many Chinese, but it does not offer an answer to the very basic questions facing the regime. Achievements in nuclear weaponry and the building of missiles are impressive but not matched by similar development in the national economy.

A country of the magnitude of China will always remain a very important factor in world politics, which no one will be able to ignore. The Chinese are patriotic and exceedingly hard-working; perhaps they will be able to overcome the present convulsions in a comparatively short period. Given moderately favorable conditions, the Chinese will continue to make headway. But there is no indication at present that it will serve in the forseeable future as a model to anyone outside China, except perhaps by the industry and the dedication of its inhabitants and other such features of national character that antedate 1949.

The Bizarre Policies of Sukarno's Indonesia

If we ignore for a moment the "cultural revolution," China has held its own during the last decade. Not so Indonesia. "Is there anything real in Sukarno's Indonesia?" one observer asked shortly before the coup—and the counter coup of 1966. And he provided this answer: "This huge and heavily armed country full of sound and fury and decay ceased years ago to belong to the world of today." The combination of verbal extremism in foreign affairs, political mysticism, and utter incompetence in domestic affairs which was so typical of Sukarno's rule, created a state of permanent chaos.

Indonesia received considerable aid from both Russia and the West—the foreign debt is now $2.7 billion. But foreign aid made no difference in respect to the economic situation; funds were spent on military equipment and prestige buildings the country could ill afford. There was no serious attempt to tackle industrial development or the country's very basic problem: agricultural resettlement. So far, 80 per cent of all Indonesians make their living from agriculture, but 60 per cent of the population is mainly concentrated on the land area of Java. A land redistribution scheme in Java and Madura was passed in 1960, but it provided land for less than 10 per cent of the landless and moreover was inefficiently applied. A real resettlement program would involve the removal of substantial sections from Java to Sumatra and Borneo. But the present resettlement rate is considerably lower than the normal population increase in Java. Inflation under Sukarno assumed fantastic proportions, the price of rice, for instance, going up sixfold within a few months in 1965.

Meanwhile "Indonesian socialism" was propagated. But beneath its veneer of revolutionary activism (to quote a close observer of the Indonesian scene) there was a deeply conservative policy idealizing a regression toward a natural economy and the social structure of the Javanese village. Basically, Sukarno was far more interested in foreign affairs, where successes (New Guinea!) were after all possible—very much in contrast to the domestic front. From Mussolini he adopted the principle of living dangerously (*tahun vivere pericoloso*). But in Italy the fascist bombast was spread by a regime that, however abominable, somehow functioned. In Indonesia there were just words that had no relation to reality.

Sukarno's personal responsibility was grave; but the failure was also that of a whole elite. The problems inherited from Dutch colonialism were grave; objective conditions such as the demographic structure of the country were, to say the least, not propitious. But was the country bound to fail? There was no inevitable logic in the retreat from rationally coping with the situation to magical incantation. Demagogic politics, human frailty and incompetence caused the breakdown in 1965–66; not predestination. Indonesia, after all, is potentially a rich country. Around the turn of the century it had been the world's main exporter of raw materials. The preconditions for an economic take-off—for primitive accumulation—existed. Indonesia had once been known as the country of Bandung and *pancha sila,* its prestige in the early 50s had been high; within a decade it had become a textbook illustration of how to ruin a country.

The Bravado of Algeria's Ben Bella

In the 1950s and early 60s, a new political force emerged— the bloc of the national-revolutionary countries of Asia and Africa. In addition to Sukarno's Indonesia there was Nasser's Egypt, Nkrumah's Ghana, Sekou Touré's Guinea, Ben Bella's Algeria, united in the struggle against imperialism and neo-colonialism. By 1967 this bloc had disintegrated, not merely as the result of outside pressure, but mostly as a consequence of inner weakness. There have been some instances of solidarity such as Sekou Touré's assistance to Nkrumah. Egypt, in a similar way, showed concern for Ben Bella after his overthrow. Attempts are still being made to reassemble the national revolutionary regimes; but since a chain cannot be stronger than its component links, these efforts are at present not very promising.

Among the leaders of the national revolutionary camp no one enjoyed greater prestige than Ben Bella. His country had won independence after a bitter and heroic seven-year struggle against France. The leaders of the FLN were a group of devoted revolutionaries, a "band of brothers." They had been trained in the French left-wing political school and had a clear anti-capitalist program. Surely, Algeria faced great structural economic and social difficulties which the protracted civil war had aggravated. But on the whole, the state of affairs was not without promise when Ben Bella took over; there existed, owing to French initiative, the basis of a modern industrial infrastructure. The return of almost a million French settlers to France and the seizure of their property enabled the Algerian government to engage almost immediately in a socialistic transformation of agriculture—not on a basis of poverty but on a relatively highly developed level. This was a chance which no other Asian or African country had. Not only were industries nationalized, but also the trade, small hotels, and cinemas. Self-management was introduced in both agriculture and industry.

A year sufficed to show that "socialism" could not be introduced by decree, that the revolutionary phraseology bore no relation to reality. Within a short time Ben Bella had deposed, exiled or imprisoned his erstwhile comrades and established one-man rule. Within an even shorter time an enormously inflated, grossly overpaid, and parasitic bureaucratic machine developed which for all practical purposes ran internal affairs. Production in most industries fell to about one-third or one-fourth of what it had been before independence. (Oil production was the one exception but this was entirely in French hands.) Output in agriculture fell, especially of wine, a vital product for export. (Ben Bella nevertheless declared that Algeria was an advanced country, that self-government in Algerian agriculture was more progressive than in Yugoslavia!) The net agricultural revenue which had been over 100 billion fr. in 1961 fell considerably in the following years.

At the same time Ben Bella decided (to quote his successor) simply for reasons of personal prestige to spend 15 billion fr. on the Afro-Asian conference that was to be held in Algiers in 1965.* While pursuing political schemes far beyond the power of his country, both in the Maghreb and all over tropical Africa, his government neglected elementary social reforms at home; unemployment in Algeria was estimated between 60 per cent (Soviet sources) and 80 per cent (Western observers) of the total labor force. Again, it cannot be too strongly stressed that disaster was not inevitable. It was the result of theoretical confusion, of demagoguery and verbal radicalism, of a regime in which there was far more corruption than sincere will to build a new society. About Ben Bella's political orientation his successor has said: "For him socialism was only a means to avenge himself on those who opposed his personal power. One day he would proclaim Castro's type of socialism; the next day he would call himself an Algerian socialist; on other occasions a Muslim socialist. . . ."

Ben Bella set out to realize his aims in a particularly inept way. But the schemes themselves were unrealistic. A

* Boumedienne in an interview with *Al Shosm*, October 9, 1965.

meaningful socialist transformation is impossible with an intelligentsia lacking the technical know-how as well as patriotic spirit and selfless devotion to serve the country. There were individuals, some of them known, others nameless and faceless, who were inspired by genuine idealism, even if their ideas all too often turned out to be mere chimeras whenever they collided with the harsh realities. But by and large it was an unedifying rush by a new elite to escape austerity, to establish itself as a privileged class, materially as well as politically.

What Hath Nkrumah Wrought?

The story of Nkrumah is not dissimilar to that of Ben Bella or Sukarno: a national leader of strong if confused left-wing convictions who acquired genuine respect and admiration in the struggle for the independence of his country, but whose subsequent rule had disastrous consequences. There is in some ways more ideological consistency in Nkrumah than in Sukarno or Ben Bella. He began as a Christian Socialist but moved steadily toward fairly orthodox Leninism (Marxism-Nkrumahism) adapted by him for African conditions.

Nkrumah's ideas have been developed in his two most recent books *Consciencism* (including an attempt to describe "positive action" in mathematical formulas) and *Neo Colonialism*. In these books Dr. Nkrumah comments at length on philosophical questions, on world affairs and world economics in general, and on the need for African unity. He hardly ever deals with his own country's problems; the Ghanaian stage clearly was not big enough for him.

Nkrumah was handed over by the British colonial administrators a country that, with all the ill effects of colonial rule, was the most developed in tropical Africa. It had the highest literacy rate by far. It received very substantial sterling holdings. But it also inherited an agriculture geared largely to monoculture and thus subject to the vagaries of world prices. (210,000 tons of cocoa in 1954–55 yielded Ghana about $240 million; 590,000 tons ten years later actually yielded Ghana less—about $210 million.)

Instead of lessening this dangerous dependence on cocoa crop exports by diversifying agricultural production, Nkrumah's government encouraged new planting which eventually led to flooding the world market. The state farms turned out badly. While 32 big state corporations were established in industry, trade, and communications, all but one steadily lost substantial money; mining and the timber industry contracted. At the same time tremendous sums were spent on prestige projects such as Nkrumah statues, sports grounds, and conference halls for meetings with African heads of state.

Many millions were allocated to promoting Nkrumah's prestige abroad and the training of political agents to be used in other parts of Africa, in pursuance of ambitious schemes for a pan-African government. The cost of living rose by 30 per cent in one year, financial resources were dissipated: holdings of about $600 million when the country attained independence in 1957 had turned into a debt of fantastic size when Nkrumah fell in February 1966.[2]

Not all this money had been squandered by mismanagement and corruption, though the famous golden bed of Mrs. Edusei was certainly not an exceptional case. Ghana had been the pace setter for tropical Africa before 1957, and it tried to live up to its reputation after independence. Nkrumah's government built many new roads and did much to develop education in Ghana. There was a real attempt to industrialize the country, and achievements such as the Volta Dam scheme ought to be mentioned. The little fishing village Tema was transformed into a big modern harbor. But most of the development schemes were undertaken

[2] The extent of the debt (and the general plight of the country) became known only after Nkrumah's fall. The misinformation about the real state of affairs in Ghana was to a considerable extent the fault of certain European and American residents—journalists, scholars, and others—unfortunately a recurrent phenomenon in many African and Asian countries. Journalists and scholars are admittedly under indirect pressure not to publish unfavorable reports about their area of study. Any violation of this unwritten rule may cause their expulsion, and thus cut them off from the subject of their specialization. As a result, the coverage of the African and Asian scene both on the scholarly and the journalistic level is often unreliable.

in the mistaken assumption that the outside world would pay for them in the end.

What is, or was, Nkrumahism?

In his saner moments Nkrumah realized that without the transformation of Ghana into a strong industrialized economy and society, "socialism" would remain a slogan and all talk of socialist progress empty chatter. And he also understood that one could not build socialism without socialists. But instead of concentrating on the basic tasks, he engaged in overambitious schemes in many directions at one and the same time. Not a very brave man at the best of times, he isolated himself in his castle, and became the "Redeemer" depicted together with Jesus Christ—the man who would live forever. He surrounded himself with self-seeking courtiers and established a dictatorial regime that antagonized the country's technical intelligentsia.

Conor Cruise O'Brien wrote that proportionately no African country had more of such people than Ghana and none lost more. Those who left or gave up did so not because they were anti-socialist or pro-colonialist—"on the contrary, they had contributed more than their share to the real progress which Ghana has made—but they experienced conditions in which it proved increasingly difficult to work effectively." The official model was a strong, disciplined party, with "democratic centralism" as its guiding principle of organization and leadership. In fact, the one-party system was simply a means to communicate commands from the top leadership to the masses—and not a very efficient and reliable means at that, as the crumbling of the party after Nkrumah's fall has shown. Only then did it emerge how little idealism and genuine conviction there had been behind the staged mass adulation of the great leader and his invincible party, how narrow his "mass basis." Nkrumah was motivated by a strange mixture of "scientific socialism" and black magic (his trust in Kankan fetishes and, to a certain extent, in witchcraft).

There was nothing specifically left-wing about this regime; one political observer has said that Nkrumah possessed more of the hysteria of Hitler and the vanity of Mussolini than of the cold genius of Lenin. Nkrumahist Ghana was "an ideological state without an ideology, a one-party dictatorship without a party." The rise of the regime meant in sociological terms the "eclipse of a bourgeoisie *manquée* by a new petty bourgeoisie of the new municipalities and local market centres" (Dennis Austin). Nkrumahism was an "indiscriminate hotch-potch of sadly familiar concepts, usually ludicrously exaggerated and invariably unsuited to Ghanaian realities. The parentage of most items is easily recognizable; manic industrialization for its own sake; the glorification of autarchy and self-help; the official slogan of 'One leader, one Party, one Nation'; the egregious cult of personality; the abuse of Western plutocracy, the doctrine of proletarian nations" (Tibor Szamueli).

Social Failures in Africa

Almost every African country has made socialism its declared policy and everyone agrees that boundless confusion has been created as the result of the indiscriminate and, on the whole, misplaced application of a Western term to African realities. "All kinds of strange notions are peddled in many parts of Africa as to the nature of a socialist society," a British Communist has written. There is Muslim socialism, Arab socialism, Neo-Destour socialism, pragmatic socialism (in Nigeria), African socialism, and so forth. But if modern history has had any lessons at all, it is that socialism presupposes a fairly high level of development—social, economic, and political. In its absence all talk about a socialist society is either meaningless or a perversion of the term.

African countries, especially those which have inscribed revolutionary socialism on their banners, have learned this to their detriment. Congo-Brazzaville, for instance, is extremely radical; it follows a pro-Chinese foreign policy, but there is nothing revolutionary about the domestic policy of a government whose power is based exclusively on a palace guard of several hundred men, many of them foreigners.

Guinea engaged in an ambitious socialist experiment in 1959–60, promising a rate of growth superior to the Soviet Union and China. Illusory plans were drawn up which failed within a very short time. Most of the national Guinean companies that had been established went bankrupt or were dissolved. Those who prepared the plans were not all aware what kind of effort was needed to carry them out. French observers of the Left (René Dumont and Charles Bettelheim) have noted the extreme disparity between the institutional superstructures and the degree of political morality: "Guineans have not been willing to bend themselves to the efforts and discipline necessary to carry out the measures they adopted even when they were advised by Communist countries (whose nationals have left Guinea quite discouraged). . . ." These are strong warnings, all the more telling, because they came from close friends and sympathizers. "To some extent, a lack of knowledge can be compensated for by complete honesty and vice versa; but a country cannot do without both."

The preconditions for development in Mali were somewhat better than in Guinea because its leaders had a better grasp of economic problems and because the peasants of Mali are among the most industrious and progressive in West Africa. However, to quote Dumont again, "when political leaders and particularly civil servants, address the Mali peasants, they give them orders in much the same way as the colonial administrators do. They do not understand rural problems and therefore cannot help the peasants efficiently." The result has been stagnation in agriculture (with the exception of cotton production which has been boosted at very high cost) and very small advance in industry.

Tanzania is one of the more hopeful countries of Eastern Africa. Like Guinea and Mali it has a one-party system and the economic sector has been gradually nationalized; about 75 per cent of the exports are government-controlled. Yet the country is beset by the same difficulties as the other "socialist" African countries: considerable—and growing—unemployment, shortage of materials, allocation of resources to unproductive purposes, lack of trained personnel. True, the population is treated to radical socialist speeches and ambitious plans as if these had any bearing on reality. As in most other African countries, enormous sums are squandered on prestige projects, expensive embassies abroad, the latest models of aircraft, etc. Far more money is spent on administration than on productive development. President Nyerere has called for hard work and austerity on the Chinese pattern, but the local elite has shown a marked lack of enthusiasm in following this appeal.

Nasser: Domestic Problems and Foreign Disaster

Compared with Algeria, Ghana, and Guinea, Nasser's Egypt (the United Arab Republic) is, with all its weaknesses, a model of purposeful achievement. From a position of a somewhat vague "Arab socialism" President Nasser has moved toward a platform of "scientific socialism." All the main industries and the banks were nationalized in the early 60s; agricultural reform, which began hesitatingly in the middle 50s, has been speeded up. Cooperatives have been developed in the Egyptian village, work on the Aswan dam has made satisfactory progress. The rate of growth in key industries, in mining and oil production has been substantial over the last few years. Yet despite this progress Egypt found itself in a state of permanent crisis even before Nasser tried his luck in brinkmanship. Most of the progress was achieved owing to massive economic help (both aid and free gifts) from West and East. The country has vastly overspent, its foreign currency reserves are exhausted, and this in turn has caused stoppage of work in certain industries. Since Egypt is unlikely to receive such huge gifts in the future, and since the war with Israel was also an economic catastrophe, its crisis has immeasurably deepened. The cost of living has risen rapidly, much faster than productivity. The population explosion continues, the cotton crop is mortgaged on arms sales for years to come.

Some of the reasons are, for the time being, beyond human control; Egypt is one of the poorest countries in the world. The odds facing Egypt in this respect are much heavier than those which the other, more primitive African countries have to overcome. Yet, Egypt has been, of course, all along far more developed: it never really was a colony. It has technical experts in almost all fields needed, so much so that it exports teachers to many Arab and African countries.

Some of the setbacks can be explained by miscalculation and overambitious schemes on the part of the government, lack of enthusiasm and willingness to work on the part of the masses. Like other Asian and African leaders, Nasser has tried to play a role in world politics out of proportion to the real strength of his country. The unsuccessful attack by Britain and France in 1956 gave him enormous political credit, which in some ways has lasted to this day. On the other hand, there have been severe setbacks in the Sudan, in tropical Africa, and Yemen; it is too early to say whether anything may come of his schemes to unite the Arab world under his leadership. He has shown realism and has learned from defeats, but there is little doubt that his ultimate ambitions have not changed over the years—to engage in a policy of expansion. Whether Egypt will ever be capable of achieving this is not certain; the outcome of the war with Israel, deliberately provoked by him, has shown all the weaknesses of a regime, the inner strength of which had been grossly overrated by many outside observers.

Basically, Egypt is as poor as it was, though poverty has been spread more evenly. Economics apart, to what extent has Egypt under Nasser advanced toward a socialist and democratic society? The attempts to establish a state party, never very energetically tackled, have not been successful: the country has been ruled by a new class, army officers (including those who were subsequently given civilian assignments), and the secret police. Among the bureaucracy and the intelligentsia there are conflicting trends: Islamic, orthodox Communist—and those favoring Marxism-Nasserism, i.e., "military socialism" which has absorbed economic and social techniques from Leninism and which in foreign affairs steers close to the Soviet camp but socially is no nearer to Soviet Communism than to France under Napoleon III or to Fascist Italy. Following the defeat in the war and the ouster of so many officers who had to serve as scapegoats, the mass basis of the regime has further narrowed. Since Nasser can now no longer be certain of the loyalty of the new class, he has to rule through his party—which hardly exists as an effective body—and, to an increasing degree, through the police. Egypt under Nasser is a more modern state than it was under Farouk and the Pashas twenty years ago. If there is a harsher dictatorship and less political freedom now than two decades ago, it is difficult to see how any semblance of parliamentary democracy could have prevailed under any effective regime. The bulk of the population, vegetating on subsistence level, totally incapable of influencing politics in Cairo, has not basically changed since Farouk—the people have no more at stake in this country than their ancestors fifty or 200 years ago. Under Nasser, Egypt has survived; but it is grotesque to think that this police-socialism, now wholly dependent on outside help, could or should serve as a model for any other country.

Dilemmas of the Third World

An interim balance sheet in 1967 of the national revolutionary regimes of the Third World shows, to put it cautiously, that the expectations of some of their prophets mentioned here have not or not yet been realized. It is one thing for the *literati* of St. Germain des Prés (and their colleagues in other parts of the world) to declare that the Third World is starting a new history of man. But facts (as Lenin among others used to observe) are a stubborn thing. Facts and figures show that the industrialized countries of the West (including, of course, Eastern Europe) have forged ahead, while the distance between them and the national revolutionary regimes of Asia and Africa has widened, not lessened.

Seen from this angle there are no major differences between the national-revolutionary regimes of Asia and Africa and those that do not proclaim a radical-nationalist policy; the problems of backwardness are common to all of them. Comparisons are always risky and often unfair; if other North African countries have done better than Algeria, it is only fair to add that Algeria, regardless of its political system, faces greater problems than its neighbors. If, on the other hand, the performance of China (or of Pakistan) and the relative stability of these countries is compared with the mounting crisis in India, the reason is not merely,

and probably not mainly, the greater inefficiency of a democratic government. Geographical, climatic, and historical
factors are at least of equal importance. Can one reasonably expect labor productivity in a tropical country like
India to be equal to that in a moderate climate? Indonesia
and Algeria have failed, but not simply as a result of their
national-revolutionary and quasi-Marxist orientation; generalizations along these lines are almost impossible because
conditions vary so much from country to country. But it
can no more be doubted that what was hailed as a panacea
—namely radical slogans—has, by and large, not worked
better than other forms of government.

The general trend in Asia and Africa is toward military
dictatorship. Some observers have regarded this as a retrograde step, others welcomed what they consider the "progressive character of military socialism." The truth is simpler:
when civilian rule breaks down, the military remains as the
only force capable of preventing chaos. Military rule which
seems likely to prevail in Asia and Africa for a very long
time is thus an *ultima ratio*. It is hardly the dawn of a new
civilization that Fanon or Sartre imagined.[8]

Since these developments come as a disappointment to
everyone, their causes ought to be discussed frankly and
dispassionately. Some have already been mentioned; they are
"objective" in character—geographical and climatic. So far,
industrial societies have developed only in the moderate
regions of the northern hemisphere and they were not
plagued by a population explosion at the time of their take-
off. With further technological progress this handicap may
eventually be overcome, but this may take many decades

[8] There is little sense in discussing in this context other predictions
that are manifestly absurd—such as the assumption that Asian and African society would be regenerated by a series of peasant wars, more or
less on the Chinese model. That such Jacqueries may occur is extremely
likely and they may be wholly justified; they may possibly be successful
in one country or another owing to local conditions. But the idea that
they will be able to achieve anything other than a redistribution of agricultural property is fanciful. Even in China, where the peasants provided
the mass basis of a revolutionary movement, it has ended, it would seem,
in a military dictatorship. Populist ideas have their attractions but they
are even less relevant now than 100 years ago.

if not centuries. Nature has made Egypt much poorer than Kuwait (as long as petroleum is needed), or than Syria and Iraq. Given the nation-state, inequality will persist. Nor is there much point in blaming neo-colonialism for the falling prices of raw materials on the world markets; world demand for most commodities is limited and cannot be artificially boosted. Something ought to be done to remedy the situation—but it is a problem likely to recur regardless of the world order.

There has been a strong inclination in Asia and Africa to blame colonialism and neo-colonialism for most, if not all, the present misfortunes. Much emotion is involved and it is difficult to separate myth from reality. That the colonial situation was an unnatural and an immoral one goes without saying. Nor does one have to repeat the whole register of colonialist crimes of commission and omission. Perhaps the most fatal omission was the failure of the colonialist powers in education—with the result that in the Belgian Congo or Indonesia, for instance, there was hardly a native intelligentsia at all to take over when these countries became independent. And in most other countries the elite was deficient both in number and quality. The political failure of Asia and Africa is therefore to a large extent the responsibility of the West.

But the proponents of the new Afro-Asian ideology go much further. They claim that the Western powers have exploited Asia and Africa all along, that modern societies in the West could only be established on the basis of this stolen wealth of the colonies. The riches of London and Paris belong therefore to the damned of the earth as well as to Englishmen and Frenchmen. Western economic aid is therefore simply a partial restitution of stolen property. These are sweeping claims, but do the facts bear them out? That the colonial powers did not acquire colonies for humanitarian reasons need hardly be elaborated, and that individuals and companies have greatly enriched themselves from them goes without saying. But in the overall balance and from a Western point of view, colonies were a prestige operation, and an expensive one at that—most of them cost the metropolitan country more than they contributed to its wealth, especially during the last fifty years.

The economics of the former European colonial powers were not ruined as a result of the loss of colonies; they prospered more than ever before. According to the classical theory of imperialism, colonies were needed by the metropolitan countries for the export of capital and the import of raw materials. The first part of the formula is not true—Western capital has never been really attracted by the colonies. And to obtain raw materials in the modern world there are cheaper ways than the establishment of colonies. The most telling charge against the Western imperialist countries is not that they robbed Asia and Africa, but that they prevented indigenous economic development.

But would these countries be more highly developed today if there had not been Western domination? The answer is by no means clear. The idea that a substantial part of the wealth of the West belongs by justice to the countries of Asia and Africa may have its attractions, seen from the capitals of these countries. The danger of passivity and self-comforting illusions is obvious.

It is in the self-interest of the West to help the countries of Asia and Africa transform themselves economically and politically into viable countries. Much of the economic aid given during the last two decades has for a variety of reasons not had the intended effect; but this is no reason at all to discontinue it. The new Afro-Asian ideology, however, is dangerous because it tries to provide the ideological justification for what is, not to mince words, a parasitical relationship, as harmful in the long run for the self-respect of the Asian and African peoples as was the colonial relationship. It has, above all, the effect of blinding the countries, and especially their elites, to their own responsibility for the present shortcomings and failures.

The Asian and African elites are overwhelmingly "socialist" in political aspiration. Yet even the most sympathetic outside observers have had to admit that more often than not this is based on the assumption that a radical socialist phraseology is sufficient to build a socialist society. That there is a relationship between socialism and work is not at all clear to those who believe that a revolution is like a magic table in the fairy tale. In the private life of these people, revolutionary phraseology is often coupled with a horror of work and an exaggerated urge for the good things in life. In this respect the African and Asian revolutionaries could no doubt learn from the Chinese example but for the fact that Peking's motivations seem not to have been altogether altruistic. (Potentially dangerous intellectuals have been sent to work in the communes; one has not heard of the party *apparatchiks* taking part in similar exercise.) This is not to say that the national revolutionary regimes ought to copy Sparta or the Puritans in every detail. But unless there is some work ethos, unless these elites begin to understand that socialism is not only high-flown oratory but that it has some direct bearing on their own lives, that selfless devotion, sacrifice, and hard work are needed, they will not make any real progress. Unless they give up their aspirations of a life of luxury, all the talk and all the literature about socialism and socialist society will remain meaningless phrase-mongering.

GUNNAR MYRDAL

Economic Development in the Backward Countries*

GUNNAR MYRDAL is a native of Sweden, where he is Professor of International Economy at the University of Stockholm. He is the author of the classic *An American Dilemma: The Negro Problem and Modern Democracy; Beyond the Welfare State;* and *Challenge to Affluence. Asian Drama,* Professor Myrdal's ten-year study of the economies of South Asia for the Twentieth Century Fund, was published in 1968.

The first question I want to raise is that of the priority to be given to industry and agriculture in the underdeveloped countries' present situation. Intellectuals in underdeveloped countries largely pin their hopes on industrialization; and I want to emphasize from the start that this article should not be construed as implying that underdeveloped countries must not do their utmost to build up industry as fast as possible.†

The need for this is particularly pressing in countries with a high population land ratio. A country like India, whose population will double before the turn of the century, cannot in the long run hope to raise the dismally low living standard of its masses, or even retain the present one, unless

* Mr. Myrdal originally presented this paper before the Italian Society for International Organizations.

† I also want to make clear that in an article dealing with so vast a subject, my remarks are necessarily limited to a few bare essentials; even these had to be simplified, as there is no space here for substantiation, differentiation, or qualification. I had to exclude from my analysis those small areas of the world where underdeveloped countries have oil and other resources, for which the demand is rapidly rising because of the advanced nations' development. I omit these not because their problems are uninteresting or unimportant, but because the vast majority of people in the underdeveloped world have no access to such resources. I should add that most of my detailed knowledge is of South Asia.

a very much higher proportion of its labor force is employed in industry. This is true regardless of whatever progress is made in Indian agriculture. More generally, without the underdeveloped countries' progressive industrialization, it will be impossible to prevent the ever-widening income gap between rich and poor countries from continuing to grow as it has done for a century.

This long-term trend is reason enough for the underdeveloped countries to give prominence to industrialization in their development plans. But, for many future decades, even a much more rapid process of industrialization than that achieved by most underdeveloped countries will not provide sufficient employment for the underutilized labor force in these countries. This is so because the additional labor demand, created by industrialization, is a function not only of the speed of industrial growth but of the low level from which it starts.

If, as is often obviously rational, investment capital and human resources (both of which will always be limited, even if the developed countries provide far more assistance than at present) are to a large extent put into fully modern, fairly large-scale industries, the additional labor demand will be small. Furthermore, when industrialization implies rationalization of earlier, more labor-intensive industries, or when these can no longer compete with the new industries, the net effect on labor demand may be negative: in this case industrialization releases more labor than it employs. From this point of view industrial development for export and for import substitution has an advantage in addition to those usually recognized. But no underdeveloped country can industrialize exclusively along these lines. This implies that in the early stages of industrialization "backwash" effects decrease, wipe out, or even reverse the efforts to create new employment.

In a study of development in the Central Asian Republic of the Soviet Union, undertaken by the Secretariat of the Economic Commission for Europe, it was found that, despite heavy industrialization, the labor force employed in manufacturing decreased for more than two decades until the industrial base became so large that its continued rapid advance brought about a correspondingly large increase in demand for labor. Similarly in India—a country which not only promoted industrialization but steered it into import substitution while protecting its traditional manufacturing— a comparison of the census figures for 1950 and 1960 shows that industrialization had hardly any effect on the proportion of the labor force earning its livelihood from agriculture.

The Population Explosion

The fact that for many future decades industrialization will not create much additional net employment in underdeveloped countries, starting from a small industrial base, must now be considered in conjunction with the fact that, over the same period, the labor force in all underdeveloped countries will increase by more than 2 per cent a year, and in some countries by very much more. It should be noted that a decrease in the birthrate, especially a gradual one, will have no effect on the size of the labor force for fifteen years, and only a very minor effect for at least three decades.

At this point it is worth noting that there will be no spontaneous decrease in fertility in the underdeveloped countries, but that such a decrease could be brought about only by a policy of government-sponsored family planning; in no major underdeveloped country has such a policy as yet been pursued with sufficient effectiveness to bring substantial results.

Moreover, the high percentage of youth in the underdeveloped countries' populations implies a tremendous momentum toward high birthrates. Even if a policy to spread birth control can have little effect on the size of the labor force for three decades, it has nonetheless immediate and beneficial effects on age distribution and, consequently, on the level of *per capita* income, savings potential, and labor productivity. To press for such a policy is therefore of the utmost importance and urgency. But it is beside the point to relate, as is only too often done, the problem of population increase to the problem of "finding employment" for the increasing labor force; the latter is a given quantity for decades ahead, almost entirely independent of what happens to fertility.

The conclusion is evident: if, for several decades, little or no new employment can be generated by industrialization, while the certainty remains that the labor force will increase by between 2–4 per cent annually, then the greater part of this increase must remain outside industry, mainly in agriculture. At this point I may be excused for expressing my surprise that these simple facts have not been recognized by economists who constantly refer to industrialization as the means by which the increased labor force in underdeveloped countries can be employed outside agriculture; indeed, they often talk about decreasing the labor force presently employed in agriculture. Industrialization is the dynamic force in an underdeveloped country's economy operating by raising the level of technical interest and knowledge, mobility, readiness for experiment and change, enterprise, and rationality even outside industry. Unfortunately, these spread effects are again a function of the levels already reached. The experience of many underdeveloped countries in the colonial era, in which great spurts of industrialization produced strange and isolated enclaves, should be warning enough that these effects are likely to be small. There is a danger that, in their efforts to pursue industrialization, many underdeveloped countries are achieving the same result of building small enclaves within a much bigger economy that remains backward and stagnant.

Agricultural Development

I want to repeat that these remarks are not an argument against industrializing as rapidly as possible. If anything, they are meant as an argument for starting as soon as possible and proceeding as fast as possible, the sooner to reach the end of the transitional period—that long period during which industrialization does not significantly serve to create employment and its spread effects remain minimal.

But, at the same time, awareness of the facts should encourage serious efforts in other directions. This is particularly necessary in the present conditions of underdevelopment, when everything must be done to prevent industrial development being frustrated and finally aborted. Indeed, in the absence of such development plans on a wider front, even the most strenuous attempts to industrialize will most probably not prevent increasing misery, particularly in the poorer countries. Agriculture is by far the largest sector in the economies of all underdeveloped countries. Always more than half—and in some underdeveloped countries anything up to 80 per cent—of the total population earn their living from the land. The immediate cause of poverty, and thus of under-development, in these countries, is the extremely low productivity of labor in agriculture. It is a dangerous illusion to believe that there can be any significant economic development in these countries without radically raising the productivity of agricultural labor.

Given the two facts of an increase in the labor force— which we can safely predict will continue to the end of this century—and of an unchanging, if not actually decreasing demand for labor caused by industrialization, we cannot avoid coming to an important policy conclusion: any realistic agricultural policy must reckon on a tremendous increase in the agricultural labor force. During the considerable period in which industrialization creates only insignificant new employment, that part of the agricultural labor surplus which takes refuge from agrarian poverty and oppression by moving to the cities will be characterized by the same under-utilization of labor as in agriculture: it will go mostly into petty trading and services of various sorts, or will swell the number of odd-job seekers, unemployed, and beggars. Urbanization on any scale in underdeveloped countries unfortunately does not, and cannot, equal industrialization.

The conclusion that planning must take into account a very rapid increase of the agrarian labor force becomes a more serious challenge in face of the fact that the present labor force is underutilized on a vast scale—a situation that is popularly termed "underemployment." Rational agricultural policy must therefore be directed toward more intensive utilization of an underemployed labor force that is constantly and rapidly increasing. We must note in passing that this is a necessity which for various reasons none of the now highly developed countries faces or ever faced during their development. Again, I am surprised that this obvious conclusion is so seldom stressed.

Land Reform

In a short article I cannot examine the implications of this conclusion for agricultural planning, except to point out that successful agricultural development requires an entirely new technology in the underdeveloped countries.

As yet no scientific basis, founded on intensive, localized research and taking into account the climatic conditions in the tropical and subtropical zones of most underdeveloped countries, has been elaborated. These countries, and the rest of humanity with them, cannot afford to fail in the task of achieving a more intensive use of a rapidly increasing underemployed agrarian labor force. There is, however, one ray of hope: the present productivity of land in the underdeveloped countries is exceedingly low. There must, therefore, be means by which a very great increase in labor input and efficiency can raise yields per acre very substantially.

When we reach this point in awareness, we have to face that the main blockage to such an advance is political and institutional. In many underdeveloped countries power is in the hands of reactionaries who have, or believe they have, an interest in preventing those changes in landownership and tenancy that would give the peasants both incentives and possibilities to exert themselves for reaching higher productivity. Even in countries who have enlightened national leaders, the landlords, money-lenders and other middlemen frequently use their power locally to subvert legislative reforms. And the peasants, sunk in apathy, ignorance and superstition which their poverty not only causes but maintains, do not protest because of their very apathy.

About this there is general agreement. The FAO (Food and Agricultural Organization of the U.N.) has studied the problem, and resolutions for land reform and similar measures are constantly being passed by the Economic and Social Council and the U.N.'s General Assembly. But in practice little is accomplished in most underdeveloped countries. With the steady increase in the agrarian labor force—which, without rapid economic development, is itself causing increased inequality—an extremely dangerous situation is developing. The reluctance among many agricultural experts to press the issue, and their tendency to evade it by taking refuge in technological questions is equally dangerous. This is another practice which stems from colonial traditions. The FAO Freedom from Hunger Campaign has underlined the extremely low productivity of labor and land in the underdeveloped countries. Countries with populations of hundreds of millions, such as India and Pakistan—both of which have more than two-thirds of their labor force employed in agriculture—are on a suboptimal level of nutrition and are increasingly dependent on American charity to feed themselves. Food production in South Asia as a whole has, in recent decades, swung from surplus to deficit. The tragic experiences in Latin America in the postwar period, its major inflations and its retarded development, are not unrelated to the fact that vested interests have so far blocked most of the major agrarian reforms on which agricultural development—and also industrial development—depends.

The FAO has calculated that close to one-half of the world's population suffers from hunger or crippling malnutrition or both—and this half lives in the underdeveloped countries. Within these countries the masses of the undernourished are peasants. Taking into account future increases in population, the FAO calculates that total food supplies must be doubled by 1980 and trebled by the year 2000 to provide a reasonable level of nutrition for the world's population. My own studies lead me to believe that this is an underestimate rather than the contrary.

Two things are clear. First, most of this increase in food production must take place in the underdeveloped countries, which implies a sharp swing against the present curve of their agrarian development. Second, failure to reach this goal implies a world catastrophe whose import is terrifying.

Superficial Planning

It is in this light that we can see the danger of considering industrialization as a cure-all for the problems of underdevelopment. The danger is all the greater because this belief serves vested interests (and many wishful thinkers) with an excuse for not facing up to the real and difficult problems involved. If the image of industrialization can be put forward as the essential requirement for what wishful thinking calls the "take-off" to "self-sustaining" growth, then these interests need not concern themselves either with the failure to change economic and social conditions on the land, or with the failure to increase agrarian productivity. It is much easier to construct factories, often with foreign aid in capital and technicians, than to change social and economic agrarian conditions and the attitudes to life and work of millions of poverty-stricken peasants. And since no one can be against industrialization, this reinforces the arguments of those in positions of influence in the underdeveloped world who often have direct personal interests in industrialization.

This mode of thought is encouraged by the tendency to superficial planning which can be observed in the prejudiced and careless reasoning about priorities. The facts I have pointed to, and the conclusions I have reached, move me, in any discussion about priorities in these terms, to give first priority to agriculture. But this mode of reasoning assumes that there is a choice in which the answers are mutually exclusive. This assumption is on the whole false or, at least, only partly true.

First, the necessary institutional reforms are costly neither in scarce capital resources nor in foreign exchange. Many of the necessary investments in agriculture are, moreover, highly labor-intensive which would mobilize underutilized labor for all sorts of permanent improvements of the land. There has been much talk about this but little action. Similarly, efforts to raise the levels of education, health, and hygiene do not require heavy expenditure of capital or foreign exchange. These efforts, in most underdeveloped countries, have bordered on the feeble, even when considered exclusively from the point of view of productivity, in their potential effectiveness of relieving the peasantry of its apathy and traditional irrationality. To the extent that these and other reforms require the investment of capital and foreign exchange, such investment serves industrialization —the construction of factories producing fertilizers and agricultural machinery—as well as any rational and productive development plan.

For those few underdeveloped countries that have reached more advanced forms of planning and have emphasized the need for industrialization, the conclusion of my analysis is, *not* that they should have chosen otherwise, but that they should direct this emphasis to maximal advantage for agricultural development, which is of paramount importance for the success or failure of their economic development. My main conclusion, however, is that industrialization alone is insufficient. Even more important is that the problem of raising—rapidly and radically—the productivity of labor and land be squarely faced. If this issue is relegated, if it is given no more than second "priority," then this type of planning is inviting its own defeat, however successful it is temporarily in constructing a few factories. I am thus asking for a larger plan—a plan designed to encompass effective agricultural reforms.

The Necessary "Double Standard"

Up to this point I have considered the issue of underdevelopment as a problem of internal, national policy. This viewpoint is essential, for the destiny of these countries will be determined principally by their own efforts of consolidating themselves as effective political units prepared to bring about the radical social and economic changes necessary for development. But much will depend on whether the advanced industrial nations are prepared to reshape their policies in such a way as to facilitate this development. Since the First World War, the underdeveloped countries' trading position has steadily worsened; while demand for their exports has lagged, their import needs have increased. Their resulting balance-of-payments gap has until now been made up by foreign grants and credits which—with the exception of relatively limited direct private investments—have not been on strictly commercial terms. The causes for the deterioration of the underdeveloped countries' trading position are permanent and will continue to dominate the development of international trade, perhaps increasingly so, as the studies made by the secretariats of the regional economic commissions have shown.

Autarchic economic development has been forced on the underdeveloped countries by the restricted scale of grants and credits; their struggle to industrialize has focused on import substitution and on applying ever stricter exchange and import controls in order to preserve their scarce foreign exchange resources for essential consumption and development. As their trading balance worsens and their planning improves, we can expect this trend to develop still further. Without enlarging on this subject, I want here only to stress again the principal conclusions I have drawn from these facts. The first is that the advanced industrial countries must now be prepared to accept what I have called *a double standard of morality in regard to commercial and financial policies*—one which, for once, gives license to the weaker instead of the stronger. If they are not to lose every chance of developing, the underdeveloped countries cannot afford to relinquish their protectionist and autarchic policies. These, in particular their import and exchange controls, are in fact less due to their own choice than forced upon them by the harsh necessities of their internal development and deteriorating international trade position.

The advanced countries can have few rational reasons for failing to recognize this necessity, since the underdeveloped countries will always use whatever foreign exchange resources they can acquire to keep their imports as high as possible. Their import restrictions, unlike those of the advanced countries, can never cause the volume of international trade to shrink.

A second conclusion is that the advanced nations must cooperate sympathetically with every attempt of the underdeveloped countries *to combine to enlarge their internal base for agricultural and industrial development* whether on a regional or world scale. Underdeveloped countries have far better reasons for joining together than the six West European countries in what they euphemistically call a "Common Market." Nonetheless the difficulties facing such policies are very great. A third conclusion is that the advanced countries must be prepared to give the underdeveloped countries preferential treatment in international trade. This means, in effect, expanding on an international scale the sort of solidarity which the advanced nations now afford to their own lagging regions and industries.

If the advanced nations were willing to accept higher price levels than the forecast averages, this would make the problem of stabilizing the prices of underdeveloped countries' traditional exports much easier to solve by commodity agreements. As the advanced nations are becoming increasingly willing to give aid, this would be both a convenient and cheap way of providing this aid in a form that directly strengthens the underdeveloped countries' economies.

If the range of the advanced nations' imports were extended not only to the underdeveloped countries' traditional exports but—within certain quotas—to new industrial goods free of tariffs and import restrictions, this would be welcomed by the underdeveloped countries which are trying to diversify their production and exports. It would be of little consequence to the advanced industrial nations, as only a few underdeveloped countries would be in a position to build up new export industries, standardize and raise their production, and develop an efficient marketing organization. Even with such preference, underdeveloped countries would face difficulties in competing with the industrialized nations which already benefit from the internal and external markets they have developed, as well as from their powerful research resources.

In most cases, moreover, it would not involve competing in those sectors where industrialized nations should be eager to expand—the sectors where technology is highly advanced and capital input particularly heavy. In the long run it would bring about an acceleration of an international division of labor that would be of advantage even to the advanced countries.

For all this, and however beneficial the results, the quantitative effects of opening up more favorable export outlets for new industries should not be exaggerated. Many underdeveloped countries, indeed probably the majority, would not be in an immediate position to make use of such preferences; this would come only later when they have achieved a higher degree of success in over-all development. In any case, they would not be able to avail themselves of such preferences on any major scale. Patterns of world trade are glutinous, rooted as they are in conditions of production that are not changed overnight.

It must not be forgotten that the overwhelming bulk of underdeveloped countries' exports is of traditional exports, and that the greater part of these consists of agricultural products which make up about 70 per cent of their total exports. It is an illusion to believe that any substantial improvement can be made in the underdeveloped countries' international trading position without tackling the problem of *defending their markets for traditional exports* which, for years and probably decades, will constitute the bulk of what they have to sell.

The main cause of the underdeveloped countries' worsening international trade position lies in a falling-off in the growth of demand for their traditional exports, and in particular for agricultural products. To the extent that this has been due to low income-elasticity of demand and technological change, the trend is irreversible. But in some part it is caused by fiscal levies which keep down consumption even of such tropical products as coffee whose imports do not compete with domestic production, and by other forms of protection which directly or indirectly are detrimental to these exports.

Two things can be asked of the advanced industrial nations which are themselves in the process of rapid development and therefore should be able to take them in their stride. First, that they be prepared to eliminate all purely fiscal duties and taxes on the underdeveloped countries' exports. Second, that they lower and finally eliminate the protective trade barriers they have erected which, directly or indirectly, limit demand for imports from the underdeveloped countries. It must be recognized that the advanced nations may need a transitional period to meet this latter demand— though not in the former—as it implies a shrinkage of domestic production. In the long run, such structural adjustments for the use of their own labor force and productive capacity would accord with their rational interests, since it is not generally to their advantage to tie up resources in these sectors of production.

A further point I wish to stress is the extreme importance of increasing multilateralization—at least to the degree of the FAO's aid in food and other agricultural products to the underdeveloped countries—so that present or potential surplus countries are *protected, indeed encouraged, to produce agricultural products for this type of export.* Their productive potentialities may otherwise remain unutilized, particularly when their natural customers are other underdeveloped countries which are short of foreign exchange. Aid in agricultural products from the U.S. and other rich countries inevitably tends to destroy their markets. They are not in a position to give away their exports. The rational solution would be to give the new experimental agency for agricultural surplus disposal, created by the FAO, the funds to pay such countries for their exports, even if these are in turn given away as aid to other underdeveloped countries.

Although the policies I have briefly recommended are in the interests of the advanced nations—interests which can only be reinforced by the international tensions created by the continual frustration of the underdeveloped countries' efforts to develop—the advanced nations cannot be expected to carry out these policies because of rationality and idealism. Pressure from the underdeveloped countries themselves is necessary. As this pressure becomes increasingly vocal, rationality will come to play a part in the policy-making of the advanced nations. But the pressure must be reasoned and accurately directed at all the important issues. Only then will new and effective policies be formulated to end the underdeveloped countries' struggle for development.

RICHARD LOWENTHAL

The Prospects for a "Maoist" International

RICHARD LOWENTHAL is best known as a political journalist. He
is presently teaching at the Free University in Berlin. He is
author of many articles and books, including *The Future of Asia*
and *World Communism: The Disintegration of a Secular Faith.*
This essay was written in 1965.

The Will to Lead

It has taken years of successive disillusionments for the
Chinese leaders to become aware of the full implications of
their sense of mission. In 1956–57, they had begun to feel
ideologically superior to Stalin's heirs, but had still wished
to keep them in the "leading role" and to guide them quietly
behind the scenes. In 1959, following a series of disappoint-
ments over Soviet policies, they had begun to criticize their
allies in the forum of the international Communist movement,
hoping to bring effective pressure to bear on them. Meeting
unexpectedly stubborn resistance, they had by late 1960
come to think in terms of a protracted factional struggle
which, after repeated compromises, would eventually enable
them to become the recognized leaders of the world movement; but they probably still thought that a split could be
avoided. It seems likely that it was only the 22nd congress
of the CPSU—the clash with the Soviet leaders over the
Albanian issue and the memory of Stalin, and the adoption
of the Soviet party's new programme—that finally convinced

Reprinted from "The Prospects of Pluralistic Communism," by Rich-
ard Lowenthal, in *Marxism in the Modern World*, edited by Milorad M.
Drachkovitch, with the permission of the publishers, Stanford University
Press. © 1965 by the Board of Trustees of the Leland Stanford Junior
University.

Mao and his team that the Soviet leaders were incurable "revisionists," and that it was the Leninist duty of the Chinese party to prepare for a split and the creation of a new, truly revolutionary International. At any rate, both the ideological output and the organizational tactics of the Chinese changed after this event: ideologically, they broadened the area of the dispute to defend Stalin's memory and attack Khrushchev's domestic policies; organizationally, they began to prepare positions for an impending break rather than for a long-term internal debate and openly strove to discredit the Soviets among the nationalists of the underdeveloped countries.

While thus looking towards a split, the Chinese leaders were still trying to avoid the onus of the initiative and also to delay the date: the longer they could work with a separate factional platform and organization inside a formally united movement, as the Bolsheviks had worked inside the Russian Social Democracy until 1913, the better, they felt, would be their chances to extend their influence—provided they did not make any more ideological concessions for unity's sake. But when the double crisis of the autumn of 1962—over the Soviet missiles in Cuba and the Sino-Indian frontier war—showed that the alliance between the two main Communist powers had been eroded to vanishing point, the course of five European Communist party congresses in the following months made it clear that the Soviets, too, now regarded a split as inevitable and would hasten it if they could. In the circumstances, the bilateral talks held in Moscow in June-July 1963 were viewed by both sides not as a last chance for reconciliation, but as a final confrontation before the break*; the Chinese published their "Proposal for the General Line of the Communist Movement," with its all-out attack on the "revisionist" CPSU program, on the eve of the talks, and the Soviets replied one month later with their "Open Letter" which contained among other charges the specific accusation that the Chinese were supporting splitting activities in various Communist parties. Ex-

---

* As the underlying factors have not been changed by the fall of Khrushchev, it is the writer's view that any new bilateral meeting following this event would have a similar, purely tactical character.

pulsions and counterexpulsions had in fact begun in a number of countries, and the time had come to justify the organizational schism on grounds of principle. After the Sino-Soviet talks had failed and the Soviets had signed the nuclear test ban agreement with the United States and Britain in late July, the Chinese were ready for it: they called the agreement a betrayal, they began to disclose parts of the secret prehistory of the conflict, and they built up the case for splitting Communist parties that had fallen into the hands of "revisionist traitors."

By the beginning of September 1963, the Chinese Communist press began to publish approving reports about the formation of anti-revisionist splinter groups in various countries; at the same time, the first clearly Peking-financed organs of Communist dissidence made their appearance outside China, after French and Spanish editions of the *Peking Review* had prepared the way several months before. Later that month, the Indonesian party leader D. N. Aidit, reporting on a two months' journey through the leading Communist capitals, on his return proclaimed the principle that true Marxist-Leninists, if expelled by a revisionist party leadership, were entitled to form a new Communist party, and that such "circles, magazines and new parties," if found to be truly Marxist-Leninist, deserved the support and solidarity of established parties under Marxist-Leninist leadership. On October 26, the deputy head of the Chinese party's propaganda department, Chou Yang, declared in a speech in Peking the splitting of revisionist-led parties by Marxist-Leninists to be an "inexorable law"—for the surprising dialectical reason that the Communist movement, like everything else, "tends to divide in two." The speech was published two months later and, more important, its principal arguments recurred in early February 1964 in the seventh of the Chinese party's official commentaries on the Soviet "Open Letter," entitled "The Leaders of the CPSU are the Greatest Splitters of All Time"; with the full authority of the Chinese party, this document took the line that in any split between "Revisionists" and "Marxist-Leninists," regardless of the factual circumstances, the political guilt rests with the revisionists—in other words, that a pro-Chinese minority cannot do wrong when it splits a pro-Soviet Communist party. During the same period, finally, the Soviet and Chinese parties had also changed roles with regard to the project of another Communist world conference: in 1962 the Chinese had urged and the Soviets evaded it, but from October 1963 it was the Soviets who sought a showdown conference to achieve a clear majority vote against the Chinese views, and the Chinese who worked to prevent it while they were building up their own new International.

The Chinese were not, in fact, explicitly speaking of the need for a new international organization; on the contrary, in their polemics against the Soviet leaders they kept stressing the independence and equality of all Communist parties, denying the right of even the most powerful outside party to interfere in any party's internal affairs and asserting that there could be no return to the times of the Comintern with its single command center. In practice, however, they behaved exactly as the Soviet leaders had behaved in the formative years of the Comintern. They used their authority to redefine the principles of revolutionary doctrine and strategy, and to decide which party or splinter group was "truly" revolutionary in accordance with those principles. They used their diplomatic missions and publishing offices in various countries to make contact with dissident revolutionary groups, to subsidize their activists by employing them, and to finance their publications.

They also indicated their willingness to combine fission with fusion: just as Lenin, in his effort to rally all militant revolutionaries, had appealed to revolutionary syndicalists even if they had no Marxist traditions and had rebuked the "intellectual arrogance" of those old-line Marxists who wished to reject them on those grounds, so the Chinese were now saying that the Algerian FLN had proved itself a more revolutionary force than the Algerian Communist party, and Castro a better revolutionary leader than the old Cuban Communists. For the new International in its initial stage, what mattered most was clearly to attract the most militant revolutionary elements of any country, regardless whether they came from inside or outside its established Communist party. This was most clearly shown in the one directly international organ that was created, also in September 1963, on the Chinese line and with Chinese money—the monthly *Revolution,* published in several languages from Paris as a magazine for Africa, Latin America, and Asia: for it based its appeal on no narrower doctrine than that of violent anticolonialism. In fact, the Chinese leaders are convinced that this must also be the main basis of the appeal of the new International as a whole.

The Primacy of the Underdeveloped Regions

Long before the factional struggle began, the Chinese had considered that their main chances of international influence lay in the underdeveloped countries of Asia, Africa, and Latin America. As early as the end of 1939, Mao had first expressed the view that the revolution in all colonial and semicolonial countries would follow the same "laws" as in China; and on the morrow of final victory in the civil war, Liu Shao-chi had proclaimed the Chinese revolution as a model for all those countries at the Peking conference of Asian and Australasian trade unionists. During the years that followed, China's authority among the Asian Communists had grown, apparently with toleration from Stalin; and after Stalin's death the Bandung conference had greatly increased China's prestige among Afro-Asian governments, and the formation of the "Afro-Asian Solidarity Committee" had given her access to a useful machinery for influencing the most militant revolutionary elements of both continents.

By the time the factional struggle with the Soviets opened in 1959–60, colonial "wars of national liberation" had become, in Peking's concept, a vital means for diverting the strength of the imperialists—above all the main enemy, the United States—and wearing them down; now they also became a useful lever for disrupting the Soviet diplomacy of "peaceful coexistence," i.e., for interfering with any plans for a Soviet-American dialogue. In the Chinese April documents of 1960, which constituted their first coherent factional platform, the need to support anti-imperialist uprisings without regard to the risk of escalation or to the consequences for overall diplomatic relations with the enemy became one of the central theses. When the Soviets advised the Algerian FLN to negotiate with de Gaulle, they could be accused of opportunism; when they supported Cuba with economic aid and demagogic threats against the United States, they could be embroiled with the Americans; when they got involved in the Congo troubles, both lines could be pursued by Peking in turn. In any violent colonial conflict, Chinese interest was clearly on the side of militancy, while Soviet interest was divided between the wish to inflict defeat on the imperialists and the need to control the risk; and the Chinese missed no chance for pointing out the difference to the Communists and sympathizers from the countries concerned. It is hardly surprising that both at the 1960 Moscow conference of 81 Communist parties and at the meetings of the World Federation of Trade Unions and the World Peace Movement, the Chinese line found a sympathetic echo chiefly among some of the delegates from the underdeveloped continents, and that support for it proved much stronger in the Afro-Asian Solidarity Organization than in any other international "front."

It is true that some of the revolutionary movements which thus received Chinese support were by no means Communist-controlled and could be described as corresponding to the "Chinese model" only in that they were anti-imperialist, peasant-based, and above all violent. But as the bulk of the Communist parties of the advanced industrial countries took sides against China in the factional struggle, it became increasingly obvious to Peking that all the chances for revolutions, be it under Communist or non-Communist leadership, were concentrated in the colonial, ex-colonial or semicolonial countries, while in the advanced countries, however large their Communist parties, there seemed to exist no immediate potential for revolutionary struggle at all. In Western Europe and North America, the Communist parties had welcomed Khrushchev's "revisionist" thesis of the "peaceful road" to power except for insignificant minorities. But the Communists of Vietnam and Laos were fighting a civil war under Chinese guidance. The Cuban Communists had, however reluctantly, joined Fidel Castro's revolution, and the Venezuelan and various other Latin American Communists were trying to imitate its partisan strategy. Strong factional opposition to the "peaceful road" strategy had developed—originally, it seems, independent of any Chinese stimulation—among the Brazilian Communists since 1957 and among the Indian Communists since 1958; while the Japanese Communists were expelling a "revisionist" group at the very moment of the 22nd congress of the CPSU. Both the early struggle for national liberation in countries where the Communist parties were weak or non-existent as in Africa, and the later Communist-led struggle against the continuing influence of the "imperialists" in formally independent countries thus seemed to offer the scene of irreconcilable, violent conflict that was required by the Chinese vision—and with it corresponding chances for Chinese leadership.

Once the Chinese had determined on preparing for a new, truly revolutionary International, it was natural that they should recognize this geographical shift in the main theatre of the world revolution. They did so by adopting, in early 1963, the formula that the countries of Asia, Africa, and Latin America now constitute "the main focus of global contradictions" and "the storm center of the world revolution," and that the struggle of their peoples would be "decisive" also for the ultimate victory of the proletariat of the advanced industrial countries; and they have since stuck to this formula in the face of all Soviet charges of "racialism" and of all warnings against weakening the colonial liberation struggle by "isolating" it from the cause of the advanced "socialist" countries and from the movement of the Western industrial proletariat. This thesis is basic for the possibility of a new, Sino-centric International in that it denies to the conflict between the Soviet-centered "socialist world system" and the imperialist powers its role as the main axis of the international class struggle. But it also constitutes the germ of a new doctrine that is incompatible with the teachings of either Marx or Lenin.

For Karl Marx, it was axiomatic that the victory of socialism would be brought about by the industrial proletariat of the most advanced countries on the basis of the highest level of economic development that capitalism could achieve. Lenin broke with this concept by seizing power in backward Russia on the ground that Russia constituted "the weakest link" in the imperialist chain, and by proclaiming the alliance between the revolutionary proletariat of the industrial West and the nationalist revolution of the colonial East; but he never left any doubt that he regarded the class struggle of the proletariat as the decisive force, compared with which the nationalist movements of the colonial and semi-colonial countries would be mere auxiliaries. The new Chinese doctrine reverses this relationship, treating in fact the working class of the advanced countries as mere auxiliaries of the peoples of the underdeveloped countries, and unreliable auxiliaries at that; it thus adopts a position that was explicitly criticized by Lenin and Stalin in the early years of the Comintern, when similar views had been expressed by Sultan Galiev and for a time also by the Indian Communist M. N. Roy. Nor can the Leninist orthodoxy of the new Chinese position be rescued by the fiction that the leading role of the proletariat in the new International will be assured by the leadership of the Chinese Communists: though Lenin himself evolved a similar fiction to justify the possibility of Soviet regimes in Asian territories without an industrial working class, he never regarded such territories as the central part of the international revolutionary front. Moreover, the Bolshevik party in Lenin's time, though in fact independent of working class interests thanks to its centralist organization, was at least based on a predominantly proletarian membership and allied with important sections of the West European proletariat, whereas in the case of Mao's party today the claim to represent the industrial proletariat has become wholly fictitious: it rests neither on its history, its composition, nor its international influence, only on the vestigial notion that whoever conducts a militant revolutionary struggle against imperialist monopoly capitalism expresses *ipso facto* the true class consciousness of the proletariat.

Yet just in its conflict with both Marxism and Leninism, Mao's new doctrine is based on some of the decisive historical facts of our time. In the forty years since Lenin died, the workers of the advanced industrial countries have become less and less revolutionary, with the result that in no such country have the Communists been able to lead a victorious revolutionary movement. By contrast, it is in the under-developed countries that huge masses of people, living in extreme insecurity on the edge of starvation, can be said to have "nothing to lose but their chains," and their despair has offered opportunities for a number of victorious revolutions, including Communist revolutions. The course of contemporary history has thus made it impossible for the Communist leaders to be faithful to Lenin's Marxist belief in the industrial working class and to Lenin's passion for revolutionary struggle at the same time, though they have tried hard not to admit the fact to themselves. Under the pressure of their conflict with the Soviets, the Chinese leaders, whose links to European Marxism and to the industrial proletariat have always been tenuous, have at last made a choice: their new International will be wholly revolutionary, but only marginally proletarian.

The Chances of "Chinese-type" Revolutions

What, then, are the chances that further revolutions of the underprivileged peoples will in fact lead to the victory of totalitarian parties committed to permanent, irreconcilable struggle against the "imperialists," and that the Chinese Communists will be able to guide the development of these new totalitarian regimes for any length of time?

In trying to answer the first part of the question, it may be useful to group the bewildering variety of pre-revolutionary crisis situations in these countries into a few main types. First, there are the few African populations still struggling against direct colonial rule or formal white supremacy. Second, there is the much larger number of politically sovereign, "semicolonial" countries whose problems of economic and social development, difficult enough in themselves, are complicated by the existence of foreign capitalist combines holding key positions in the national economy—combines that often have no positive interest in the overall development of the country concerned and sometimes are directly opposed to it. Third, there are the newly independent countries whose regimes, quite apart from any influence of foreign capital, are proving for various reasons unable to create a functioning administration and a sense of national loyalty, yet are continuing to enjoy Western "imperialist" support simply because they are in power and often appear as the only available alternatives to Communist victory.

In the first type of situation, Communist leadership has hitherto been exceptional: only in the Vietnamese uprising against French rule did the Communists lead from the start. The Chinese Communists themselves emphatically recognize that such a contingency, however desirable, should not be a condition for their support of an anti-imperialist revolt: for years they have gone out of their way to extol the Algerian FLN, despite its non-Communist ideology and leadership, as a model for other oppressed nations; and while hoping for stronger Communist influence among the underground movements in South Africa and the Portuguese colonies, they will similarly support them in any case. Yet the FLN in power has shown no desire to continue militant conflict with the West for conflict's sake; whether it will eventually return to such conflict will neither depend on the memories of its heroic period nor on Chinese advice, but on the obstacles it encounters in trying to develop its country and on the ability of its leaders to cope with them. Generally speaking, the "first phase" of the anticolonial revolution—the struggle for political independence—is unlikely to result in Communist regimes of any kind.

The second type of prerevolutionary situation is widespread both in Latin America and in the Middle East, and examples occur in all underdeveloped regions. The histories of Mossadegh's rule in Persia and of Kassem's Iraqi revolution as well as of Nasser's Egypt, and of Peron's Argentina as well as of the Bolivian and Venezuelan revolutions, offer examples of the political explosions that may result if independent national development has to be achieved against the joint resistance of native oligarchies and foreign capitalist interests. So far, Fidel Castro's Cuban revolution has been the only one of this type that has actually issued in Communist rule, yet it seems to have greater potentialities as a model than that of Ho Chi Minh among the first type; for while non-Communist movements for political independence have almost universally succeeded, many of the non-

Communist revolts against "semicolonial" dependence have failed. Now regardless of Castro's cautious maneuvering in the Sino-Soviet conflict, the close affinities between the "Fidelist" guerrilla strategy as taught by Guevara and Mao's type of partisan warfare are notorious, and throughout Latin America today the influence of the Fidelist and the Chinese model tend to merge. On the whole, the prospects that further revolutions against "semicolonial" dependence may turn Communist are serious, because here the link between nationalism and anti-capitalism is inherent in the situation; they can be reduced only if the Western powers, and particularly the United States, go out of their way to dissociate themselves from the vested interests of Western private corporations in those countries.

Yet there are indications that the "classical" chances for Chinese-inspired Communist revolutions arise in the third type of crisis: the one that occurs where the leaders of a newly independent country fail, for whatever reason, to create a viable state and, *a fortiori,* to solve the problems of economic development—particularly if those leaders, after successfully conducting the original struggle for independence, have meanwhile been accepted by the West. After all, Mao's original conquest of China was the victory of such a "second wave" revolution, due to the failure of the once revolutionary Kuomintang to cope with the immense difficulties of Chinese unification and modernization after decades of war and civil war. Today, comparable failures are offering opportunities for a variety of promising strategies to Chinese-oriented Communist parties in several Southeast Asian countries. The Indonesian Communists are seeking to profit from the administrative and economic ineffectiveness of Sukarno's "guided democracy" by first collaborating with him, involving him in conflict with the West, infiltrating his machinery of government and finally inheriting his power; the Vietnamese Communists have profited from the different, but equally marked ineffectiveness of the bureaucratic-military regime in South Vietnam to expand their guerrilla warfare in the teeth of all American support for their opponents. These "second wave" opportunities are not identical with the "second phase" of the anticolonial revolution foreseen by

Leninist theory: just as in China in the 40s, they arise not from the class struggle of the proletariat against the rule of the "national bourgeoisie," but from mass despair in a climate of general political decay. (The Chinese do not even hesitate to exploit the weakness of some of the new states by promoting purely tribal revolts, as now in the Congo!) But as China's own case has shown, the chances of the "second wave" revolution are none the less real for not fitting into the traditional Leninist schema.

The Limits of Chinese Control

We must thus reckon with the prospect that further totalitarian revolutions of a more or less "Chinese" type may be victorious in various parts of the underdeveloped world, and we can be sure that Mao's China will give them any aid and encouragement of which it is capable. But it does not follow that the regimes emerging from such totalitarian movements, or even the movements themselves before the seizure of power, will be willing to submit to Chinese leadership in the way in which all Communists submitted to Soviet leadership for several decades. There are, in fact, at least three major obstacles to this. First, the revolutionary movements on which the Chinese tend to lean are much more strongly nationalist than those with which Lenin built the Third International: after all, the Comintern arose from a reaction to the "betrayal of internationalism" by the official socialist parties in World War I, whereas the new "Sinintern" is to be largely based on the "betrayal of the national liberation struggle" by the Soviets. Second, for many of the movements in question, China is not the only available, nor even a sufficient, source of support: Castro may well regard China as more reliable than Russia—but he has to rely on Russia nevertheless, because the Soviets can offer him so much more of what he needs. Third, Russia was the unique model for all Communists until at least 1949. Now Russia has lost her uniqueness—but that does not mean that China has automatically gained it, even in the eyes of those Communist parties and governments that incline to her side of the schism.

The Chinese Communists themselves are sufficiently aware

of these limitations to disclaim any thought of returning to a "world party" with the rigid, single-centered discipline of the Comintern. They may in fact exert close organizational control over the pro-Chinese splinter groups in the West that depend on them for funds and publicity, and over such traditionally dependent Communist underground parties as those of Malaya and Thailand, most of whose members are Chinese. Their influence may be dominant in helping the left wing of the Indian and, of course, the Nepalese Communists to organize their separate parties, and traditionally strong with the Communist party of Japan; but they could not afford to interfere in the least with the autonomy of the powerful Communist party of Indonesia, which made a point of taking its time and listening to both sides before it officially joined the "Chinese camp." Again, North Korea may have become some kind of a Chinese satellite, but the Communist rulers of Albania have joined the Chinese cause by their free decision and have made an independent contribution to the dispute, and North Vietnam, for all her dependence on Chinese backing in her military struggle in the South, could not simply be ordered to take the Chinese position but had to be slowly won over.

But while the Chinese Communists can and do renounce any claim to disciplinary subordination in their new International, they cannot renounce the claim to ideological leadership: they have always believed that no united international movement is possible without a recognized ideological authority, and as we have seen, the schism means to them that they have now to play this role. The logic of this claim to ideological leadership has not only driven them to elaborate their version of the Communist doctrine more and more thoroughly, just as the Leninist version of Marxism was thoroughly elaborated only in the context of the worldwide break with the democratic Socialists; it has also compelled them to find a doctrinal justification for their own claim to uniqueness—as the only great power actually engaged in building socialism and eventually Communism.

It is in that context that Mao's latest charges about the "restoration of capitalism" not only in Yugoslavia, but also in Russia itself, acquire their true international significance.

They serve not only to denounce the "Khrushchev clique" and to explain to the Chinese Communists that they must in the future stand alone without counting on the Soviet alliance, but also to "prove" to the Communists and revolutionary nationalists of the underdeveloped regions whom China wants to lead that there is no alternative. If Russia is going capitalist again thanks to the alliance between the re-emerging private businessmen and kulaks, the corrupt bureaucrats and grafters and the "revisionist traitors" at the top who tolerate and protect them; if Russia's new spirit of less visible controls and increased emphasis on material incentives and comforts is a capitalist spirit, as Mao's latest document maintains, then the schism is not merely about questions of strategy and tactics, not even merely about orthodoxy versus heresy: it is a conflict between a socialist and a capitalist power. The Soviet Union is not merely an unreliable ally—it is ruled by traitors who have joined the enemy camp. To China, as the only great power still following the true path of socialism, has fallen the task to carry the banner; henceforth, to struggle for socialism means to accept China's leadership.

The Repercussions on China

Yet this argument for the uniqueness of China contains both dangers to her own development and weaknesses from the viewpoint of her international attraction; for it depends on a rigidly egalitarian and military concept of the road to socialism that rejects all privileges for scarce technical, economic, and administrative cadres and deprecates any belief in material incentives in favor of a cult of collective enthusiasm and heroic poverty. Unless this dogma is radically revised (which might conceivably occur after Mao's death), it will add to the many objective difficulties of China's economic development a self-made obstacle that may well prove insurmountable; indeed, one is tempted to wonder whether it does not really express a half-conscious tendency of the Chinese leaders to give up the near-hopeless struggle for industrializing China without major foreign aid and to seek instead to conserve their political order on the present low economic level by glorifying its social justice and collective discipline.

But such a "socialism" of "high-minded but hungry people sitting around an empty table in complete equality," as Khrushchev once expressed it, would lack one of the main attractions hitherto exerted by the Communist bloc on the intelligentsia of the underdeveloped countries—the attraction of a model for quick modernization. Indeed, the passion to catch up with Western productivity and power implies at least a partial acceptance of Western values; conversely, Mao's increasingly complete rejection of those values is incompatible with that obsession with material productivity which the Bolsheviks took over from their Western teacher Karl Marx, and the new nations from their former imperialist rulers. It is, of course, conceivable that the Chinese reversal of the order of priorities will appeal to some political elites in Asia and Africa, particularly in countries where the problems of economic development appear increasingly insoluble; Communism of the Chinese type would then become not a model for development, but a model for accepting its failure and reacting by a final extrusion of the influence of Western civilization. But short of either such a generalized withdrawal from the present fascination with economic development, or a radical change in Chinese economic and social doctrine, it would appear that Communist China's chances of being accepted as a guide for "building socialism" in developing countries are much poorer than its chances of serving as a guide for the revolutionary seizure of power.

If this is true, it limits severely the prospects of maintaining Chinese authority in a new International. For it means that while revolutionary movements in the underdeveloped world will gladly accept Chinese ideological guidance along with other forms of support, successful revolutionary governments will, unless physically dependent on China, tend to keep their own counsel and refuse to recognize Peking's "leading role." Whenever possible, they will continue to accept support from both Russia and China, as Cuba is doing and Vietnam would have wished to do; and if forced to make a choice, those who are not in China's physical power sphere may well prefer the protector that demands least ideological conformity and offers most material help. This means that Castro's Cuba, despite its interest in guerrilla revolutions, is unlikely to join a Chinese-led International. It also means that though the Indonesian Communists may be expected to become one of the most important founder members of such an International, a Communist-governed Indonesia would hardly submit to China's ideological authority for long. The Chinese effort to build up a new International may have an important stimulating effect on Communist and semi-Communist revolutionary movements in the underdeveloped world, but the new body itself will be unstable, and may decay much more rapidly than its parent.

BENJAMIN SCHWARTZ

Chinese Visions and American Policies

BENJAMIN SCHWARTZ is professor of history and government at Harvard University and has traveled extensively in the Far East. He is the author of several books, among them *Communism in China and the Rise of Mao; A Documentary History of Chinese Communism* (with Conrad Brandt and J. K. Fairbank); and *In Search of Wealth and Power: Yen Fu and the West.*

Washington is, of course, aware of Peking's hopes for the future; one is tempted to add, only too well aware. What might be called Mao Tse-tung's optimum global vision has only recently been called to our attention once more in Lin Piao's widely publicized article, "Long Live the Victory of People's Wars."* Here we find Asia, Africa, and Latin America enveloped by "wars of national liberation" strictly modeled on the classical pattern of the Chinese revolution. The ingredients of this classical model can be clearly enumerated. The war must first of all be led by a genuine Marxist-Leninist party (which now means a party oriented to Peking); the party must rely primarily on peasant support and establish rural base areas; the peasant-based people's armies must fight a type of guerrilla war which draws its basic inspiration from Mao's maxims on this subject; the people's war must also be supported by a broad united front of "all those with whom one can unite" which will, however, remain firmly under Communist control. In this way the main enemy will be effectively isolated. In spite of Peking's continuing denunciations of Moscow's effort to "wave the baton" in the Communist world, one

Reprinted from *Commentary*, by permission; © 1966 by the American Jewish Committee.

* See "China's Strategy—A Critique" by Donald S. Zagoria in the November 1965 *Commentary*—Ed.

need not doubt that the Chinese themselves dream of waving the baton decisively in a world Communist movement reconstituted through the Maoist strategy and now centered on Peking.

In the face of assertions that Lin Piao's statement represents a newly-proclaimed Chinese *Mein Kampf,* and in the interest of historical perspective, it is important to point out that all the essential features of this statement were contained in Liu Shao-ch'i's famous speech in 1949 to the meeting of the Asian and Australian wing of the WFTU. At the time, to be sure, the message was delivered within the limits imposed by a seemingly monolithic international Communist movement led by Moscow. Liu could, in fact, deliver the speech only because the Kremlin was for the moment itself lending a certain hesitant and suspicious support to the notion—rendered plausible by certain developments then current in Vietnam, Indonesia, India, and Malaya—of the applicability of the Chinese model to other areas of the non-Western world. It was made entirely clear, however, that the center of world Communist authority lay in Moscow. Since then, the inhibitions have been removed, and Peking has been able to proclaim its vision in all its imposing amplitude.

Nevertheless, that vision was probably more unambiguously plausible in 1949 than it has ever been since. The rapid retreat of the Western empire had just begun and by no means seemed inevitable (from the Communist perspective least of all). The isolated cases of Indian and Philippine independence could easily be dismissed by both Moscow and Peking as a bourgeois sham, and the hope that rising nationalism would everywhere come under Communist leadership was vivid and reasonable. Ho Chi Minh was even then the paradigm of the popular nationalist leader who was also a convinced Marxist-Leninist.

The rise within the next few years of new states under non-Communist auspices and the failure of various Communist efforts in Asia subsequently led both Moscow and Peking to adjust their sights to a world which neither had foreseen. Out of this experience, there emerged the famous Bandung policy of cultivating Asian, African, and Latin American states already in being, whatever the nature of their internal polity. Bandung is often depicted as a triumph of Chou En-lai's suave diplomacy. If it was a triumph, however, it was a triumph of massive adjustment to an unlooked-for situation—hardly a triumph of the vision projected by Liu in 1949. Since Bandung, Peking's policies toward the third world have oscillated within the range of possibilities lying between the optimum vision and the Bandung line, while certain particular policies toward particular states can be explained quite satisfactorily in terms of the most conventional power politics. No doubt, the optimum vision remains the "esoteric" doctrine closest to Mao's heart. Yet there have been considerable stretches of time when the vision has been discreetly thrust into the background for the very solid reason that it is difficult to cultivate the existing states of Asia, Africa, and Latin America while simultaneously calling for their overthrow by "genuine" Marxist-Leninist wars of liberation.

In the Lin Piao statement the optimum vision does, to be sure, reemerge to the surface in full clarity—perhaps to encourage patience in Hanoi by stressing the "protracted" nature of the classical people's war; perhaps because at a time when the Bandung approach is generally not flourishing, a reaffirmation of the faith seems necessary; perhaps, again, because of the continuing need to distinguish Peking's "pure" line from the adulterations of Moscow. But whatever the real motive behind the restatement of the original vision at this time, a careful scrutiny of Lin Piao's article reveals the odd fact that, side-by-side with the maximum projection, ambiguities and ambivalences can be found which leave the doors wide open to alternative approaches. For example, having asserted that "national democratic" revolutions must be led by *genuine* "proletarian parties," having declared that *genuine* independence can be wrung from the imperialists only by "people's wars," and having contemptuously dismissed the socialist claims of all states not ruled by *genuine* Communist parties, Lin Piao avoids going on to draw any concrete conclusions. That is, he sedulously refrains from assigning the existing states of Africa, Asia (with the exception of India), and Latin America to the ranks of the "lackeys of imperialism"; nor is he likely to do so, as long as Peking continues to cherish hopes of a "Bandung" type conference in which it would play a leading role.

The Lin Piao document simultaneously gives expression to the optimum vision and to diluted versions of it. The original united-front doctrine—the doctrine of "uniting with whom one can unite"—was meant to apply *within* given societies. In the diluted version, entire established nation-states are brought into the doctrine. Thus, the theme of the class struggle between rich and poor has been extended to "rich nations" and "poor nations." Very recently, even this conception was diluted by Mao's further extension of the doctrine to the not-so-poor nations of the "second intermediary zone" (Western Europe, Canada, etc.) which might conceivably be included in a vast united front against the main enemy—the United States.

While all this may appear to represent an enormously clever extrapolation of Mao's maxims, the fact remains that uniting with "poor nations" is not the same thing as uniting with the poor. The genius of the Maoist united-front strategy lay in its ability to combine absolute discipline and clarity of purpose in the core organization—the Chinese Communist party—with a maximum of maneuverability *vis-à-vis* other social and political groups *which it could effectively control*. The notion that the established states of Africa, Asia, and Latin America—no matter how poor—are as subject to direction from Peking as were the peasants of North China or the "Democratic League" during the late 40s, is based on a false analogy between incomparable entities. On its immediate periphery China may, of course, exert the same types of coercive pressure which other great powers exert toward their weaker neighbors. This does nothing, however, to demonstrate the demonic effectiveness of the Maoist strategy. Indeed, in dealing with the whole "first intermediate zone," Peking has already discovered that a simple appeal to common poverty and to a colonial past will not automatically lead existing states with their own concrete conceptions of national interest, their own specific histories and preoccupations, and their own sensitive pride, to accept Peking's "hegemony" in any international united front. Nor will it be at all easy to convince states which have had little experience with the United States in the past, to think of it as Chinese patriots thought of Japan in the 30s and 40s.

The ambiguities created by such dilutions pervade the Lin Piao document. Does the sensational assertion that North America and Europe now constitute—"in a sense"—"the cities of the world," while Asia, Latin America, and Africa constitute the "rural areas," refer only to the vast peasant masses of those latter regions, or does it also refer to the established regimes there? The answer is left in what is probably an intentional haze. No doubt, any regime willing to accept Peking's slogans will at least provisionally be included in the category of "rural areas" even if its polity be that of a feudal monarchy.

Even the concept of "war of national liberation" is subjected to dilution by Lin Piao. After stating flatly that people's wars must be led by the "proletariat," Lin Piao concedes, in passing, that "various classes [that is, non-Communist political elites] may lead people's wars against imperialism." Thus, in his list of countries which have undergone genuine "people's wars," Lin Piao is able to include Algeria and Indonesia (the Indonesia of the period before the recent coup), despite the fact that neither of these cases fits the classical model outlined elsewhere in the same article. In Algeria, it is true, the elements of armed revolution, guerrilla warfare, and base areas were present, but the most vital ingredient of all—the leading role of a "Marxist-Leninist party"—was missing, as it certainly was also in the case of Indonesia.

"War of national liberation" has become, then, one of those accordion-like terms which can be given either a strict or broad construction. Even states which have achieved independence by the most innocuous and pacific means may qualify as members of the anti-imperialist camp so long as they express the correct attitudes toward U.S. imperialism. A fortiori, Peking is likely to apply the term "war of national liberation" to almost any revolution or rebellion anywhere in the third world on the assumption that any violent disturbance can only propel the Chinese wave of the future and weaken the United States. It is one of the great triumphs of Peking's propaganda that Washington has come to agree with this view. If Washington had been in the same frame of mind with respect to "wars of national liberation" during the Algerian revolt, the United States would no doubt have thrown its full support behind the French policy of suppression.

In sum, then, the Lin Piao article simultaneously restates Peking's maximum hopes and reflects all the adjustments which Peking has had to make to a world which—with the notable exception of Vietnam—has so far failed to shape itself to Chinese expectations.

But what of the future? The idea that the whole third world will easily succumb to China's infallible strategies has won ready acceptance among a large assortment of C.I.A. operatives, Pentagon strategists, professional Communist experts, games-theoreticians, political scientists, and others. Only yesterday, we had an enormous literature designed to show that the Soviet model and Soviet strategies would prove irresistible in the third world. It having since been discovered that Moscow must cope with a world as unpredictable and refractory to its own purposes as it is to ours, the same style of thought has now been transferred to China.

It would, of course, be utterly presumptuous to predict that the Chinese optimum strategy may not succeed in this place or that. The pressing question at the moment, however, is: which is the more dangerous—to predicate American policy on the fear that the whole third world is ripe for a "Chinese take-over" via the Maoist strategy, or to base it on the assumption that the third world is likely to develop in ways infinitely more varied and complex than anything dreamt of in Mao's philosophy? One would, at the very least, expect that arguments weighing against the Chinese projection would be given equal weight with arguments tending to support it. The great receptivity to the Chinese projection seems to rest, at least in part, on a theory which many of us share with the Chinese themselves—namely that the third world (whether it be described as "the rural areas" or the "underdeveloped" ones) is so homogeneous in its essential features that any political strategy which succeeds in one sector of this world may be expected to succeed in another. What is true of one underdeveloped, agrarian society is true of any other.

From some points of view, the features which all these societies have in common may indeed be of overriding importance. It is, however, extremely doubtful that the political destiny of any one of them can simply be deduced from the characteristics shared by all. The emergence and ultimate success of the Maoist strategy in China itself, for example, were made possible by certain very specific conditions existing in China during the 30s and 40s—primary among them the failure of the Nationalist government to achieve firm military control within its own territory. This special feature of the Chinese political landscape, which helped to create and shape the Maoist strategy (as Mao himself has often admitted), is by no means universally present in the states of the "underdeveloped" world. Whatever may be their failures in other areas, many of these states (India for one) have proven quite capable of creating fairly unified and disciplined national armies. Apart from this, there is the fact that China, particularly North China, was subject during the 40s to the Japanese invasion and that Japanese military power was subsequently dispersed in many directions; and there is the fact that Mao Tse-tung and his group not only developed their strategy, but were also superb implementers of it. The very combination of Marxism-Leninism and nationalism that characterized Mao and his group was itself a product of certain peculiarities of Chinese history during the 20s and 30s—peculiarities which there is no compelling reason to expect will be duplicated in the Nigeria of the 60s.

The Vietnamese case offers little real basis for generalizing, for the striking thing about Vietnam is that it has, to a unique degree, shared some of the characteristics of the Chinese situation. While the proximity to China must be given its own due weight in the history of Vietnam since 1945, the decisive point is the emergence of a shrewd, able, and ruthless Vietnamese Communist group which succeeded in gaining fairly effective control of a genuine Vietnamese nationalist movement. As indicated above, even in 1949, Ho Chi Minh's movement represented the only Communist operation in existence which closely approximated Liu Shao-ch'i's model. This movement continued to find support in certain segments of the population of the South who identified with it out of nationalist motives. Above all, it was able to apply its strategies against a regime which suffered from some of the same weaknesses as the Nationalist government in China. There was vast rural discontent, which Diem proved incapable of handling; there was his inability to unify and control his own military elite; and there were bitter communal divisions within the society which, while not resembling anything which had existed in China, produced effects similar to the regional fragmentation of power there.

But what of the other countries of Southeast Asia? They are all within geographical proximity of China, and none can afford to ignore the Chinese reality or the possibility of direct Chinese military intervention. To the extent, however, that Chinese hopes in this area still rely on the efficacy of the Maoist strategy, is it inevitable that Thailand—to take one case—must follow the path of Vietnam? In recent months there have been many reports suggesting that Peking is now "turning on" its strategy in Thailand. Behind all such reporting, of course, lies the assumption that the success or failure of the strategy depends on buttons pressed in Peking, even though we have little evidence to show that the spectacular rise of the Vietcong during the last few years has, in fact, had anything to do with immediate direction from Peking, however welcome it may have been to the Chinese. In assessing the potentialities of the strategy in Thailand, therefore, it is the following questions which have to be examined. Does the Thai government effectively control its own armed forces and are these forces reasonably cohesive? Is there acute discontent in the countryside (outside of the much-discussed Northeast)? Is the direction of the incipient "people's war" in the hands of Thai leaders, or are Laotians, Vietnamese, and Chinese (in the South) playing a dominant role? These are the relevant questions, whatever the Chinese may wish and however the war in Vietnam may go.

It may, of course, be argued that even if the Chinese are not able to export Communism by exclusive reliance on their own revolutionary strategy, they will prove flexible enough to use other methods to achieve the same end. To do this, however, they will need more than those few precariously pro-Peking Communist groupings now in existence; a whole host of new Marxist-Leninist movements under effective Chinese control in places where they do not now exist will have to be created. The view that they will easily be able to create such a vast movement rests again on an unflagging belief in an ongoing entity called "world Communism" or "international Communism" which somehow has a life of its own over and above the sum total of actual Communist states and parties, and which remains unaffected by the vicissitudes of its constituent "detachments."

Involved in all this is a refusal to take the crisis which has erupted in the Communist world in recent years with real seriousness. Only yesterday, the phrase "world Communism" was generally used to describe an ostensibly monolithic power system centered on Moscow and based on the unquestioned authority of the Kremlin; the phrase referred not to a disembodied set of ideas, but to an organized movement. Now, however, one often encounters among those who speak of "world Communism" a view which conceives of Communism as a kind of homogeneous unchanging substance which is, to be sure, subject to shattering but whose inner essence remains unchanged even after fragmentation. Since the substance remains the same the shattered parts may again be reassembled and resolidified at any moment (this time, presumably, under the leadership of Peking). Furthermore, the expansive capacity of the substance also remains unaffected by the experience of fragmentation. (It is no accident, incidentally, that many who argue most strongly for this particular view of "world Communism" were among those who most strongly insisted in the past that the system was monolithic and unbreakable.) However much they may come to differ, we are told, all Communist states share the aim of achieving Communism.

But what is Communism? Theoretically, the power to define what it is remains the exclusive prerogative of the

Communist party. In Communist ideology, the party is not merely a political organization: it is the embodiment of all those transcendental qualities which Marx attributed to the industrial proletariat. Whatever the good society may be, it can only be attained by the Communist party, for it is the Communist party which alone has access to the inner secrets of history and which can therefore apply infallibly correct solutions to the unfolding problems of history. As the embodiment of the general will of the proletariat, the party should be trans-national and immune to inner conflicts of interest. These attributes of infallibility, universality, and unanimity have been the inner essence of the Communist party as the ultimate mystery of Marxism-Leninism. Can one say that this mystery has remained unaffected by the recent crisis in the Communist world?

The Chinese, to be sure, have found a comforting precedent for the crisis in the history of Communism. Lenin, they say, often found himself in the minority within the Russian Social-Democratic movement. He did not hesitate to break with the majority when the majority was wrong, and in the end his truth prevailed. Here again we find ourselves in the realm of false analogies. Can the relationship between vast Communist nation-states be compared with that between warring factions among Russia's Marxist intelligentsia? Will China be able to deal with the USSR and its ideological claims in the manner in which Lenin disposed of the Mensheviks after October 1917? Will China be able, in any foreseeable future, to suppress the claims to Communist legitimacy of the Yugoslavs, the Poles, the Rumanians, or the Italian Communist party? The hard fact is that for all its pretensions (some quite spurious) to a purer Marxist-Leninist doctrine, Peking is doing quite as much as Moscow to undermine the transcendental status of the world Communist movement. The famous doctrine that the decisions of any given Communist party (i.e., that of the USSR) are not universally binding on other Communist parties subverts not only Moscow's claims of central authority but *all* future claims of other potential centers of world Communism. It need hardly be pointed out that the slavish obedience to Moscow's line by foreign parties during Stalin's lifetime was not based on reasoned judgments that Stalin was always right, but precisely on the doctrine of the infallible authority of the Kremlin. Even if the Chinese do manage to create new pro-Peking Communist movements in Africa and Latin America, can they ever expect to exercise the type of authority over these groups which the Kremlin formerly exercised over the Communist world?

What is actually happening behind all the polemics is that the nation-state is asserting its primacy over the transnational claims of Marxism-Leninism while the very concept of an ultimate authority decays. To be sure, this still leaves open the possibility of the elaboration of national varieties of "Communism." The Maoist vision of the good society is one such variety; the day has passed, however, when one variety of national Communism is accepted without question as the mandatory image of the future even by "Marxist-Leninist" groupings.

The question of whether there can any longer exist an ultimate seat of authority in the "Communist world" and who— if anyone—will occupy this seat has now become the very heart of the Sino-Soviet conflict. It is probably not a question which can be resolved by compromises and agreements on the substantive issues which occupy the foreground of the polemics. But could it be resolved—as some have argued—by a reversal for the United States in Vietnam which would prove the Chinese contention that the U.S. is "a paper tiger" unable to cope with local "people's wars," disprove the Soviet position that American power must be respected even in this area, and convert the whole of "world Communism" to China's outlook? Even this is highly doubtful. For if it is meant that Moscow will itself be converted to Peking's outlook, it must be pointed out in the first place that Moscow's ideological position on "wars of national liberation" has by no means been as consistently "revisionist" as Peking would have us believe. Even now there is some question as to whether Moscow is, or is not, willing to lend support to Cuban-sponsored wars of national liberation in Latin America. In the improbable event that Moscow were to acknowledge Peking's correctness on this issue, Peking has guaranteed itself against the necessity of reconciliation by imposing on Moscow a whole catalogue of impossible conditions on other issues. As for the East-European Communist states and the Communist parties of Western Europe, which have adopted a generally "anti-Chinese" stance, they have done so for solid political reasons of their own, and they are not likely to be swayed into the "Chinese camp" by debaters' points. And finally, Peking's ability to create strong new Chinese-oriented Communist parties throughout the third world will continue to depend on local conditions within that world and not merely on the "demonstration" effect of Vietnam.

In sum, the Sino-Soviet conflict has—to use a term employed in the polemic—become a "hegemonistic" conflict. The two principal actors have grown more concerned with the question of who shall prevail than the question of who is right. But this does not mean that either one or the other must prevail, for both the Communist states and the Communist parties lying between the two are probably less and less interested in having an ultimate source of infallible authority anywhere.

In emphasizing the enormity of the present crisis in the Communist world, I have no intention of implying that the world is "going our way," if by "our way" we mean the imminent universal enthronement of American-style liberal democracy or European social democracy. The retreat of empire has produced neither the Communist floodtide nor the "Western" or "American" century. The major drift has been in the direction of what might be called, for lack of a better term, populist-nationalist dictatorships. Whether their power rests on a single party or on the armed forces, the leaders of such states invariably claim to incarnate the will of the "people-nation." On many issues, no doubt, they are closer to the Communist world than to ours. They generally profess adherence to "socialism," their anti-colonialism often draws on the Leninist vocabulary, and they often find it expedient to denigrate the mere "machinery" of political democracy in favor of "organic" theories of representation.

One need not conclude, however, that this development is in any sense "inevitable." Some societies may avoid it.

All one can say is that circumstances in many areas have been favorable to it. Nor need one gratuitously idealize it as do some elements of the "New Left," on the grounds that it is revolutionary and "socialist": some of these states may prove abominably corrupt, exploitative, and ineffective; others may be fairly effective in important areas and reasonably decent. Nor, again, need one be led by a dogmatic liberal-ism to assign them all to the Communist camp and refuse to coexist with them. The same development might well have occurred if Marx and Lenin had never lived, since the basic fund of ideas on which these leaders draw was, in fact, fully available in certain Left Jacobin-nationalist tendencies emerging out of the French Revolution. Ultimately, indeed, these ideas may turn out to be hardier than the more spectacular hybrid, Marxism-Leninism. Given the infinitely less intense and less transcendental nature of the ideologies governing the new states, there is a good chance that they may not go the whole way to totalitarianism, that they will prove more relativistic and technical-pragmatic in their eco-nomic approaches, and that they may also perhaps prove open in the long run to demands for personal freedom. Above all, one must remember that the overruling passion of these leaders is the passion to remain masters in their own house-holds. This involves the refusal to accept any claims to hegemony—including spiritual claims—from outside. Since we, on our side, are presumably unburdened (or are we?) by an official philosophy which imposes on us the duty to universalize our own system, one would think that it would be a great deal easier for us than it would be for either Moscow or Peking to live with this passion for national autonomy.

It has, of course, been argued that all these regimes are simply halfway houses to Communism, and that the Chinese need but wait a little longer before an unstable third world—faced with enormous economic, demographic, and social problems—succumbs to Maoist strategies. No doubt, a mini-mum requirement for the survival of these states is that they show some movement in the direction of solving their problems, but it is far from certain that they must "solve" all of them immediately in order to remain viable. As a minimal *sine qua non,* they must demonstrate their power to maintain basic political and military control of the areas under their jurisdiction. But even where a given regime is overthrown, there is no reason to think that its successor will be less passionately concerned to maintain its own independence and autonomy. The notion that the Communist world possesses simple formulae for solving economic, demographic, and social problems which will prove irresistible in the third world is daily confounded by the growing diversity of "models" within the Communist world. The Chinese model (itself in a state of flux) no longer follows the Soviet model and does not resemble either the Yugoslav or even the Polish model. Fidel Castro, in spite of his adherence to Marxism-Leninism, has yet to find anywhere in the Communist world a ready-made model adequate to the concrete problems which confront him. Furthermore, while it continues to be represented as an ultimate and inevitable apocalypse or nemesis, the very nature of Communism has become highly problematic. Marxism-Leninism itself is proving a kind of halfway house to types of national "socialism" which oddly approximate some of the tendencies in the third world. There may arise in the future spiritual and social movements capable of bursting through the tough integuments of the nation-state framework, but one may strongly doubt whether the Communism we have known and experienced in the past can qualify any longer as such a movement.

I would suggest, then, that it is mistaken and dangerous to base American policy on the expectation that the whole third world is about to behave in a manner corresponding to Peking's optimum hopes for the future. It must be stressed again that these hopes are grounded not on the exportability of Chinese soldiers, but on the exportability of Chinese revolutionary strategy. Peking may staff its embassies with huge contingents of experts in "people's war" who will try to manipulate the "natives," but it has yet to be shown that the embassy staffs are quite that clever, or that the natives are quite that manipulable. Even in Southeast Asia where the Chinese can, and may yet, intervene with troops, Peking still fervently wishes to rely on the salability of its strategy. In Vietnam the strategy has, with adaptations, been quite effective—not because of buttons pressed in Peking or because of huge embassy staffs, but because of the very particular political history of Vietnam. Its effectiveness in other countries of Southeast Asia remains a function of internal situations in those countries, particularly if we assume the ongoing presence of American and Soviet power in the area.

Is Peking capable of adjusting to a world which does not correspond to its maximum hopes? Granted that in the mind of Mao and those closest to him the hopes are still active and real, the fact is that the process of adjustment has long since begun. The Bandung line of 1955 represented a major retreat from Liu Shao-ch'i's line of 1949. The current effort to cultivate commercial and even political relations with states of the Western world and with Japan can only be squeezed into Maoist categories by stretching these categories to the breaking point. Even the extraordinary concession which Peking has felt obliged to make to the principle of national independence and autonomy within the Communist world in the course of its polemics with Moscow, constitutes an unacknowledged adjustment. In the eyes of Mao, these adjustments may represent temporary expedients which will soon be rendered unnecessary by the true wave of the future. There is, however, no need for us to accept Peking's assessment of their significance.

It nevertheless remains true that a minimum condition for Peking's adjustment to a world as recalcitrant to her most grandiose ambitions as it is to the ambitions of the rest of us, is the recognition of China's status as one of the great world powers: a willingness—nay, an eagerness—to move as far as we can to involve and enmesh China, however harsh and unaccommodating its behavior may be, in whatever precarious structure of world order we have.

There is a reasonable possibility that, as a recognized great power, China would in the end come to accept its position in a world of nation-states large and small. To some, it may seem foolhardy to predicate foreign policy on "reasonable possibility" rather than on "policy science." I would simply urge that what we have on the other side is not science but unthinking extrapolation of the Chinese maximum vision, and a host of ill-considered clichés and stereotypes (put forth by people on various sides of the policy debate). We have, for example, the notion that whereas the Russians are "Western" (although they were considered "Oriental" by many only yesterday), the Chinese are occultly Oriental, or Asiatic. What conclusions one is expected to draw from this distinction, I do not know. A candid survey of the span of Chinese history leads to no firm conclusions on the question of whether the Chinese are more or less belligerent or more or less fanatical than Westerners: certainly, the imperial state was not more aggressive than the Czarist empire. We have the further stereotype that with its vast population, China must of necessity achieve world hegemony. From this, some have drawn the conclusion that we ought to recognize Chinese hegemony as quickly as possible, while others have called for the immediate dispatch of a few well-placed missiles. Then we have the notion that "Asia" must inevitably form part of a Chinese empire either because China controlled "Asia" in the past (which is false), or because Asians are all alike culturally or peculiarly prone to submit to those of superior strength. While China will undoubtedly play a leading role in Asian, and indeed world, politics, the fact is that Asia is not a political, and certainly not a cultural, entity: there are many states in Asia as little anxious to form part of a Chinese empire as states on other continents and probably as resourceful in avoiding this fate as others.

Finally, there is the more serious argument that the Chinese leaders still think of China as the center of civilization in a world of barbarians. Here I would point out that the cosmology of Chinese universal kingship on which this faith was founded has collapsed along with the world which made it plausible; that while Peking does regard itself as the center of an international faith, it is not the same faith which animated "sinocentrism" in the past (it is, in fact, a faith many of whose tenets are not even Chinese); and that the China of the present finds itself in a world which will continue to reject its "sinocentric" claims. These are all considerations, it seems to me, which may be quite sufficient to overcome the pull of mental habits inherited from the past.

I have not here attempted to put forth solutions to our Vietnamese dilemmas. Obviously, whether we regard Vietnam as the first "test case" in a chain reaction leading to a realization of the Chinese optimum vision, or whether we accept the reasonable possibilities suggested above, is a question which bears very strongly on the price—military, political, and moral—we are willing to pay to maintain our present position in that unhappy land.

PART III

———◆———

ROBERT L. HEILBRONER

Counter-revolutionary America

ROBERT HEILBRONER is an adjunct professor at the graduate faculty of the New School for Social Research and is the author of a number of books, including *The Making of Economic Society, The Great Ascent,* and, most recently, *The Limits of American Capitalism.*

Is the United States fundamentally opposed to economic development? The question is outrageous. Did we not coin the phrase, "the revolution of rising expectations"? Have we not supported the cause of development more generously than any nation on earth, spent our intellectual energy on the problems of development, offered our expertise freely to the backward nations of the word? How can it possibly be suggested that the United States might be opposed to economic development?

The answer is that we are not at all opposed to what we conceive economic development to be. The process depicted by the "revolution of rising expectations" is a deeply attractive one. It conjures up the image of a peasant in some primitive land, leaning on his crude plow and looking to the horizon, where he sees dimly, but for the *first time* (and that is what is so revolutionary about it), the vision of a better life. From this electrifying vision comes the necessary catalysis to change an old and stagnant way of life.

Reprinted from *Commentary,* by permission; © 1967 by the American Jewish Committee.

The pace of work quickens. Innovations, formerly feared and resisted, are now eagerly accepted. The obstacles are admittedly very great—whence the need for foreign assistance —but under the impetus of new hopes the economic mechanism begins to turn faster, to gain traction against the environment. Slowly, but surely, the Great Ascent begins.

There is much that is admirable about this well-intentioned popular view of "the revolution of rising expectations." Unfortunately, there is more that is delusive about it. For the buoyant appeal of its rhetoric conceals or passes in silence over by far the larger part of the spectrum of realities of the development process. One of these is the certainty that the revolutionary aspect of development will not be limited to the realm of ideas, but will vent its fury on institutions, social classes, and innocent men and women. Another is the great likelihood that the ideas needed to guide the revolution will not only be affirmative and reasonable, but also destructive and fanatic. A third is the realization that revolutionary efforts cannot be made, and certainly cannot be sustained, by voluntary effort alone, but require an iron hand, in the spheres both of economic direction and political control. And the fourth and most difficult of these realities to face is the probability that the political force most likely to succeed in carrying through the gigantic historical transformation of development is some form of extreme national collectivism or Communism.

In a word, what our rhetoric fails to bring to our attention is the likelihood that development will require policies and programs repugnant to our "way of life," that it will bring to the fore governments hostile to our international objectives, and that its regnant ideology will bitterly oppose capitalism as a system of world economic power. If that is the case, we would have to think twice before denying that the United States was fundamentally opposed to economic development.

But is it the case? Must development lead in directions that go counter to the present American political philosophy? Let me try to indicate, albeit much too briefly and summarily, the reasons that lead me to answer that question as I do.

I begin with the cardinal point, often noted but still insufficiently appreciated, that the process called "economic development" is not primarily economic at all. We think of development as a campaign of production to be fought with budgets and monetary policies and measured with indices of output and income. But the development process is much wider and deeper than can be indicated by such statistics. To be sure, in the end what is hoped for is a tremendous rise in output. But this will not come to pass until a series of tasks, at once cruder and more delicate, simpler and infinitely more difficult, has been commenced and carried along a certain distance.

In most of the new nations of Africa, these tasks consist in establishing the very underpinnings of nationhood itself —in determining national borders, establishing national languages, arousing a basic national (as distinguished from tribal) self-consciousness. Before these steps have been taken, the African states will remain no more than names insecurely affixed to the map, not social entities capable of undertaking an enormous collective venture in economic change. In Asia, nationhood is generally much further advanced than in Africa, but here the main impediment to development is the miasma of apathy and fatalism, superstition and distrust that vitiates every attempt to improve hopelessly inefficient modes of work and patterns of resource use: while India starves, a quarter of the world's cow population devours Indian crops, exempt either from effective employment or slaughter because of sacred taboos. In still other areas, mainly Latin America, the principal handicap to development is not an absence of national identity or the presence of suffocating cultures (although the latter certainly plays its part), but the cramping and crippling inhibitions of obsolete social institutions and reactionary social classes. Where landholding rather than industrial activity is still the basis for social and economic power, and where land is held essentially in fiefdoms rather than as productive real estate, it is not surprising that so much of society retains a medieval cast.

Thus, development is much more than a matter of encouraging economic growth within a given social structure. It is rather the *modernization* of that structure, a process of ideational, social, economic, and political change that requires the remaking of society in its most intimate as well as its most public attributes.* When we speak of the revolutionary nature of economic development, it is this kind of deeply penetrative change that we mean—change that reorganizes "normal" ways of thought, established patterns of family life, and structures of village authority as well as class and caste privilege.

What is so egregiously lacking in the great majority of the societies that are now attempting to make the Great Ascent is precisely this pervasive modernization. The trouble with India and Pakistan, with Brazil and Ecuador, with the Philippines and Ethiopia, is not merely that economic growth lags, or proceeds at some pitiable pace. This is only a symptom of deeper-lying ills. The trouble is that the social physiology of these nations remains so depressingly unchanged despite the flurry of economic planning on top. The all-encompassing ignorance and poverty of the rural regions, the unbridgeable gulf between the peasant and the urban elites, the resistive conservatism of the village elders, the unyielding traditionalism of family life—all these remain obdurately, maddeningly, disastrously unchanged. In the cities, a few modern buildings, sometimes brilliantly executed, give a deceptive patina of modernity, but once one journeys into the immense countryside, the terrible stasis overwhelms all.

To this vast landscape of apathy and ignorance one must now make an exception of the very greatest importance. It is the fact that a very few nations, all of them Communist, have succeeded in reaching into the lives and stirring the minds of precisely that body of the peasantry which constitutes the insuperable problem elsewhere. In our concentration on the politics, the betrayals, the successes and failures of the Russian, Chinese, and Cuban revolutions, we forget that their central motivation has been just such a war *à l'outrance* against the arch-enemy of backwardness—not alone the back-

* See C. E. Black, *The Dynamics of Modernization.*

wardness of outmoded social superstructures but even more critically that of private inertia and traditionalism.

That the present is irreversibly and unqualifiedly freed from the dead hand of the past is, I think, beyond argument in the case of Russia. By this I do not only mean that Russia has made enormous economic strides. I refer rather to the gradual emancipation of its people from the "idiocy of rural life," their gradual entrance upon the stage of contemporary existence. This is not to hide in the smallest degree the continuing backwardness of the Russian countryside where now almost fifty—*and formerly perhaps eighty*—per cent of the population lives. But even at its worst I do not think that life could now be described in the despairing terms that run through the Russian literature of our grandfathers' time. Here is Chekhov:

> During the summer and the winter there had been hours and days when it seemed as if these people [the peasants] lived worse than cattle, and it was terrible to be with them. They were coarse, dishonest, dirty, and drunken; they did not live at peace with one another but quarreled continually, because they feared, suspected, and despised one another. . . . Crushing labor that made the whole body ache at night, cruel winters, scanty crops, overcrowding, and no help, and nowhere to look for help.

It is less certain that the vise of the past has been loosened in China or Cuba. It may well be that Cuba has suffered a considerable economic decline, in part due to absurd planning, in part to our refusal to buy her main crop. The economic record of China is nearly as inscrutable as its political turmoil, and we may not know for many years whether the Chinese peasant is today better or worse off than before the revolution. Yet what strikes me as significant in both countries is something else. In Cuba it is the educational effort that, according to the New York *Times,* has constituted a major effort of the Castro regime. In China it is the unmistakable evidence—and here I lean not alone on the sympathetic account of Edgar Snow but on the most horrified descriptions of the rampages of the Red Guards—that the younger generation is no longer fettered by the traditional view of things. The very fact that the Red Guards now revile their elders, an unthinkable defiance of age-old Chinese custom, is testimony of how deeply change has penetrated into the texture of Chinese life.

It is this herculean effort to reach and rally the great anonymous mass of the population that is *the* great accomplishment of Communism—even though it is an accomplishment that is still only partially accomplished. For if the areas of the world afflicted with the self-perpetuating disease of backwardness are ever to rid themselves of its debilitating effects, I think it is likely to be not merely because antiquated social structures have been dismantled (although this is an essential precondition), but because some shock treatment like that of Communism has been administered to them.

By way of contrast to this all-out effort, however short it may have fallen of its goal, we must place the timidity of the effort to bring modernization to the peoples of the non-Communist world. Here again I do not merely speak of lagging rates of growth. I refer to the fact that illiteracy in the non-Communist countries of Asia and Central America is increasing (by some 200 million in the last decade) because it has been "impossible" to mount an educational effort that will keep pace with population growth. I refer to the absence of substantial land reform in Latin America, despite how many years of promises. I refer to the indifference or incompetence or corruption of governing elites: the incredible sheiks with their oildoms; the vague, well-meaning leaders of India unable to break the caste system, kill the cows, control the birthrate, reach the villages, house or employ the labor rotting on the streets; the cynical governments of South America, not one of which, according to Lleras Camargo, former president of Colombia, has ever prosecuted a single politician or industrialist for evasion of taxes. And not least, I refer to the fact that every movement that arises to correct these conditions is instantly identified as "Communist" and put down with every means at hand, while the United States clucks or nods approval.

To be sure, even in the most petrified societies, the modernization process is at work. If there were time, the solvent acids of the twentieth century would work their way on the ideas and institutions of the most inert or resistant countries.

But what lacks in the twentieth century is time. The multitudes of the underdeveloped world have only in the past two decades been summoned to their reveille. The one thing that is certain about the revolution of rising expectations is that it is only in its inception, and that its pressures for justice and action will steadily mount as the voice of the twentieth century penetrates to villages and slums where it is still almost inaudible. It is not surprising that Princeton historian C. E. Black, surveying this labile world, estimates that we must anticipate "ten to fifteen revolutions a year for the foreseeable future in the less developed societies."

In itself, this prospect of mounting political restiveness enjoins the speediest possible time schedule for development. But this political urgency is many times compounded by that of the population problem. Like an immense river in flood, the number of human beings rises each year to wash away the levees of the preceding year's labors and to pose future requirements of monstrous proportions. To provide shelter for the three billion human beings who will arrive on earth in the next forty years will require as many dwellings as have been constructed since recorded history began. To feed them will take double the world's present output of food. To cope with the mass exodus from the overcrowded countryside will necessitate cities of grotesque size—Calcutta, now a cesspool of three to five million, threatens us by the year 2000 with a prospective population of from thirty to sixty million.

These horrific figures spell one importunate message: haste. That is the *mene mene, tekel upharsin* written on the walls of government planning offices around the world. Even if the miracle of the loop is realized—the new contraceptive device that promises the first real breakthrough in population control—we must set ourselves for at least another generation of rampant increase.

But how to achieve haste? How to convince the silent and disbelieving men, how to break through the distrustful glances of women in black shawls, how to overcome the overt hostility of landlords, the opposition of the Church, the petty bickerings of military cliques, the black-marketeering of commercial dealers? I suspect there is only one way. The conditions of backwardness must be attacked with the passion, the ruthlessness, and the messianic fury of a jehad, a Holy War. Only a campaign of an intensity and single-mindedness that must approach the ludicrous and the unbearable offers the chance to ride roughshod over the resistance of the rich and the poor alike and to open the way for the forcible implantation of those modern attitudes and techniques without which there will be no escape from the misery of underdevelopment.

I need hardly add that the cost of this modernization process has been and will be horrendous. If Communism is the great modernizer, it is certainly not a benign agent of change. Stalin may well have exceeded Hitler as a mass executioner. Free inquiry in China has been supplanted by dogma and catechism; even in Russia nothing like freedom of criticism or of personal expression is allowed. Furthermore, the economic cost of industrialization in both countries has been at least as severe as that imposed by primitive capitalism.

Yet one must count the gains as well as the losses. Hundreds of millions who would have been confined to the narrow cells of changeless lives have been liberated from prisons they did not even know existed. Class structures that elevated the flighty or irresponsible have been supplanted by others that have promoted the ambitious and the dedicated. Economic systems that gave rise to luxury and poverty have given way to systems that provide a rough distributional justice. Above all, the prospect of a new future has been opened. It is this that lifts the current ordeal in China above the level of pure horror. The number of human beings in that country who have perished over the past centuries from hunger or neglect, is beyond computation. The present revolution may add its dreadful increment to this number. But it also holds out the hope that China may finally have been galvanized into social, political, and economic attitudes that for the the first time make its modernization a possibility.

Two questions must be answered when we dare to risk so favorable a verdict on Communism as a modernizing agency. The first is whether the result is worth the cost, whether the possible—by no means assured—escape from underdevelopment is worth the lives that will be squandered to achieve it.

I do not know how one measures the moral price of historical victories or how one can ever decide that a diffuse gain is worth a sharp and particular loss. I only know that the way in which we ordinarily keep the books of history is wrong. No one is now toting up the balance of the wretches who starve in India, or the peasants of Northeastern Brazil who live in the swamps on crabs, or the undernourished and permanently stunted children of Hong Kong or Honduras. Their sufferings go unrecorded, and are not present to counterbalance the scales when the furies of revolution strike down their victims. Barrington Moore has made a nice calculation that bears on this problem. Taking as the weight in one pan the 35,000 to 40,000 persons who lost their lives—mainly for no fault of theirs—as a result of the Terror during the French Revolution, he asks what would have been the death rate from preventable starvation and injustice under the *ancien régime* to balance the scales. "Offhand," he writes, "it seems unlikely that this would be very much below the proportion of .0010 which [the] figure of 40,000 yields when set against an estimated population of 24 million."*

Is it unjust to charge the *ancien régime* in Russia with ten million preventable deaths? I think it not unreasonable. To charge the authorities in pre-revolutionary China with equally vast and preventable degradations? Theodore White, writing in 1946, had this to say: . . . "some scholars think that China is perhaps the only country in the world where the people eat less, live more bitterly, and are clothed worse than they were five hundred years ago."†

I do not recommend such a calculus of corpses—indeed, I am aware of the license it gives to the unscrupulous—but I raise it to show the onesidedness of our protestations against the brutality and violence of revolutions. In this regard, it is chastening to recall the multitudes who have been killed or mutilated by the Church which is now the first to protest against the excesses of Communism.

* *Social Origins of Dictatorship and Democracy,* p. 104.
† *Thunder Out of China,* p. 32.

But there is an even more terrible second question to be asked. It is clear beyond doubt, however awkward it may be for our moralizing propensities, that historians excuse horror that succeeds; and that we write our comfortable books of moral philosophy, seated atop a mound of victims—slaves, serfs, laboring men and women, heretics, dissenters—who were crushed in the course of preparing the way for our triumphal entry into existence. But at least we are here to vindicate the carnage. What if we were not? What if the revolutions grind flesh and blood and produce nothing, if the end of the convulsion is not exhilaration but exhaustion, not triumph but defeat?

Before this possibility—which has been realized more than once in history—one stands mute. Mute, but not paralyzed. For there is the necessity of calculating what is likely to happen in the absence of the revolution whose prospective excesses hold us back. Here one must weigh what has been done to remedy underdevelopment—and what has not been done—in the past twenty years; how much time there remains before the population flood enforces its own ultimate solution; what is the likelihood of bringing modernization without the frenzied assault that Communism seems most capable of mounting. As I make this mental calculation I arrive at an answer which is even more painful than that of revolution. I see the alternative as the continuation, without substantial relief—and indeed with a substantial chance of deterioration—of the misery and meanness of life as it is now lived in the sinkhole of the world's backward regions.

I have put the case for the necessity of revolution as strongly as possible, but I must now widen the options beyond the stark alternatives I have posed. To begin with, there are areas of the world where the immediate tasks are so far-reaching that little more can be expected for some decades than the primary missions of national identification and unification. Most of the new African states fall into this category. These states may suffer capitalist, Communist, Fascist, or other kinds of regimes during the remainder of this century, but whatever the nominal ideology in the saddle, the job at hand will be that of military and political nation-making.

There is another group of nations, less easy to identify, but much more important in the scale of events, where my analysis also does not apply. These are countries where the pressures of population growth seem sufficiently mild, or the existing political and social framework sufficiently adaptable, to allow for the hope of considerable progress without resort to violence. Greece, Turkey, Chile, Argentina, Mexico may be representatives of nations in this precarious but enviable situation. Some of them, incidentally, have already had revolutions of modernizing intent—fortunately for them in a day when the United States was not so frightened or so powerful as to be able to repress them.

In other words, the great arena of desperation to which the revolutionizing impetus of Communism seems most applicable is primarily the crowded land masses and archipelagoes of Southeast Asia and the impoverished areas of Central and South America. But even here, there is the possibility that the task of modernization may be undertaken by non-Communist elites. There is always the example of indigenous, independent leaders who rise up out of nowhere to overturn the established framework and to galvanize the masses—a Gandhi, a Marti, a pre-1958 Castro. Or there is that fertile ground for the breeding of national leaders—the army, as witness Ataturk or Nasser, among many.*

Thus there is certainly no inherent necessity that the revolutions of modernization be led by Communists. But it is well to bear two thoughts in mind when we consider the likely course of non-Communist revolutionary sweeps. The first is the nature of the mobilizing appeal of any successful revolutionary elite. Is it the austere banner of saving and investment that waves over the heads of the shouting marchers in Jakarta and Bombay, Cairo and Havana? It most certainly is not. The banner of economic development is that of nationalism, with its promise

* What are the chances for modernizing revolutions of the Right, such as those of the Meiji Restoration or of Germany under Bismarck? I think they are small. The changes to be wrought in the areas of greatest backwardness are much more socially subversive than those of the 19th century, and the timespan allotted to the revolutionists is much smaller. Bourgeois revolutions are not apt to go far enough, particularly in changing property ownership. Still, one could imagine such revolutions with armed support and no doubt Fascistic ideologies. I doubt that they would be any less of a threat than revolutions of the Left.

of personal immortality and collective majesty. It seems beyond question that a feverish nationalism will charge the atmosphere of any nation, Communist or not, that tries to make the Great Ascent—and as a result we must expect the symptoms of nationalism along with the disease: exaggerated xenophobia, a thin-skinned national sensitivity, a search for enemies as well as a glorification of the state.

These symptoms, which we have already seen in every quarter of the globe, make it impossible to expect easy and amicable relations between the developing states and the colossi of the developed world. No conceivable response on the part of America or Europe or, for that matter, Russia, will be able to play up to the vanities or salve the irritations of the emerging nations, much less satisfy their demands for help. Thus, we must anticipate an anti-American, or anti-Western, possibly even anti-white animus from any nation in the throes of modernization, even if it is not parroting Communist dogma.

Then there is a second caution as to the prospects for non-Communist revolutions. This is the question of what ideas and policies will guide their revolutionary efforts. Revolutions, especially if their whole orientation is to the future, require philosophy equally as much as force. It is here, of course, that Communism finds its special strength. The vocabulary in which it speaks—a vocabulary of class domination, of domestic and international exploitation—is rich in meaning to the backward nations. The view of history it espouses provides the support of historical inevitability to the fallible efforts of struggling leaders. Not least, the very dogmatic certitude and ritualistic repetition that stick in the craw of the Western observer offer the psychological assurances on which an unquestioning faith can be maintained.

If a non-Communist elite is to persevere in tasks that will prove Sisyphean in difficulty, it will also have to offer a philosophical interpretation of its role as convincing and elevating, and a diagnosis of social and economic requirements as sharp and simplistic, as that of Communism. Further, its will to succeed at whatever cost must be as firm as that of the Marxists. It is not impossible that such a philosophy can be developed, more or less independent of formal Marxian conceptions. It is likely, however, to resemble the creed of Communism far

more than that of the West. Political liberty, economic freedom, and constitutional law may be the great achievements
and the great issues of the most advanced nations, but to the
least developed lands they are only dim abstractions, or worse,
rationalizations behind which the great powers play their imperialist tricks or protect the privileges of their monied classes.

Thus, even if for many reasons we should prefer the advent
of non-Communist modernizing elites, we must realize that
they too will present the United States with programs and
policies antipathetic to much that America "believes in" and
hostile to America as a world power. The leadership needed
to mount a jehad against backwardness—and it is my main
premise that only a Holy War will begin modernization in our
time—will be forced to expound a philosophy that approves
authoritarian and collectivist measures at home and that uti-
lizes as the target for its national resentment abroad the tower-
ing villains of the world, of which the United States is now
Number One.

All this confronts American policy-makers and public opinion with a dilemma of a totally unforeseen kind. On the one
hand we are eager to assist in the rescue of the great majority
of mankind from conditions that we recognize as dreadful and
ultimately dangerous. On the other hand, we seem to be committed, especially in the underdeveloped areas, to a policy of
defeating Communism wherever it is within our military capacity to do so, and of repressing movements that might become Communist if they were allowed to follow their internal
dynamics. Thus, we have on the one side the record of Point
Four, the Peace Corps, and foreign aid generally; and on the
other, Guatemala, Cuba, the Dominican Republic, and now
Vietnam.

That these two policies might be in any way mutually incompatible, that economic development might contain revolutionary implications infinitely more far-reaching than those
we have so blandly endorsed in the name of rising expectations, that Communism or a radical national collectivism might
be the only vehicles for modernization in many key areas of
the world—these are dilemmas we have never faced. Now I
suggest that we do face them, and that we begin to examine in

a serious way ideas that have hitherto been considered blasphemous, if not near-traitorous.

Suppose that most of Southeast Asia and much of Latin America were to go Communist, or to become controlled by revolutionary governments that espoused collectivist ideologies and vented extreme anti-American sentiments. Would this constitute a mortal threat to the United States?

I think it fair to claim that the purely *military* danger posed by such an eventuality would be slight. Given the present and prospective capabilities of the backward world, the addition of hundreds of millions of citizens to the potential armies of Communism would mean nothing when there was no way of deploying them against us. The prospect of an invasion by Communist hordes—the specter that frightened Europe after World War II with some (although retrospectively, not too much) realism—would be no more than a phantasm when applied to Asia or South America or Africa.

More important, the nuclear or conventional military power of Communism would not be materially increased by the armaments capacities of these areas for many years. By way of indication, the total consumption of energy of all kinds (in terms of coal equivalent) for Afghanistan, Bolivia, Brazil, Burma, Ceylon, Colombia, Costa Rica, Dominican Republic, Ecuador, El Salvador, Ethiopia, Guatemala, Haiti, Honduras, India, Indonesia, Iran, Iraq, Korea, Lebanon, Nicaragua, Pakistan, Paraguay, Peru, Philippines, the UAR, Uruguay, and Venezuela is less than that annually consumed by West Germany alone. The total steel output of these countries is one-tenth of US annual production. Thus, even the total communization of the backward world would not effectively alter the present balance of military strength in the world.

However small the military threat, it is undeniably true that a Communist or radical collectivist engulfment of these countries would cost us the loss of billions of dollars of capital invested there. Of our roughly $50 billion in overseas investment, some $10 billion are in mining, oil, utility, and manufacturing facilities in Latin America, some $4 billion in Asia including the Near East, and about $2 billion in Africa. To lose these assets would deal a heavy blow to a number of large corporations, particularly in oil, and would cost the nation as a whole the loss of some $3 to $4 billion a year in earnings from those areas.

A Marxist might conclude that the economic interests of a capitalist nation would find such a prospective loss insupportable, and that it would be "forced" to go to war. I do not think this is a warranted assumption, although it is undoubtedly a risk. Against a Gross National Product that is approaching ¾ of a trillion dollars and with total corporate assets over $1.3 trillion, the loss of even the whole $16 billion in the vulnerable areas should be manageable economically. Whether such a takeover could be resisted politically—that is, whether the red flag of Communism could be successfully waved by the corporate interests—is another question. I do not myself believe that the corporate elite is particularly war-minded—not nearly so much so as the military or the congressional—or that corporate seizures would be a suitable issue for purposes of drumming up interventionist sentiment.

By these remarks I do not wish airily to dismiss the dangers of a Communist avalanche in the backward nations. There would be dangers, not least those of an American hysteria. Rather, I want only to assert that the threats of a military or economic kind would not be insuperable, as they might well be if Europe were to succumb to a hostile regime.

But is that not the very point?, it will be asked. Would not a Communist success in a few backward nations lead to successes in others, and thus by degrees engulf the entire world, until the United States and perhaps Europe were fortresses besieged on a hostile planet?

I think the answer to this fear is twofold. First, as many beside myself have argued, it is now clear that Communism, far from constituting a single unified movement with a common aim and dovetailing interests, is a movement in which similarities of economic and political structure and ideology are more than outweighed by divergencies of national interest and character. Two bloody wars have demonstrated that in the case of capitalism, structural similarities between nations do not prevent mortal combat. As with capitalism, so with Communism. Russian Communists have already been engaged in skirmishes with Polish and Hungarian Communists, have nearly come to blows with Yugoslavia, and now stand poised at the threshold of open fighting with China. Only in the mind of the *Daily News* (and perhaps still the State Department) does it seem possible, in the face of this spectacle, to refer to the unified machinations of "international Communism" or the "Sino-Soviet bloc."

The realities, I believe, point in a very different direction. A world in which Communist governments were engaged in the enormous task of trying to modernize the worst areas of Asia, Latin America, and Africa would be a world in which sharp differences of national interest were certain to arise within these continental areas. The outlook would be for frictions and conflicts to develop among Communist nations with equal frequency as they developed between those nations and their non-Communist neighbors. A long period of jockeying for power and command over resources, rather than anything like a unified sharing of power and resources, seems unavoidable in the developing continents. This would not preclude a continuous barrage of anti-American propaganda, but it would certainly impede a movement to exert a coordinated Communist influence over these areas.

Second, it seems essential to distinguish among the causes of dangerous national and international behavior those that can be traced to the tenets of Communism and those that must be located elsewhere. "Do not talk to me about Communism and capitalism," said a Hungarian economist with whom I had lunch this winter. "Talk to me about rich nations and poor ones."

I think it *is* wealth and poverty, and not Communism or capitalism, that establishes much of the tone and tension of international relations. For that reason I would expect Communism in the backward nations (or national collectivism, if that emerges in the place of Communism) to be strident, belligerent, and insecure. If these regimes fail—as they may—their rhetoric may become hysterical and their behavior uncontrolled, although of small consequence. But if they succeed, which I believe they can, many of these traits should recede. Russia, Yugoslavia, or Poland are simply not to be compared, either by way of internal pronouncement or external behavior, with China, or, on a smaller scale, Cuba. Modernization brings, among other things, a waning of the stereotypes, commandments, and flagellations so characteristic of (and so necessary to) a nation engaged in the effort to alter itself from top to bottom. The idiom of ceaseless revolution becomes less relevant—even faintly embarrassing—to a nation that begins to be pleased with itself. Then, too, it seems reasonable to suppose that the vituperative quality of Communist invective would show some signs of abating were the United States to modify its own dogmatic attitude and to forego its own wearisome clichés about the nature of Communism.

I doubt there are many who will find these arguments wholly reassuring. They are not. It would be folly to imagine that the next generation or two, when Communism or national collectivism in the underdeveloped areas passes through its jehad stage, will be a time of international safety. But as always in these matters, it is only by a comparison with the alternatives that one can choose the preferable course. The prospect that I have offered as a plausible scenario of the future must be placed against that which results from a pursuit of our present course. And here I see two dangers of even greater magnitude: (1) the prospect of many more Vietnams, as radical movements assert themselves in other areas of the world; and (2) a continuation of the present inability of the most impoverished areas to modernize, with the prospect of an eventual human catastrophe on an unimaginable scale.

Nevertheless, there *is* a threat in the specter of a Communist or near-Communist supremacy in the underdeveloped world. It is that the rise of Communism would signal the end of capitalism as the dominant world order, and would force the acknowledgement that America no longer constituted the model on which the future of world civilization would be mainly based. In this way, as I have written before, the existence of Communism frightens American capitalism as the rise of Protestantism frightened the Catholic Church, or the French Revolution the English aristocracy.

It is, I think, the fear of losing our place in the sun, of finding ourselves at bay, that motivates a great deal of the anti-Communism on which so much of American foreign policy seems to be founded. In this regard I note that the nations of Europe, most of them profoundly more conservative than America in their social and economic dispositions, have made their peace with Communism far more intelligently and easily than we, and I conclude that this is in no small part due to their admission that they are no longer the leaders of the world.

The great question in our own nation is whether we can accept a similar scaling-down of our position in history. This would entail many profound changes in outlook and policy. It would mean the recognition that Communism, which may indeed represent a retrogressive movement in the West, where it should continue to be resisted with full energies, may nonetheless represent a progressive movement in the backward areas, where its advent may be the only chance these areas have of escaping misery. Collaterally, it means the recognition that "our side" has neither the political will, nor the ideological wish, nor the stomach for directing those changes that the backward world must make if it is ever to cease being backward. It would undoubtedly entail a more isolationist policy for the United States *vis-à-vis* the developing continents, and a greater willingness to permit revolutions there to work their way without our interference. It would mean in our daily political life the admission that the ideological battle of capitalism and Communism had passed its point of usefulness or relevance, and that religious diatribe must give way to the pragmatic dialogue of the age of science and technology.

I do not know how to estimate the chances of affecting such deep-seated changes in the American outlook. It may be that the pull of vested interests, the inertia of bureaucracy, plus a certain lurking fundamentalism that regards Communism as an evil which admits of no discussion—the anti-christ—will maintain America on its present course, with consequences that I find frightening to contemplate. But I believe that our attitudes are not hopelessly frozen. I detect, both above and below, signs that our present view of Communism is no longer wholly tenable and that it must be replaced with a new assessment if we are to remain maneuverable in action and cogent in discourse.

Two actions may help speed along this long overdue modernization of our own thought. The first is a continuation of the gradual thawing and convergence of American and Russian views and interests—a rapprochement that is proceeding slowly and hesitantly, but with a discernible momentum. Here the initiative must come from Russia as well as from ourselves.

The other action is for us alone to take. It is the public airing of the consequences of our blind anti-Communism for the underdeveloped world. It must be said aloud that our present policy prefers the absence of development to the chance for Communism—which is to say, that we prefer hunger and want and the existing inadequate assaults against the causes of hunger and want to any regime that declares its hostility to capitalism. There are strong American currents of humanitarianism that can be directed as a counterforce to this profoundly anti-humanitarian view. But for this counterforce to become mobilized it will be necessary to put fearlessly the outrageous question with which I began: is the United States fundamentally opposed to economic development?

DENNIS H. WRONG

Economic Development and Democracy

DENNIS WRONG is professor of sociology at New York University. He is the author of *Population and Society,* chapters in several books, and numerous articles and reviews in academic journals and in *Commentary, Dissent, Scientific American, Partisan Review, The New York Review of Books, Book Week,* and others.

Robert Heilbroner's foregoing essay, "Counter-revolutionary America," is the most intelligent and forceful statement of a point of view widely held by writers on economic development in the Third World. Although Heilbroner is an economist, his conclusions rest only to a minor degree on economic expertise. Both in the article and in his earlier book-length essay, *The Great Ascent,*[1] he fully recognizes that economic development necessarily involves massive social and political changes in addition to the changes in the techniques and the organization of production that the term in its narrow sense connotes. Heilbroner's argument, anticipated in his earlier book but stated far more strongly and without qualification in the more recent article, is that the obstacles posed to rapid economic development by traditional values and old established ruling elites are so great that a revolution bringing to power a Communist-type totalitarian dictatorship can alone be expected to overcome them and proceed with the urgent task of modernizing backward societies.

It is worth reviewing step by step the reasoning by which Heilbroner reaches this conclusion. The essentials of his position are shared by many other writers—indeed, some of them have become virtual commonplaces in discussions of economic

[1] Robert L. Heilbroner, *The Great Ascent,* New York: Harper Torchbooks, 1963.

development. By summarizing the argument as schematically as possible, shorn of Heilbroner's considerable eloquence and richness of allusion, it should be possible to see its main structure and to separate the truths from the assumptions and hypotheses contained in it.

Only the starting point of the argument involves an economic proposition: namely, that the task of initial capital accumulation in underdeveloped countries requires the holding down for a time of the living standards of the peasants, who constitute the mass of the population; not until the "infrastructure" of a modern economy has been built will it be possible for the resulting gains in productivity to be widely distributed.

But strictly economic considerations are transcended as soon as we ask what groups and agencies in contemporary underdeveloped countries are capable of organizing and directing the economic task of drawing a portion of the peasantry off the land to build capital and collecting part of the agricultural produce of the remaining peasants to feed this new nonagricultural labor force. The absence of rising commercial and entrepreneurial classes resembling the European bourgeoisie, or of any group imbued with an ethos favoring, as the Protestant ethic favors, hard work and the sacrifice of present material gains for the future, means that the state alone can play the necessary role in today's backward countries. Most experts on economic development concede (in the large at least) that the state must assume the entrepreneurial function in the majority of the nations of the Third World and that these nations are therefore likely to adopt some form of collectivism or "state socialism." Only a handful of neoclassical economists disagree. The state must be a strong state if it is to initiate successful programs of economic development. That is, it must, in the first instance, possess the power and the will to coerce or buy off traditional elites who resist modernizing measures. But, more important, it must command the allegiance of a significant portion of the population.

There is little in this analysis so far that is likely to arouse much disagreement. The next step in Heilbroner's argument, however, goes beyond the limits of general consensus. In order to win the support of the masses, the argument runs, the state must promote a new ideological creed that will penetrate their minds and hearts, win them away from traditional habits, beliefs and loyalties—"reach and rally them," as he puts it—and induce them to acquiesce in the sacrifices and rigors of the period of capital accumulation. Such a creed is bound to be intolerant of all dissent and is likely to contain a strong negative component, branding foreigners, in particular the West, as carriers of evil and actual or potential supporters of oppositionists at home. Clearly, this description is matched most closely by a revolutionary regime which has seized power after mobilizing a sizable segment of the population against the old order or foreign imperialists, or, most probably, a combination of both. Only a militant revolutionary state can make the sharp break with the past and impose the strict totalitarian discipline on a sprawling agrarian society that are needed to begin "the Great Ascent" to the heights of modernization.

Heilbroner's rejection of the belief or hope that democratic, constitutional governments, preserving and fostering the political liberties of the individual citizen, are capable of achieving economic development is presented in less detail than his reasons for thinking that some form of totalitarian collectivism can do the job. But his case against democratic government is implicit in much of his argument and has been more fully stated by other writers who share his general outlook. I shall draw on some of them to flesh out his thesis.[2]

Most of the states in the Third World are far from being genuine nations. Democratic institutions and practices, it is held, can only delay the task of nation-building by encouraging all the diverse ethnic, religious, tribal and linguistic groups that make up the populations of the new states to articulate their distinctive values and interests. The new states must create an overriding sense of national purpose and identity transcending parochial group loyalties if they are to carry out effective economic development programs. A democratic multi-party system will perpetuate and even accentuate the

[2] For a critique resembling in some respects the present one of prevalent assumptions about modernization in the Third World, see Charles C. Moskos, Jr. and Wendell Bell, "Emerging Nations and Ideologies of American Social Scientists," *The American Sociologist*, 2 (May 1967), pp. 67–72.

fragmentation of their populations. This argument has been applied most widely in defense of one-party dictatorships in Africa. It makes a specifically *political* case against democracy in the Third World, seeing nation-building as the prime requisite for the strong state that is in turn a prime requisite for economic development.

Unlike Africa, most Asian and Latin American nations do not confront the immediate necessity of welding together collections of tribal peoples who have often been traditional enemies and have never acknowledged any central political authority. The case against democracy in Asia and Latin America rests less on the alleged requirements of nation-building than on the contention that democratic governments cannot succeed in breaking the resistance to far-reaching social reform offered by old classes and elites—parasitic landlords, village moneylenders, *compradore* merchants, corrupt military and bureaucratic cliques, hoary priestly oligarchies. Democracy is likely to be no more than a façade behind which these groups retain full power, occasionally lulling the masses with token reforms.

A more general argument against democracy in the Third World, one that is more closely linked to the initial prerequisites for economic development, holds that the masses are likely to vote themselves welfare state benefits, opting for immediate improvements in their standard of living rather than for capital investment and thus defeating long-range development programs. Argentina under Perón, and particularly the persistence of Perónist sympathies among the industrial workers long after the dictator's fall from power, are frequently cited as the standard horrible example.[3] There is an obvious contradiction between the assertion that democracy in the Third World is doomed to be a mere façade manipulated by the traditional ruling classes and the expressed fear that it will result in the mass electorate voting for immediate, "uneconomic" gains in income, but we shall let this pass for the moment.

Such in broad outline is Heilbroner's thesis, omitting only his observations on the probable attitude of the United States

[3] Heilbroner, *The Great Ascent,* p. 100.

to revolutionary regimes in the Third World, which I shall discuss very briefly later. The thesis, both in Heilbroner's and in other versions of it, has evoked vigorous objections from liberals and democrats unwilling to accept the necessity and inevitability of the totalitarian trend it postulates. Their reactions, however, have usually failed to go beyond ringing reaffirmations of democratic and humanitarian values, and expressions of moral outrage at the apparent readiness of so many Western writers to regard violence and repressive government as the unavoidable price of modernization. Heilbroner is entitled to reply to such protests—indeed, he has already so replied (see the correspondence columns of the July 1967 *Commentary*[4])—"don't blame me for being the bearer of bad news. To refute me you must first show that the news is not as bad as I've reported, that my analysis is mistaken, and this you have failed to do."

The Heilbroner thesis outlines certain social prerequisites for economic development and maintains that democratic institutions are bound to present obstacles to fulfilling them. Since democracy runs the risk of promoting anarchic factionalism, may permit privileged classes to retain covert control over the government, and encourages all groups to seek to use the state to advance their material interests, the thesis possesses an immediate plausibility. This plausibility carries over to the next step in the argument, where it is asserted that a government lacking democratic features will be able to avoid the problems of democracy and meet the requirements of modernization. But what if we start by asking what are the difficulties that a totalitarian revolutionary regime is likely to face in carrying out development programs? These difficulties are conceded in passing by Heilbroner, but they fail to receive the attention they deserve because of the initial critical focus on the difficulties apt to be encountered by "mild," democratic governments.

To begin with, the inflammatory nationalism, the xenophobia, and the exaltation of the state, which, according to Heilbroner, are invariable ingredients of the "mobilizing appeal" of revolutionary elites, lead to the investment of con-

[4] *Commentary*, 43 (July 1967), pp. 18–20.

siderable resources in armaments and the maintenance of large standing armies. Such expenditures are, of course, an utter waste from the standpoint of economic development. If demonstration steel mills and airlines are to be regarded as economically irrational national status symbols, how much more so are jet planes, tanks and well-drilled armies? True, the desire for national strength and military glory may powerfully motivate a nation to modernize its capital equipment and thus lay the foundation for eventual increases in productivity that will wipe out mass poverty and improve every citizen's material lot. A nation that can send sputniks into outer space is presumably capable of mass-producing shoes and automobiles, although the Soviet Union has yet to confirm this. However, underdeveloped nations are more likely to purchase the sinews of war from the advanced nations by intensifying their production of staple raw materials—the very condition that is part of the whole syndrome of their economic backwardness. Moreover, the trouble with large defense expenditures is that they tend to become self-perpetuating, not merely because they create vested interests, but because they persuade insecure neighbors to arm themselves and thus make the claim that a large military establishment is necessary for national security —a claim that tends to become self-fulfilling. Surely, those nations that have followed most closely Heilbroner's prescription —Russia, China, Egypt, Sukarno's Indonesia—have diverted enormous human and material resources from peaceful economic development to military uses.

In addition, the enhanced importance of the army makes a military takeover more probable should the revolutionary regime falter. If any "wave of the future" is discernible in the Third World at the present moment, it is in the direction of military dictatorships rather than Communist revolutions. Since 1960 revolutionary national socialist or left-nationalist reformist regimes have been overthrown in Argentina, Brazil, Bolivia, Algeria, Ghana and Indonesia, and have been discredited—to put it mildly—in Egypt and Syria. It is still altogether possible that in China, Mao's "cultural revolution" will be terminated by an army takeover. Military dictatorships have also replaced shaky democratic civilian governments in Nigeria, the Congo, Greece and a number of smaller

African nations. A few of these new regimes are national socialist and even pro-Communist in ideological orientation (e.g. Algeria); a larger number are right-wing, strongly anti-Communist or even proto-fascist (e.g. Argentina, Brazil, Greece, Indonesia).

Finally, aggressive nationalism and militarism may induce nations to seek territorial expansion, causing wars that risk spreading to engulf entire subcontinents, if not the world.

Barrington Moore, Jr., observes that military defeat in World War II was part of the price paid by Japan for following a conservative-fascist path to modernization.[5] In other words, the dead of Hiroshima and Nagasaki, the Tokyo firebomb raids, and the Pacific islands campaigns must be cast into the balance against the "preventable deaths" from starvation and injustice under the old regime in toting up the costs of Japanese modernization.[6] Should not the Soviet Union's enormous losses in World War II be assessed, along with the victims of Stalin's purges and enforced collectivizations, as part of the price of totalitarian Communist modernization? Stalin's army purges, his opportunistic foreign policy toward Germany and his unpopularity with the peasants who first hailed the Nazi invaders as liberators stemmed from his totalitarian rule and contributed to Russian military defeats in the early stages of the war.

Some Western nations also went through a military-expansionist phase in the course of their modernization. But in the present century technology has made even so-called "conventional" warfare far more destructive than in the past. If, as Heilbroner argues, greater population growth and density make economic development more urgent in the Third World today than in the West in the last century, then the changed scale of warfare and a more unstable international environment should also be taken into account if militaristic regimes are to be recommended as archmodernizers.

What countries have achieved economic development to date as a result of nationalist-Communist revolutions? Let us concede the case of the Soviet Union, although the entire issue

[5] Barrington Moore, Jr., *The Social Origins of Dictatorship and Democracy*, Boston: The Beacon Press, 1966, p. 271.

[6] Ibid., p. 104; Heilbroner, "Counter-revolutionary America," p. 248.

of whether the Bolshevik October revolution as distinct from the February revolution, let alone Stalin's totalitarian rule, was necessary for Russian economic development remains highly debatable among economists and historians. Heilbroner tells us that for himself he would rather be "an anonymous peasant" in China or Cuba than in India, Peru or Ecuador.[7] But by his own admission "it may well be that Cuba has suffered a considerable economic decline" since Castro took power, and "we may not know for many years whether the Chinese peasant is better or worse off than before the revolution."[8] He praises Cuba for its educational effort, and China for having freed its youth from the bondage of the traditional family system. However, these achievements—assuming their reality—at most facilitate economic development rather than constituting development itself. Heilbroner might also reflect that the peasants of India and Peru evidently do not share his view of their prospects, having rejected in large numbers the opportunity to vote for Communist parties in free elections. In short, with the ambiguous exception of the Soviet Union, the Communist promise of rapid industrialization remains no more than a promise.

Heilbroner's case for the necessity of totalitarian ruthlessness to achieve modernization rests ultimately on his conviction of the enormous urgency of the problems of the backward countries. They cannot proceed according to the more leisurely timetable of past Western industrialization; they must take a giant step forward within the next three or four decades or mass famine and internal chaos are sure to be their fate. Essentially, Heilbroner sees the continuing population explosion as imposing the need for an all-out attack on backwardness which must have priority over other values and objectives. Not the entire Third World, but "primarily the crowded land masses and archipelagos of Southeast Asia and the impoverished areas of Central and South America" must look to revolutions led by modernizing elites to rescue them from deepening poverty. The extent to which Heilbroner's argument rests on the population explosion is striking, considering that,

[7] Heilbroner in *Commentary*, 43 (July 1967), p. 20.

[8] Heilbroner, "Counter-revolutionary America," p. 245.

though there are many exceptions, economists as a rule are more optimistic than demographers in their estimates of the prospects of economic development in backward countries. Economists perceive the economic job to be done and are impressed by the ample technical resources—including their own counsel—available to do it, while demographers, horrified by the floods of additional people indicated by extrapolated population growth rates, insist that without birth control any development program is doomed to founder.

But are Communist countries likely to check population growth? Heilbroner refers patronizingly to India's failure to control the birth rate, but there is not the slightest evidence that China has had any greater success. Indeed, China's leaders lag behind India's in their awareness of the need for an anti-natalist population policy. The relatively sparsely settled Soviet Union never faced a population explosion comparable to that of Southeast Asia—a further reason, incidentally, for questioning the necessity of totalitarianism for Russian economic development. The doctrinal anti-Malthusianism of Communist ideology imposes a special handicap on Communist countries with regard to birth control. Nor do non-Communist revolutionary elites imbued with aggressive nationalism and anti-Western fervor seem promising candidates to assign high priority to diffusing family planning over building steel mills and armies.

But what if birth rates should turn downward *before* the "take-off" point in economic development has been reached? In a recent article in *Public Interest,*[9] Donald Bogue, the University of Chicago demographer, departed from the conventional pessimism of his colleagues[10] to predict the imminent end of the population explosion in the Third World. There is good reason to believe, he insists, that by the end of the present decade the efforts of government and private agencies promoting family planning will at last pay off and birth rates in India and several other Asian countries will begin unmistakably to decline. Bogue is unable to present decisive evidence

[9] Donald Bogue, "The End of the Population Explosion," *Public Interest,* 2 (Spring 1967), pp. 11–20.

[10] Including myself. See, for example, Dennis H. Wrong, "Population Myths," *Commentary,* 38 (November 1964), pp. 61–64.

supporting his forecast—he claims that the "catching on" of new birth control methods in peasant populations is still too recent to have been statistically recorded. His main tangible evidence is based on studies in several countries, the most impressive of which was conducted in South Korea, showing that peasant women have in surprising numbers adopted in an exceedingly short space of time such recently developed contraceptive methods as intra-uterine devices and even pills. Maybe Bogue will turn out to be a false prophet, but it is worth recalling that sharp reversals of demographic trends have happened before simultaneously in a number of quite different countries. There is no reason why sudden mass adoption of family planning resulting in lower birth rate might not occur in large areas of the Third World. Writing about Latin America, another demographer, J. Mayone Stycos of Cornell, also expresses cautious optimism in a recent book reporting his research in Peru and several Caribbean nations.[11]

I have argued that, though the difficulties faced by democratic governments in carrying out economic development are real ones, totalitarian revolutionary regimes also face difficulties peculiar to them that Heilbroner and others tend to slight. Military dictatorships, a third and at present the most common type of regime in the Third World, have not been notoriously successful modernizers either.[12] One might conclude in an even more pessimistic vein than Heilbroner that neither democracy, revolutionary collectivism nor military rule are capable of achieving modernization and that it is therefore unlikely to take place at all. Yet such a conclusion would clearly be unjustified. In the past there have been a variety of paths to modernization: it has been achieved by essentially conservative regimes in Germany and Japan, by postrevolutionary bourgeois democracies in England and France, under a pure bourgeois democracy in the United States and by Communist dictatorship in Russia; even a few military regimes have made considerable progress, as in Turkey and Mexico.

[11] J. Mayone Stycos, *Population Control in Latin America*, Ithaca, New York: Cornell University Press, 1967.

[12] See William McCord, "Armies and Politics: A Problem in the Third World," *Dissent*, 14 (July–August 1967), pp. 444–52.

There is apparently no intrinsic connection between economic progress and formal political institutions. The pace of economic development has also varied greatly, particularly among smaller nations free from the tensions of international rivalry.

Democratic institutions such as parliamentary government, elementary civil liberties and the rule of law, though not—except in the United States—universal suffrage, preceded economic development in the Western bourgeois democracies. Why should it be so widely assumed that democracy can only emerge in the Third World after modernization has been carried out by authoritarian governments? Those who argue this confuse the *strong* state that is indeed required for economic development with a monolithic, authoritarian state. The skeptics about democracy, with all their talk of avoiding ethnocentric evaluations of the institutions of non-Western peoples, often project the experience of Western democracies into the different social context of backward societies when they contend that Asian and African electorates will use the ballot to advance their short-term interests like voters in the West accustomed to governments whose rationalized welfare and service functions have succeeded, as Michael Walzer has argued, in demystifying the very idea of the state itself. Actually, the demands of the masses in underdeveloped areas are likely to be too modest rather than excessive from the standpoint of stimulating development.[13] Democracy, moreover, may take many different forms: ancient village communal bodies like the old Russian *mir* and the Indian *panchayats* can serve as two-way communication channels between modernizing elites and the base of the social structure, giving rise to a kind of "democratic centralism" that is a reality rather than a façade for unilateral dictation by the leadership. Also, even after universal suffrage was in effect in the Western democracies, the political organization and mobilization of the lower classes was a long, slow process. The masses in the Third World are not going to leap at once into the political arena to make shortsighted and selfish immediate group demands. There is no reason why they cannot be trusted to accept the guidance of enlightened

[13] Moskos and Bell, op. cit., p. 69.

modernizing elites that truly consult them and give them a sense of participation in the process. It is precisely such a sense of participation that Heilbroner sees as the forte of Communist revolutionaries, but there is no inherent reason why they alone should be capable of instilling it.

What about American policy toward the Third World? Although a secondary issue, this was ostensibly the main subject of Heilbroner's essay. Heilbroner to the contrary notwithstanding, the United States has not been consistently anti-revolutionary nor indeed consistently anything except opposed to states that have directly aligned themselves politically and militarily with the Soviet Union or China. The United States has given aid to Communist Yugoslavia; to nationalist, pro-Communist and anti-American states such as Ghana under Nkrumah, Algeria and Egypt; as well as to non-Communist revolutionary regimes such as Bolivia in the 1950s. Admittedly, the bulk of American aid has gone to such "client states" ruled by conservative dictatorships as South Korea, Taiwan and South Vietnam. But American policy has on the whole been shortsightedly opportunistic rather than ideologically consistent, willing to support almost any government, left or right, that is not a direct dependency of Russia or China. When Heilbroner suggests that the United States is unlikely to allow any nations in the Third World to remain neutral in the Cold War[14], he seems to be taking seriously Dulles's rhetoric of a decade ago—even then the rhetoric did not correspond to American practice. More probably, he has in mind the war in Vietnam, but the flimsy American justification for the war rests on the assumption that China is the "real" enemy, not the Viet Cong or Hanoi. The United States accepted, after all, a neutral government in Laos.

Latin America, however, is obviously the area where Heilbroner's label "Counter-revolutionary America" is most applicable. Not only do the pocketbook interests of American businessmen have a greater influence on government policy there than elsewhere in the world, but the fall-out in domestic politics of victories by Communist or proto-

[14] Heilbroner in *Commentary*, 43 (July 1967), p. 20.

Communist revolutionaries is bound to be far greater. The Dominican tragedy reveals the panic which may strike an American administration if it persuades itself that there is even the slightest possibility of a repetition of the Cuban experience. It is indeed hard to imagine the United States passively tolerating *any* anti-American, revolutionary government in this hemisphere.

Finally, let us suppose that American policy-makers accept Heilbroner's analysis and become convinced that modernization of the Third World is possible only under Communist or authoritarian left-nationalist auspices. The results may be curious indeed. *The New Republic* of July 8, 1967, reports that a privately distributed newsletter subscribed to by Wall Street insiders suggests that it may very well be in the American national interest to allow the Third World to go Communist. The United States will save money in economic aid as the new Communist regimes seek development by sweating their own peasantries, whose labor will have to carry the whole burden of capital accumulation. If they fail, the United States cannot be blamed. If they succeed, they will in a decade or two become moderate and "bourgeois" in spirit like the Russians and not only can we live in peace with them but we can engage in mutually profitable trade with them. Such a view may very well spread among those whom C. Wright Mills once called "sophisticated conservatives" and become more influential than the anger and frustration at the failure of American capitalism to convert the world that Heilbroner imputes to our leaders. And, as is so often the case in politics, the diagnosis may become self-confirming if America reduces instead of expands its aid to the Third World in expectation of a wave of totalitarian revolution. The Heilbroner thesis might thus ironically help bring about the conditions it claims to deplore in counseling us to resign ourselves to their inevitability.

Rebuttal by Robert Heilbroner

I am grateful to Dennis Wrong for his thoughtful and carefully argued reply to my article and to *The Great Ascent*. Here and there I disagree with him on small points, most of which will emerge below. But in the main I feel that somehow even Wrong, who so scrupulously avoids the rhetoric of outrage, has failed to come squarely to grips with the contentions on which my point of view is based. Let me therefore attempt to answer him by restating my position and emphasizing where I think the issue lies between us.

A. The essential starting point must be whether or not one believes that modernization will take place under the aegis of *present* governments in most of Latin America, Southeast Asia, and the Near East.[1] I have made it clear that I do not think it will. What is more, I rather doubt that Wrong would disagree with this pessimistic appraisal, although he would no doubt wish to see it qualified. If this is so, then economic development will have to wait until the regimes that now seem incapable of mounting a successful modernization program are replaced by other regimes. The question is, what kinds will they be?

B. Are the chances propitious for the emergence of democratic governments as the modernizing forces in these areas? I do not think so for the following reasons, some mentioned by Wrong and some not:

1. In many states only a revolutionary party will be able to oust the incumbent regimes.

2. In most nations the tradition of democratic opposition is unknown or thinly held, and the tradition of "strong man" government very widely accepted.

[1] I omit the Western and Eastern parts of Africa, where the problems of nation-building are now all-important. Nation-building can occur under many kinds of regimes.

3. The changes needed to bring modernization are not only political, but economic, social, intellectual, and even religious. Such deep-seated changes are extraordinarily difficult to achieve under the best of circumstances. I suspect that only authoritarian regimes can impose them.[2]

Against these doubts Wrong suggests some counterarguments. One of these is that "democracy" is capable of many guises. This is certainly true and some measure of "democracy" in a *consultative* sense (e.g., the Russian soviets, at least in theory) may exist even under dictatorships. What cannot, I think, be tolerated is a recognized and potentially powerful *opposition party.*

A second counterargument of Wrong's is that the Western nations have climbed to modernity under various sorts of governments, including a number of democratic (although not always very consultative) ones. This is of course so. The question then arises as to the relevance of Western (or Japanese post-Meiji) experience to the critical areas of the underdeveloped world. I think the relevance is slight for the following reasons:

1. The population crisis enjoins a much greater degree of haste for the contemporary backward world.

2. There has been no period of preparation comparable to the three centuries of European commercialization.

3. The backward world is handicapped by the deformations of imperialism.

Thus I hesitate to apply the lessons of the West to the East and South. However, if Wrong is merely arguing that the developing elites need not display the worst forms of totalitarianism; that a degree of tolerance is compatible with a strong modernization movement; and that a measure of freedom may be functional rather than otherwise, I would not dis-

---

[2] And they will be *imposed.* Modernization is a kind of cultural imperialism that is forced upon the masses. Hence it means little to claim, no doubt correctly, that the peasants do not like Communists. They will not like any zealous modernizers. And no other kind will succeed.

agree. Much depends on the personalities of the development leader and his opposition, on the tradition and circumstances of the country, etc. Nonetheless, I would argue (and again I doubt that Wrong would disagree) that strong tendencies must exist for extending and deepening the control of leadership, not only over political and economic life but into social and intellectual life as well. Perhaps I should point out, although Wrong has been good enough to do so for me, that in making this prediction I am not saying what I wish to have happen, but only what I think will happen, whether I wish it or not.

C. Taking off from these premises, I go on to state that left-authoritarian regimes, very likely, although not necessarily Communist, probably offer the best chance for a breakthrough in the backward areas. Here several points are to be examined:

1. Is such a breakthrough needed? Will not a slower process of change suffice?

As Wrong points out, my prognosis rests heavily on the urgency of the population program. It is this above all that sets the timetable. If Bogue is right, the timetable may be much extended and the necessity for rapid and radical action accordingly reduced. But is Bogue right? I am certainly far from convinced, and evidently neither is Wrong. Moreover, even if population growth *slows down,* will the deceleration come in time to avert economic and social crisis? Do not forget that populations will double in the most impoverished areas by the year 2000.

2. Will a revolutionary regime succeed in "breaking through"?

One cannot be sure. As Wrong points out, a Communist government may be ideologically unable to institute birth control. Or its ideological fervor, etc., may fall on deaf ears. Or it may just make terrible mistakes. In that case, I should think the probable outcome would be that mentioned at the end of his piece—there will be *no* modernization, and the future will be one of gradual deterioration, starvation, etc. I consider this an entirely possible state of affairs for the next generation. Yet one must ask, what is the chance for modernization if there is not an all-out revolutionary effort? This brings us back to my initial two premises.

3. Is there any evidence that the Communists can mount a successful development effort?

Wrong states that the Communists have so far delivered no more than promises. I would reply that promises are better than nothing. But are they only promises? Russia, to be sure, is a great mystery—is her development due to Communism or to pre-1913 industrialization? I would suggest that without Communism Russia would today be a kind of Brazil, with the extremes of Sao Paolo and the San Francisco Valley. But that is only a guess. The evidence as to Cuba buttresses my feeling that Castro has instituted a genuine and deeply-rooted change. Reston's *New York Times* articles (written after my initial piece) provide grist for my mill. As for China, who knows? What matters is the outcome after the present power struggle is resolved. I am impressed by Edgar Snow's observation in *The Other Side of the River* that whatever one may think of the Communist effort, there is no doubt that China has been profoundly and irreversibly changed. It is this kind of change that I believe to be an absolutely necessary condition for development; and at the base of my argument is my belief that among the existing political forces in the world only Communism is likely to be able to administer such a change. What other force does anyone suggest?

D. Wrong emphasizes the destructive side of authoritarianism and its penchant for war.[8] There is something to be said for this, although I fear that democracy provides no guarantee of peace. (Do I dare mention India and Goa; England and Suez; France and Algeria; and the U.S. and its military adventures?)

But once again I am forced back to choosing between ugly

[8] Let me object in passing that armies are not "utter waste" in backward areas. They are often very useful as a means of performing labor tasks, educating the peasants, and instilling morale.

alternatives. Revolutionary regimes bring a ruthless will and a desire to change "everything"; nonrevolutionary regimes seem unable to change even the few things that cry out for it. *If* we could have the best of both worlds—the enthusiasm, the dedication, the clear-cut program of the revolutionary, and the tolerance, open-mindedness, and decency of the gradualist—who would not welcome it? But I fear that in the existing condition of things we will have to make a far less palatable choice. If so, I opt for the party of "total" change. I repeat that if I had to take my chances here and now as an anonymous particle of humanity in China or India or in Cuba or' Brazil, I would unhesitatingly choose the Communist side. Furthermore, I suspect Wrong would too. (To be sure, if I could choose to be an intellectual in both nations I would opt for the other side. But only a tiny few of the particles of humanity are intellectuals.)

E. Last, I am not much alarmed over the possibility of my counsel becoming a self-fulfilling prophecy.[4] Even if it were, I would prefer the difficulties of living in a world that was largely Communist in the backward areas and isolationist here in the U.S., to one that threatens to go Communist and that evokes from us the military response of a Vietnam. But in the end I am interested in making a historical forecast, not in preparing a blueprint for action. My forecast is that if modernization takes place in the backward world (and again I caution that it may not), it will be because of the efforts of revolutionary, and very likely Communist, regimes. I forecast as well that the successes of milder, democratic government in bringing modernization to the peoples of Latin America, Southeast Asia, and the Middle East will be small, if any. Let us wait ten or twenty years and see which of us is right.

[4] If I may be allowed one more footnote, I would also suggest that the temper of revolutionary regimes will be affected to some extent by our own attitudes. Certainly one reason for their bellicosity (I do not say the only reason) has been our own intransigent opposition to them.

Surrebuttal by Dennis H. Wrong

I am glad Robert Heilbroner finds that I have correctly understood and presented his views. He has done as well with mine. Hopefully, the absence of rhetoric and polemical flourishes in our exchange will clarify the issues between us.

Heilbroner reiterates his conviction that left-authoritarian or communist movements "offer the best chance for a breakthrough in the backward areas." Whether he is right or wrong in this belief, he fails fully to confront the prior question of how likely in the near future such movements are to come to power at all and win the chance to show what they can do. Far from foreseeing any upsurge of democratic modernizing forces in the Third World, I argued that the present trend was toward the overthrow of *both* democratic governments and left-authoritarian regimes by the armed forces. Heilbroner is more hopeful—given his assumptions—than I am that there will be successful Communist revolutions; I am more hopeful than he that some modernization will take place under a variety of political regimes. He apparently regards such recent events as China's declining prestige in the Third World, the turmoil inside China, the overthrow of left-nationalist "strong men" in Indonesia, Algeria, and Ghana, the misadventures of "Arab socialism," and the repeated failures and defeats of Cuban-sponsored guerrillas in Latin America, as mere eddies in a broad historical current favoring revolutionary authoritarian regimes and movements. I, on the contrary, think that the Viet Cong may be the leaders of the last Communist-directed "war of national liberation" rather than the forerunners of a new revolutionary wave.

But if Heilbroner is right and Communist revolutions do take place in much of the Third World, can they achieve modernization? Communists have won power primarily by their own efforts in only five countries: Russia, Yugoslavia, China, North Vietnam, and Cuba. None of the three conditions Heilbroner adduces for doubting relevance of past Western experience to the contemporary underdeveloped world was fully present in Russia or Yugoslavia, so their record is scarcely more pertinent to the argument than the successful modernization achieved under democratic auspices by England and the United States. As to China, I agree with Heilbroner—who knows? China may indeed have been "profoundly and irreversibly changed," but such change may or may not in the end facilitate the particular kind of "profound and irreversible change" we call modernization. In its exaltation of an ascetic, chiliastic revolutionary brotherhood, Mao's "cultural revolution" appears to be directed *against* assigning high priority to economic development and the materialism it inevitably brings rather than the reverse. North Vietnam has been involved in wars for over a decade. Cuba, a partially modernized country before Castro, has at most established some of the prerequisites for balanced modernization (e.g. mass literacy) while undergoing actual economic decline. I agree that promises are better than nothing, but Communists are not the only people in the Third World promising modernization.

The very polycentrism of the Communist world that makes nonsense out of the anti-Communist slogans invoked by Washington to justify the Vietnam war reduces the likelihood that future national Communist regimes will be the ruthless modernizers Heilbroner expects them to be. Would Egyptian national communism differ in any important way from Nasser's regime? Would an Algerian revolution create a state markedly different from the Ben Bella and Boumedienne dictatorships? Revolutions led by hard-bitten, Moscow-trained Stalinist orgmen might have a chance of successfully using totalitarian methods to impose the drastic surgery of modernization on a recalcitrant peasantry. So might revolutions led by men like Mao's original cadres. So might revolutions led by orthodox Marxist-Leninists like most of the national Communists of Eastern Europe. But post-Stalinist Moscow no longer tightly controls the Communist parties in the Third World (or, indeed, anywhere), and Maoism today has little in common with traditional Marxist-Leninist doctrine. Revolutionary movements in the Third World are likely to be shaped to a greater extent by national character traits than was the case in past Communist revolutions and such traits have usually been an obstacle—though by no means the only one—to modernization. The degree to which Communist parties in the Third World base themselves on dissatisfied ethnic, religious, and caste minority groups in their struggle against existing governments has been documented by Donald Zagoria. Can we really expect such parties, should they win power, to be as relentlessly future-minded as the puritanical, iron-willed Bolsheviks who are the prototypes for our model of totalitarian modernization?

If Heilbroner is right that Communist revolutions offer the only hope for modernization and I am right in doubting that there will be many successful revolutions in the near future, then the obvious conclusion is that there may be little or no modernization and that economic deterioration and political fragmentation are likely results. I agree that this is an entirely possible outcome for the next generation. It seems to me much more probable that disciplined, authoritarian revolutionaries will be able to seize power under conditions of mass famine and chaos than that they will succeed in overthrowing present governments which are maintaining some degree of order and economic progress, painfully slow though the latter may be. After all, in four of the five countries where indigenous communist movements have triumphed (Cuba is the one exception), the Communist seizure of power occurred during or immediately after devasting wars and foreign invasions that had disrupted agricultural life and destroyed the control of the previous governments over much of their territories. In such circumstances, determined revolutionary movements have their best chance of succeeding. But this possibility is not what Heilbroner has in mind: he sees Communist revolutions as a way of *averting* political and economic collapse rather than as an eventual consequence of collapse.

The issue of the timetable for modernization is really the crucial one. I agree that none of the existing regimes in the Third World, neither the formal democracies, the collectivist one-party states, nor the military dictatorships, have achieved full modernization. But "when we look at the positive side of our ledger sheet, we perceive an astonishing fact. Against all the obstacles to development that we have described, economic progress has in fact been taking place, and at a pace which by comparison with the past amazes us with its rapidity." So writes Robert Heilbroner on page 89 of his book *The Great Ascent*. He immediately observes that both the gains already achieved as well as future gains risk "being washed out by population growth."

Now I am indeed not fully convinced that Donald Bogue is right in predicting the imminent end of the population explosion. Who can have complete confidence in any forecast of something that has never happened before, like the mass adoption of birth control by peasant populations within a decade or two? But the probability of this happening seems to me somewhat greater than the probability of a wave of Communist revolutions in the Third World followed by the rapid achievement of modernization by the revolutionary regimes. The populations of the advanced countries, including Japan, have altered their childbearing habits in very short periods of time and without having been exposed to large-scale, state-directed campaigns urging them to do so. Since I wrote my original article, another leading American demographer, Frank Notestein, president of the Population Council, has expressed in the October, 1967 *Foreign Affairs* qualified optimism over the prospect of new birth control methods spreading in the underdeveloped world and reducing current rates of population growth before the end of the century. If this should happen it will not remove entirely the urgency of the need for rapid modernization in the larger, more densely-populated areas, for even a rate of growth that is half the present one (and this Notestein considers possible) will still be an economic burden. But slower population growth will certainly make it easier for any regime committed to modernization to make some progress and will allow a wider margin for retrievable error.

I am aware that Heilbroner is making a forecast rather than advocating a course of action. But forecasts can become self-fulfilling if those who possess power are persuaded by and act on them. I too would prefer a Communist

Third World and an isolationist United States to a succession of Vietnams; but is Heilbroner really prepared to give up all hope that the United States and the West in general can have any constructive influence on the economic development of the backward areas? Did the author of *The Future as History* mean by that phrase that it is as futile in the end to reflect on what still might be as it is to mourn over what might have been?

PART IV

———◆———

IRVING HOWE

The Politics of Disaster

Like many other people, I have been reading the recent literature on the history and politics of Vietnam. It is a depressing experience, and it bears out once more de Tocqueville's remark that "a true but complicated idea has always less chance of succeeding than one which is false but simple."

For political mythologists, Vietnam presents an unambiguous picture. The spokesmen for Washington, fixated upon their anti-Communist crusade, and the apologists for Hanoi, fixated upon the vocabulary of anti-imperialism, tell pretty much the same kind of story: monolithic, brute, devoid of those complexities we know to be the texture of political life wherever it can emerge with some freedom. The more one reads about Vietnam, the more one is tempted to cry out, "How appalling they have been on both sides!" So I write here not at all as an expert, but as someone trying, no doubt with errors, to scrape some meaning from what the experts report.

AUTHOR'S NOTE: The essay which follows is not meant as an exhaustive analysis of the Vietnam situation, nor as a discussion of proposals for bringing that ghastly war to an end. The exhaustive analysis appears in a number of books, some of them mentioned in the essay; the discussion of proposals for peace has been recently a major topic in the periodical press. What I have tried to do here is to outline certain of the political problems which arise as a result of the increasing role of the United States in Asian affairs. And that is difficult enough. —I.H.

1946

Looking back upon the history of modern imperialism, one cannot avoid the ironic reflection that even among oppressors there are crucial distinctions. The British in India were economic cut-throats and racialist snobs, yet somehow, even if involuntarily, another side of British experience and thought got through to the Indians. Partly because of the penetration of British radicalism (the London School of Economics served as a preparatory school for the Indian nationalists), and partly because of the training provided by the British Civil Service, the Indians were able to create an indigenous political movement, the Congress party of Gandhi and Nehru, which sank its roots into the countryside and gained the assent of the intelligentsia.

Why did not the same thing happen in the French colonies, or even in certain other British colonies? I am not quite sure, but I would speculate that in France there has always remained a segment of a military-social elite which could not reconcile itself to the idea of a democratic republic and found an outlet in the colonies for its authoritarian energies. While not as racialist as the British, the French colonial overseers established themselves in greater independence from the home governments in Paris and could therefore rule more freely in accord with their fundamental outlook— an outlook that combined repressive authoritarianism with a measure of cultural proselytizing.

French colonialism found its rationale in fantasies of glory; British colonialism in fantasies of uplift. Both were self-deluding, yet the differences would prove to be important. Fantasies can become or shape realities. Something of British democracy seeped past British imperialism into Indian society, whereas in Indochina, despite an intensive cultural "Frenchifying" among the landowners and intellectuals, there was not permitted even a feeble carbon of the democratic process. In Indochina, specifically, the colonialists formed a semi-feudal caste free to exploit the country.

A disaster; and now, as hostages of history, we pay for it.

The Vietnamese, as they emerge from the pages of Fall, Scigliano, Hammer, Lacouture, and Buttinger seem a marvelously attractive people: subtle, charming, clever. They have a history of repeated struggle against French imperialism, from the late 19th century until the Second World War, and a far longer history of resistance against Chinese imperialism. They have thrown up obscure figures of heroism, romantic nationalists who remind one a little of the 19th-century Polish nationalists in doomed revolt against the Czar. For the Vietnamese, as for the Poles, nationalism became a mystique, and from a mystique it could easily decline into a cabal. The plots of the Vietnamese nationalists, most of them sons of mandarins and middle bourgeoisie, fail repeatedly, and most of all, because they do not reach the Vietnamese people, either the peasants or the urban population.

For this failure to strike social roots there are at least two reasons. The French circumscribe Vietnamese nationalism into the desperate isolation of café and exile, thereby preventing it from taking on the breadth and maturity of Indian nationalism. The French succeed in keeping the nationalists cut off from their own nation—without realizing that thereby the nation will be driven to rise up without, and even against, the nationalists.

The other reason for the claustrophobic, pre-modern character of Vietnamese nationalism has to do with Vietnam itself. The aristocratism of the mandarins, like that of the Polish landowners in the late 19th century, dominates the political style of Vietnamese nationalism. There are in Vietnam few, if any, *narodnik* or populist inclinations; the nationalists mean to act for, but not through, the nation. And what is more, by the 20th century Vietnam is barely a coherent and functioning nation, any more than Poland could be said to be a coherent and functioning nation at the turn of the century. Vietnam is a hope for a nation, to be established once the French are driven into the sea. But meanwhile the nationalist intelligentsia lacks social roots, popular support, authentic experience. It knows little of the lessons absorbed by Gandhi, Nehru, and, in a perverted way, even Sukarno. These Vietnamese nationalists are trapped in their traditional dependence

on mandarin elitism; their ingrained respect for Chinese
and French culture; their oscillation between careers in the
French civil service, which can be fairly comfortable, and
sudden outbreaks of rebellion, which can lead to prison and
exile. All through the 1920s and 1930s the French colonialists
and Vietnamese nationalists play by more or less fixed rules
—with the proviso that one side has the power and the
other not.

There is a further tragedy. The Vietnamese nationalists,
often men of heroism and purity, see in their nationalism . . .
nothing but nationalism. It is virtually without social content,
authentic or false social content; without, say, the village
democracy of Gandhi or the humanitarian socialism of
Nehru. Again, like the 19th-century Polish nationalists, their
bias is unconsciously conservative: they cannot even imagine
anything else, and they fail to see the deep connection between
French rule and the privileges of the native elite from which
most of them derive.

Historically they are squeezed in a nutcracker between the
colonialism of yesterday and the totalitarianism of tomorrow.
They have nothing to offer against these, except the martyred
cry of their nation, and soon enough the Communists take
over even this, for at the very least the Communists understand that for the national goal to be reached it must contain
more than mere nationalism. The tragedy of the Vietnamese
nationalists is that they are 19th-century nationalists trying
to move from the 17th century into the 20th century, while
their French masters and teachers are 18th-century absolutists.

Let us avoid mythology. Brilliant leader that he would
become, Ho Chi Minh was deeply implicated in the fiascos and
deceits of Stalinist policy in Asia during the 1920s and 1930s.
But history—by which, concretely, I mean first the French
and then the Vietnamese nationalists—would give him and
his party the rare privilege of a second and then a third
chance. For as it turned out, the Communists were the only
political force in Vietnam that functioned according to the
premises of modern politics. They alone saw the need to
speak to the quiescent mass of the people and to stir them with
slogans blending national and social goals. They alone created

cadres that would combine a monolithic discipline from above with the manipulation of an untutored population below.

Against such competition, the apolitical Vietnamese nationalists, for all their sincere parochialism, were helpless. And it is probably this parochialism which explains their failure to throw up a true national hero: for none of their leading figures, whatever his ability, could break past French restraints and grow into the role of national leadership.

The decisive moment occurs immediately after the collapse of Japanese domination at the end of the Second World War. Communist leaders in exile quickly make their way home, especially in North Vietnam, to join their cadres in the villages, with whom they had maintained a functioning underground organization during the war; while the nationalist leaders remain exiles in China, wasting precious weeks until they will return with the hated Chinese armies. The delay proves fatal. And more than fatal: it is profoundly symptomatic. For the Communists alone grasp the need for building a movement with extensive social roots in the countryside, and beginning now, as well as through the war against the French, they transform themselves into a popular movement by means of their identification with the national cause. That they will gain the support of a majority of Vietnamese may be doubted, and has, in any case, never been demonstrated through a free election; but that they will soon be the most powerful Vietnamese movement, with strong popular support, cannot be doubted.

The French, too, contribute to the growing strength of Vietnamese Communism. In an appalling miscalculation they look upon Ho Chi Minh as "reasonable" and upon the non-Communist nationalists as intractable, and proceed to intermittent cooperation with the Communists in breaking the back of the nationalist and Trotskyist groups.

The Trotskyists, quite strong in the Saigon region and the winning party in the 1939 Cochin China election, are now, in the spring of 1946, brutally decimated by the Viet Minh, the Communist-led resistance movement. In the summer of 1946 the French supply Ho Chi Minh's second-in-command, General Giap, with artillery to wipe out pockets of resistance, led by the nationalist Dai Viet party against Communist domination in North Vietnam. The French in Hanoi also surround a section of the city to prevent members of the nationalist group VNQDD from coming to the aid of their leaders who, elsewhere in the city, are being rounded up by the Communists.

These are facts. And they are facts that ought to be considered by those Americans who cultivate the legend of "Uncle Ho," the benign leader.

Yet the irony of it all is that not Ho Chi Minh but the French broke the alliance between Communists and colonialists. During the late forties and fifties, the Viet Minh, rebuffed by the French, becomes the dominating force in the Vietnamese resistance; Ho Chi Minh, part of whose power was connived in by the French, now turns it against them. Yet in thereby helping liberate the nation, the Communists also destroy, at least in the North, its components of diversity and freedom, through a systematic liquidation of non-Communist nationalists. Creating an independent Vietnam, they create also an independent police state.

1954–56

Was there ever, after the Geneva Agreement, a significant chance for establishing South Vietnam as a viable country that would be non-Communist yet devoted to at least a measure of democratic freedom and social reform? Concerning such questions we of the democratic left have our ready answers—answers, as our critics point out, not always to be distinguished from our fervent hopes. And we cannot in honesty be at all certain that our answers are always relevant. For clearly there are situations in which anti-democratic pressures from both right and left are so enormous, that the frail shoots of freedom cannot flourish or survive. The more I have read about Vietnam, the more convinced I have become that in its decisive particulars the situation there was sharply different from that of any other underdeveloped country. The nature of French imperialism; the political-social weaknesses of traditional Vietnamese nationalism; the accession to leadership in the resistance movement by the Communists (something that happens nowhere else); the open and hidden cooperation of the French and the Communists in slaughtering political dissidents immediately after the Second World War; and then the years of struggle between the Viet Minh and the French, brought on by the blindness and cupidity of the latter and leading to results that can only favor the former—all of this militates against a democratic outcome.

But one thing is certain: the failure to try a mixture of political liberty and social reform in South Vietnam made all but inevitable a victory for the Communists.

Here we ought to gain a clearer sense of Diem, a man who, with good reason, has been portrayed as a despot, but also, it should be remembered, a man about whom Ho Chi Minh once said that "he too in his way is a patriot." He never collaborated with the French, and though, like Sukarno, he did accept Japanese protection against the French, he never became a Japanese puppet either. Nor was Diem ever accused of personal corruption. As Ellen Hammer remarks in *The Struggle for Indochina:*

> For some twenty years Diem had remained aloof from the political scene, and, as a symbol of Nationalist intransigence . . . a certain legend had grown up around his name. . . . Unfortunately he came to power at a time when nationalism was no longer sufficient and nothing short of political genius would be enough to cope with the situation. . . .

In 1954, when an effort was made, largely under the aegis of the United States, to establish an independent South Vietnam, Diem defined himself politically not only as an anti-Communist but also as an authentic and progressive nationalist leading the opposition to the pro-French and Bao Dai elements in Saigon.

At this point, then, the United States extended support to Diem because it seemed that he, unstained by collaborationism, spoke for those Vietnamese nationalists who wanted an independent country in the South, a country that would be tied neither to the Communists in Hanoi nor to the French and their agents. Later the representatives of the State Department would refuse or be unable to grasp the need for intensive social reform as a precondition for the survival of South Vietnam; but they did at least understand that, unless there were an

untainted nationalist at the head of the Saigon regime, there
was not even a possibility that the new country could be
established.

In 1954–5 Diem also won tentative support among whatever left-liberal elements remained in Saigon; also the support
of the 900,000 refugees, mostly Catholic peasants, who came
from the North;* and even the support of certain non-
Communist Vietnamese who had fought in the Viet Minh
against the French but could not stomach the prospect of Ho's
totalitarian state. The attitude of the bulk of the population in
South Vietnam toward the Diem regime in 1954–5 is not
easily determined. Obviously, there was no great enthusiasm,
nor any reason for it. The impression of the most cautious
observers is that a sizable portion of the people was at least
prepared to wait and see what Diem would do before it took
any decisive stand for or against him.

What South Vietnam did not yet have was the kind of institutional and economic infrastructure which a modern state
needs, be it democratic or not. Nor did South Vietnam have
the developed political movements a democratic society requires. The nationalist groups remaining in South Vietnam
were small, broken, isolated from the countryside, and, above
all, unsure of which course to follow. For all the reasons I
have touched upon, there was neither a liberal nor social democratic movement which might have become the agent pressing
for the reforms necessary in this new country—though there
were elements holding to liberal and social democratic ideas
which, had there been a reasonable interval of peace and an
atmosphere of political freedom, might have grown into parties and movements.

At the outset Diem seemed on the way toward improvising a
nation-state. He established a national administration; he began

* Ellen Hammer writes about this migration: "The religious factor
was undoubtedly an important one in their decision to leave, but it
would seem that revulsion against forced labor and the tight economic
and political controls and heavy levies imposed upon them by the Communists weighed heavily among refugees . . . It was clear not only that
the exodus constituted a serious popular indictment of the northern
[Communist] regime, but that it would have been multiplied several-
fold had the refugees been permitted to leave freely."

the physical reconstruction of the country; he managed to sub-
due the various private armies, some mere rackets and others
a strange blend of racket and religious sect. It cannot be said
that Diem had any strong social base in the country as a whole
or any significant popular movement behind him; given the
chaotic conditions of the past several decades, no political
tendency in South Vietnam except the Communists could or
did. But insofar as Diem's task was that of a pure and simple
nationalist, he did—up to a point—fulfill his perspective.*

But the central fact was that Diem did not merely face the
problem of nation-building; he had also to face an enormous
social upheaval, a countryside that had been stirred into consciousness and revolt during the struggle against the French.
He could thus satisfy his national ambitions *only if* he simultaneously undertook a social program—only, that is, if he acted
against certain immediate economic interests of the landown-
ing class from which many of his supporters came. It would
have been far cheaper, in any effort at even a modest land reform, to compensate the landowners for property appropriated
than to do what in effect was done:—a counterfeit "land reform" which did not seriously affect the relationship of power
in the countryside but which led the peasants, rightly enough,
to feel hostile toward the Saigon regime. This failure to abolish
the burden of rent was all the more disastrous since the peasants had actually stopped paying rent during the recent years
of turmoil; so that the Diem regime not merely withheld an
improvement they expected but reinstated a burden they believed themselves rid of.

* It soon became clear that there could be no free or even rigged-
cum-free election in the Communist North. Since the North had a majority of the population, this meant that even if something like a free
election took place in the South and even if the Communists won only a
small percentage of the vote, they would—with the mechanical majori-
ties rolled up in the North—be bound to win in a nation-wide poll, *regardless of whether they really had the support of a majority of the
people.*

On the other hand, if the regime in Saigon had been truly progressive
and thereby able to garner some popular support, a call for a nation-
wide election, both North and South, might have been politically advantageous. For by 1956 Ho Chi Minh, harrassed by a serious food
problem and deeply in trouble with a recalcitrant peasantry, was apparently not at all eager for a genuine vote.

Now it can be said, with obvious cogency, that the class ties and outlook of the Diem regime made such reform unlikely. That is quite true. Yet we have witnessed several instances during the past half-century in which land reform of varying effectiveness has been carried out by non-socialist regimes partly against the interests of sections of the ruling classes. Land reform, after all, does not mean the socio-economic liquidation of a ruling class; it means an incursion upon, or limitation of, and sometimes merely a redirection of its economic power. In Mexico, India, Formosa and Japan there have been programs of land reform—all countries with sharply different circumstances, yet all granting some landless peasants at least some satisfaction of their hunger for land. After achieving independence India undertook a program of acquiring the vast properties owned by the petty princes; these properties then became subject to the laws of the Indian states limiting the amount of land individuals could own and distributing surpluses. The national program for land redistribution was enacted under the guidance, as it happens, of a conservative bourgeois politician, Sardar Patel, who understood that if India was to survive, at least some redistribution of the land was necessary. I am not saying that the results have been satisfactory, or that there do not remain large numbers of landless peasants in India; but what was done in India could have been tried in South Vietnam, where the political need for such measures was even greater.

As for Japan and Formosa, the land reform programs there were more thorough-going than in most countries that have been troubled by a land problem. The relevance of these experiences is somewhat limited, since in both countries land reform was instituted by military occupations, the U.S. in Japan and Chiang Kai-Shek in Formosa, so that it was possible to override the objections of the old landowners and ignore their political influence. But in South Vietnam during the Diem period the U.S. probably had almost as decisive a voice as it did in Japan during the MacArthur occupation. And what is crucial is that, despite platonic commitments to land reform and paper programs in behalf of it, the U.S. did not press Diem in this direction. On the contrary, it enabled Diem to stay in power through a virtually unqualified commitment of money and military aid, and by threatening his opponents that if they overthrew Diem such aid would be withdrawn. Apart from whether one approves of such a relationship between an immense power and a tiny nation, the fact remains that the U.S. might have pressured the South Vietnamese into land reform but failed to do so.

The real issue in South Vietnam during the years 1954 through 1956 was whether a nationalist leadership which had managed precariously to establish the beginnings of nationhood would have the social intelligence to see that if it did not institute some reform, even its national aspirations would be frustrated. If it did not act to limit and confine certain class interests with which it was linked, then both the class and the national leadership would lose everything.

Was the Indian Patel more generous or humanitarian than the Vietnamese Diem? I doubt it—and what does it matter? Patel, however, grasped the critical fact that for the survival of a newly-independent country like India under Congress party rule, the interests of the princely landowners had to be clipped. Diem lacked this kind of understanding. There were, to be sure, obvious and enormous differences in their situations: the Indians were not faced with a Communist competitor commanding a network of underground agents and enjoying popular support. Which was all the more reason for Diem, simply out of nationalist commitment, to take bold social steps and transcend the limitations of his political outlook. There were people both in Vietnam and abroad who kept urging this upon the regime; but their advice was not taken.

What I wish to stress here is that there was nothing historically ordained in this failure, either on the part of the South Vietnamese or the United States. Historical reasons for it, historical pressures in behalf of it, historical probabilities pointing toward it—yes. But choices there were, choices involving social imagination and political grasp. Even if the right course had been taken, with liberty in the cities and land reform in the countryside, the odds would still have been heavily against the survival of an independent South Vietnam. But there would have been a decidedly better chance.

More than class interest was involved in the failure of the Diem regime. It was in the grip of a narrow social outlook derived from its mandarin origins; and this narrow outlook made it both intensely devoted to its image of the national interest and utterly incapable of grasping the central fact of modern politics: that whether democratic, totalitarian or authoritarian, *modern politics is a mass politics.* The masses may be aroused to participate democratically, or through totalitarian ritual and mock-action; but participate they do. Diem, still in the grip of mandarin paternalism as well as an old-style Catholic absolutism, could not act upon such an understanding of modern politics even to the extent that figures like Sukarno and Nasser could.

Since, however, the social issues churning in Vietnamese life were not to be brushed aside; since they co-existed with problems of nation-building, and indeed were indistinguishable from them; Diem's failure to confront these social issues meant that he was in effect cutting himself off from the people. It meant that his idea of the nation could be imposed only by suppressing the social issues—that is, by establishing an authoritarian regime. At its most serious, before it degenerated into a mere family oligarchy and racket, Diemism signified an utterly doomed effort to fulfill a 19th-century vision of nationalism in a context where the social problems of the 20th century had burst into full bloom. Diem therefore had no alternative —given his political outlook—but an imposition of *a politics from above.* He would create a nation despite and then in opposition to the people. The rationale Diem gave for suppressing democracy was not very different from that offered by dictators like Nkrumah or quasi-Maoists like Paul Sweezy: that the conditions were not yet "ripe" for anything else.

To all of this, one qualification needs to be added. Diem and his clique did try—since they had some glimmer of awareness—to impose an ideology of sorts upon South Vietnam. They imported a version of Left-Catholic "personalism" from France, which they then twisted into authoritarian channels; they set up organizations along semi-corporatist lines, borrowing the techniques which Chiang had tried in China during the thirties and which had in turn been copied from Mussolini;

they created the appearance of participation (mass rallies, re-education centers, etc.). How then were they different from the Communists? In at least two ways. The Diemists lacked the tried and selfless cadres which the Communists had built up over decades: men idealistic, ruthless and corrupt, devoted to the mystique of totalitarianism and the language of equality. And secondly, the Diemists had nothing to offer the peasants, as by contrast the Communist-led Viet Minh did. In short, Diemism could enjoy neither the moral advantages of democracy nor the practical advantages of totalitarianism. Thus, Diem was forced to ape the repressive methods of the Communists without being able to copy those of their methods that won them the allegiance of peasants and intellectuals.

Moreover, Diem soon launched a campaign of repression in the countryside against the former Viet Minh fighters and thereby contributed to a resumption of civil war. By the end of 1956 it was clear that for the scatter of democrats in South Vietnam there was no honorable course but opposition to Diem. But of one thing I am convinced: that the idea of trying in the mid-fifties to create a democratic-reformist alternative—however precarious and difficult—to both Ho Chi Minh and the puppet Emperor Bao Dai was in the interests of the Vietnamese.

This conviction has been fortified by reading Jean Lacouture's book, which makes clear that in South Vietnam during the middle and late fifties there were nascent political forces —if only they had been given time to regroup and mature!— which might have provided the kind of leadership the country needed. For it is not true, it is a falsehood perpetrated by the apologists for Hanoi, that the country was totally polarized between Ho and Diem. Intermediary political groups in the South were weak and confused; they would be crushed before they had a chance to go through any experience of political clarification; but they did exist. If Diem antagonized the peasants, he also destroyed those political elements in the cities that had a more intelligent approach to the peasants. Lacouture offers a description of the various groups, ranging from the Cao Dai sect to the trade unions which, like the Buddhists, did not know where to turn.* Still, what one can see in South Vietnam during these years was an effort to improvise an uneasy union of Eastern tradition and Western ideas. Had South Vietnam been able to enjoy twenty years of relative peace, there might have developed equivalents to Nehru or Betancourt or Mehta—why not? The Vietnamese had the intelligence and sophistication. But everyone with power, from Ho to Diem, from France to the United States, made certain that no such development would occur. Together they created the tragedy of Vietnam.

Coda: *The writing of history is, among other things, the description of missed opportunities. To look back upon the last two decades of Vietnamese life is to annotate the wastage of possibilities. How large or real were those possibilities? Was it probable or even likely that a South Vietnam initiating some land reform and allowing for a modest democratic life could have become a viable society? I do not see how such a question can be answered with any assurance. A few things, however, can be said:*

a) Time is of the essence. *A land reform in 1955 would have been worth ten times as much as a land reform in 1965. A free political life in 1955 might have done for South Vietnam what a free political life could no longer do in 1965.*

b) Retrospective wisdom is valuable, *if only because it may possibly prevent the repetition of disaster. Even if the peculiar conjuncture of circumstances in South Vietnam made a democratic course unlikely, there was the possibility, at the outset, of building on narrow foundations and then, with international help, of creating a more solid infrastructure of political and social institutions. Slender as that possibility may seem—and both the realpolitik Right and authoritarian Left gloat in minimizing the possibility—it is the political and moral*

---

* An editor of *Dissent*, scrutinizing an earlier version of this essay, raised the question: "But you yourself said it was necessary to suppress the para-military forces of the Cao Dai and Hoa Hoa sects; can you then propose that they then be allowed to function freely as part of the national life?" Yes, precisely. To create a modern nation it was necessary to suppress the particularistic *military* power of the sects. Yet once this was done, the sects remained, and had to remain, an important element in the country's life. In his own distorted way, even Diem understood that they had now to be absorbed and allowed to participate in the social-political life of the country; but he did this in an authoritarian and destructive way. To have done it democratically would obviously have been difficult, extremely difficult; *but then, so was everything in South Vietnam difficult!*

obligation of radical democrats to keep stressing that the possibility was there.
c) There are no guarantees in politics, *only chances for better or worse.*

1956–66

The aspect of the Vietnam conflict that is least thoroughly discussed in the studies thus far written is the role of the United States. At least in respect to the earlier years, it is hard to find a pattern of American interventionism that conforms to a coherent master plan, either benevolent or malicious. So far as one can tell—later investigations may change the picture—U.S. involvement in Vietnam came about mainly as the result of drift and without much awareness of likely consequences. I very much doubt that when U.S. troops began to be sent to Vietnam in 1961, there was a clear understanding in Washington of the ultimate consequences.

The motivating ideology behind this interventionist drift was, however, much firmer in nature: it was the kind of anti-Communism which, with variations, has been U.S. policy since the Truman Administration. The U.S. intervention in Vietnam was thus, from the beginning, seriously complicated by the cold-war struggle with China. There can be no question that the idea of "stopping the Chinese" and perhaps of establishing bases in proximity to Communist China gave U.S. intervention in Vietnam a "hard" military character, in which lip service was paid to the need for social reform but the local requirements of Vietnamese society were subordinated to the big-power confrontation.

In Vietnam itself U.S. diplomacy continued its traditional policy of relying upon established power, which in this case meant Diem. Some of the policy-makers in Washington would no doubt have preferred a more liberal regime in Saigon, but they acted according to the view appropriate enough in a stable world or in a pre-modern politics, that power is a visible reality which has to be accepted wherever and however it exists. That an apparently stable structure of power can disintegrate rapidly, they surely knew as well as we do; but by training, temperament, and tradition they were not equipped to act upon this knowledge. Between what some of them knew intellectually and the way in which most of them acted practically, there was a chasm.

At one point there were drawn up by certain U.S. technical experts plans for land reform in South Vietnam similar to the one successfully introduced in Japan. These came to nothing, partly because the political figures under whom the experts worked failed to grasp that in South Vietnam the problem of land reform was far more than a technical-administrative matter; it had become a burning political issue. And partly these plans came to nothing because the U.S. embassy, both during the time it kept Diem in power and after it drove him out, had no authentic conviction that such things matter crucially. The idea of land reform took on a decorative function—as later, in the rhetoric of Johnson and Humphrey, it would be reduced to absurdity. Like most decorations, it depreciated in value through careless use. Once the balance of power in the U.S. "presence" within South Vietnam shifted increasingly to the military and the CIA, there was a predictable inclination to rely still more heavily upon military "realism"—which meant upon those Vietnamese generals who, while political cretins, spoke the language of blunt might.

By 1961, it now seems clear, the jig was up. The political situation had deteriorated disastrously, and, as usual, the United States tried to undo political failure with military might —of which the consequences would be a magnification of the failure and a new phase in the shedding of blood. Once American troops began to be sent, that signified the decisive failure of American policy. And the sending of troops was to lead, in effect, to a deepening of the political crisis and a worsening of its consequences. I do not hold to an unqualified opposition to military interventionism under any and all circumstances, but the predisposition of radical democrats should be *strongly* against military intervention, on the ground that it almost always comes as a last-ditch effort to rescue a failed and/or deplorable policy. Such was the case in 1961, the small beginning of a large disaster.

Now it may be argued that the inadequacy of U.S. policy consisted in the fact that it either intervened too much or not enough. Obviously the U.S. made its power felt; given the relationship of forces, it was impossible for anything else to happen. But the U.S. never chose, in a decisive fashion, to pressure South Vietnamese governments for a policy of reform. Such a course would have meant, in practice, to exert an increasing political influence, but it might also have been a way of escaping the disintegration which would prompt the Johnson Administration to decide upon military intervention.

As it was, U.S. policy gained the fruits neither of appropriate pressure nor of genuine non-involvement—either of which would have been better, both in terms of democratic values and practical necessities, than what actually took place.

The result of the policy actually pursued by the U.S. has been twofold: first, that whichever clique held power for a time in Saigon could pretty much count on American acquiescence (the one exception apparently being a short-lived semi-neutralist cabinet of the civilian Dr. Quat); and second, that each Saigon regime could assume that, because of the political limitations the U.S. representatives had imposed upon themselves, they were not finally going to exert the kinds of pressures that might discommode their clients in Saigon. Diem and Ky were puppets, yet puppets can sometimes act with a notable freedom of maneuver.

For left-liberal critics of U.S. policy, all this poses some difficult problems. If, for example, you chose to attack the U.S. for having supported Diem, is not this to imply that you would have wanted the U.S. to support another regime, say that of Mr. X? But to have supported the regime of Mr. X might have meant a deeper political involvement—and it is simply disingenuous not to recognize that deeper political involvement carries with it a risk of military intervention, even if the former is justified as a way of obviating the latter. (For example, to give economic support to Zambia in the present Rhodesian crisis *does* involve a risk of military intervention at a later point.) Now it is possible to say, as do certain leftists, that anything the U.S. might do in Vietnam or anywhere else had, ineluctably, to be reactionary. But to say that is, in effect, to limit radical criticism to a "demand" for socialism: highly desirable but not quite immediately to the point. And it is also to make incomprehensible the fact that even the most ultra-

radicals do in fact make demands upon—that is, proposals for
—U.S. foreign policy.

I see no choice but to acknowledge the inescapability of
U.S. economic and political power, which is to say, the inescapability, within the framework of the world as it now is, of
U.S. economic and political influence. Saying this, I would immediately add that democratic radicals ought to have a strong
predisposition against military intervention. Yet there cannot
really be, in the present situation, a policy of absolute isolationism, and the people who argue for it at one point are usually
among the first to deplore it at another. What matters, within
the boundaries of inherently unsatisfactory relationships, is the
political content, character, limitation, and decorum of the
influence.

The problems remain very sticky, and you can discard them
either by resorting to a Humphrey type of rhetoric, which is
to justify whatever is done by the men in power, or by shouting
"imperialist," which too often justifies whatever is done by
other men in power. But for radical democrats it is necessary
to acknowledge, even if we cannot solve, such problems as
these:

> *Is our criticism of U.S. policy in Vietnam that it tried to
> influence the direction of that country's economic and social
> policies or that it did so in a reactionary way?*

> *Assuming that one would have favored a policy of advocat-
> ing reforms in Vietnam during the late fifties, can one seriously
> have expected conservative generals and politicians to carry
> them through? Can revolutionary changes be effected by
> non-revolutionists?*

The first question I have already discussed briefly. As to the
second, our answer is, obviously, no. But the term "revolution" is bandied about a little too much these days in academic
circles. What was needed in South Vietnam during the late
fifties was not a socialist revolution, for which neither the
economy nor the politics of the country was ready, but a policy of serious reform, both on the land and in the cities. Toward this end, pressure was possible. For example, in the elections for the national assembly held in Saigon in 1959, the
Diemists were roundly beaten in Saigon but an opposition

candidate was nevertheless denied his seat. (They ordered these things more efficiently in the North.) Precisely this kind of outrage could have been privately and publicly attacked by the U.S., as in fact it was attacked by liberals and democratic radicals at the time.

What happened instead everyone knows, and since we have discussed recent Vietnamese events in many issues of Dis-SENT and I am not pretending to write a full-scale political account, I need not here go into detail. The U.S. chose repeatedly to throw its weight behind one or another right-wing group or military junta which promised stability and prosecution of the war. Having decided that Diem had outlived his usefulness, the U.S. had him replaced; but because it had acquiesced in his earlier destruction of the political life of South Vietnam, there were no popular leaders to replace him, and the U.S. found itself accepting generals even less acceptable than Diem. Then, having decided upon massive military steps, the U.S. "had" to pursue military tactics which meant indiscriminate bombings of the civilian population, because it lacked the political support among the people of the countryside which would have enabled it to cope with guerrillas in any other way; but then, because it adopted these tactics, it no doubt further alienated large numbers of Vietnamese. Having stumbled, then raced, into a military adventure from which there seems no ready exit, the Johnson Administration began to develop a rationale of blatant imperialist ideology, a sort of Monroe Doctrine for Asia.

Behind this policy was a complex of motives and forces: ingrained U.S. conservatism, contempt for non-whites, simplistic anti-Communist mania, political ineptitude, native moralism, and more. It can lead only to further bloodshed and perhaps enlarged warfare. Is there any reason to suppose that the outcome of the recent U.S. policy of support for Ky and against the Buddhists will come to anything else? Once again, as in the 1950s, there seemed a possibility of sorts that an indigenous political life could be nurtured in South Vietnam, a political life that is ultimately the only bulwark—if any bulwark remains—against indefinite U.S. occupation or a Communist victory. And once again the U.S. acquiesced in the policy of the generals.

Any democrat who reads the histories of modern Vietnam cannot avoid a feeling of profound depression. That this martyred country can have a future in which it will either not be napalm-bombed into extinction or subdued to the ghastly silence of totalitarianism now seems unlikely. The crimes of the past reverberate; error multiplies; deceit abounds. Perhaps, through failure and blindness, it is too late for freedom in South Vietnam; then, at least, let there be some kind of peace.

MICHAEL   WALZER

Moral Judgment in Time of War

MICHAEL WALZER is on the editorial board of *Dissent* and teaches political theory at Harvard University. He is the author of *The Revolution of the Saints: A Study in the Origin of Radical Politics,* published in 1965.

> *When you resorted to force as the arbiter of human difficulty, you didn't know where you were going. . . . If you got deeper and deeper, there was just no limit except what was imposed by the limitations of force itself.*

Dwight Eisenhower, at a press conference, January 12, 1955

> *I have said to these young men that they make too much of American brutality. The Viet Cong is equally brutal. Whether one is among the battling Pakistanis and Indians, or in Watts, or in warfare anywhere, the law of violence is such that each side becomes equally vicious. To try to distinguish which is more vicious is to fail to recognize the logic of war.*

Bayard Rustin, in *Civil Disobedience,* an occasional paper of the Center for the Study of Democratic Institutions, 1966

From opposite sides of the spectrum of American politics, Eisenhower and Rustin suggest the same general theory of moral judgment in wartime. They both suggest that only one judgment is possible. War itself (Rustin is a pacifist), or some particular war, can be called just or unjust. But apparently nothing whatsoever can be said about morality *in* war, about justice or injustice in the midst of the strife, because the "logic of war" imposes brutality equally on all participants. Once war begins, there are no moral limits, only practical ones, only the "limitations of force itself" and of the "law of violence." This is a very common American view and one sufficiently serious to warrant careful refutation. I want to argue that it is profoundly wrong and that what the old lawyers called *jus in bello* (justice in war) is at least as important as *jus ad bellum* (the justice of war). War is indeed ugly, but there are degrees of ugliness and humane men must, as always, be concerned with degrees. As we watch the continued escalation of the war in Vietnam, this truth is driven home with especial force. Surely there is a point at which the means employed for the sake of this or that political goal come into conflict with a more general human purpose: the maintenance of moral standards and the survival of some sort of international society. At that point, political arguments against the use of such means are overshadowed, or ought to be, by moral arguments. At that point, war is not merely ugly, but criminal.

There are limits to what can be done in wartime, even by men convinced that they are pursuing justice. These limits are never easy to specify, and it may be that they need to be newly specified for every war. It may be that morality in war is a discretionary morality. But that does not absolve us from making judgments. It only requires that we be undogmatic, pay close attention to the facts, and struggle to grasp, as best we can, the anguish of each concrete decision.

There is an immediate improbability about Rustin's statement which is worth noting at the outset. If brutality is something that can be measured and apportioned, as he seems to suggest, then there are an infinite number of possible apportionments, and it is extremely unlikely that equality will ever be attained. In every war, the likelihood is that one side is more brutal than the other, though often the differences are too small to matter much, even to the most scrupulous of moralists. But in the case of Vietnam, where the destructive powers of the two protagonists are so radically unequal, a casual insistence on equal brutality cannot satisfy even the least scrupulous of moralists.

But perhaps what Rustin means is that each side is as brutal as it can be, given its relative power. Brutality stops only when force is limited or when it encounters superior force. That is presumably also Eisenhower's meaning. But then what the two men are talking about is, so to speak, the logic of intentions and not of behavior. Even here, however, they are probably not right. In many wars it is possible to say that different degrees of brutality are intended by the different sides. Sometimes these different intentions are an inherent part of different strategies, sometimes of different military situations. It is fairly obvious, for example, that armies fighting in friendly territory are likely to intend less brutality—whatever the limits of their power—than armies fighting amidst a hostile population. Insofar as wars are territorially limited (most wars are), one side probably has to be more brutal than the other. There are moral as well as strategic disadvantages to fighting wars in other peoples' countries.

Even if there is an identity of brutal intentions, however, it does not follow that the judgments we make of the two sides should be the same. Military decisions are guided by a kind of reciprocity: one side must do, or thinks it must do, whatever the other side does. In every war, however, there exist agreements, mostly informal, which rule out certain actions. Such agreements are usually enforced by mutual deterrence, though self-restraint also plays a part. Sometimes mutual deterrence doesn't work; perhaps one side is so strong that it need not fear retaliation from the other, whatever it does. Then self-restraint may break down also, and the agreements will be violated. After all, it might be said, the purpose of soldiers is to escape reciprocity, to inflict more damage on the enemy than he can inflict on them. Soldiers can never be blamed for taking advantage of superior strength. But that is not so, for there are many different ways of taking advantage of one's strength. In every case where superiority is attained and the war escalated beyond some previously established set of limits, a hard judgment has to be made. If the escalation breaks down limits useful not merely to the enemy, but to humanity generally, if precedents are established which make it likely that future wars will be more brutal than they would otherwise be, the initiating party can and must be condemned. This is so even if it can plausibly be said (for it can always be *said*) that the other side would have done the same if it could. Men are guilty of the crimes they commit, not the ones they are said to have wished to commit.

When we speak of brutality in wartime, we do not mean the killing of enemy combatants. It is generally recognized that virtually anything can be done to combatants. They have every reason to expect the worst and presumably are trained to defend themselves. It is their business to kill others until they are themselves killed. That is a brutal business when compared to peacetime pursuits; nevertheless, it involves behavior which is appropriate in time of war. Brutality begins with the killing of prisoners and non-combatants.

In the case of prisoners, the line between legitimate and illegitimate behavior is fairly easy to draw, in part because the condition which makes a man a prisoner is fairly easy to specify. A prisoner is an ex-combatant, helplessly in the hands of his enemies. He is entitled (according to explicit international conventions) to benevolent quarantine for the duration of the war. There has been a tendency in recent years to deny the quarantine and maintain a state of warfare, a struggle for the minds of the prisoners, even in the prison camps themselves. This is indeed a struggle limited only by the nature of available force: confessions and conversions cannot be won by killing prisoners. Virtually every form of violence short of murder, however, has been used. (See "The Destruction of Conscience in Vietnam," by Marshall Sahlins, DISSENT, January–February, 1966, for a description of ideological warfare against Vietcong prisoners; the theories behind this warfare and the methods employed in it seem to have been adapted from the Chinese Communists.) All this is criminal brutality. There is surely nothing in the "logic of war" that requires it.

With regard to non-combatants, the theoretical problems are much more difficult. This is so for a great number of reasons, several of which have been brought forward in recent months as justifications for American actions in Vietnam. First of all, modern military technology makes it very difficult to limit the damage one inflicts on enemy soldiers alone or even on military installations. Even if a decision is made not to wage a full-scale campaign of terror against civilian populations, civilians are bound to be hurt and killed by what are called necessary efforts to prevent the production and transportation of military supplies. The function of the word "necessary" in arguments of this sort is worth examining. It serves to foreclose the very possibility of moral protest. Bombing is legitimate in war, the argument goes, whenever it is necessary to victory (or stalemate, or attrition, or whatever purpose is being pursued). Military necessity cannot justify wanton destruction; at the same time, moral principles cannot invalidate necessary destruction. In effect, necessity is the only standard, and the trained officers and strategists of the armed forces are the only competent judges. They solemnly conclude that civilian deaths are part of the inevitable ugliness of war.

They are sometimes right; but the argument does not hold in every case. It does not hold, for example, against all efforts to limit the geographic areas within which military judgments can apply. Rearward areas are not always subject to the same political jurisdiction as are the armies at the front. In the past, serious attempts have been made to recognize different degrees of neutrality for such areas and to admit the possibility of benevolent neutrality short of war—the kind of position the U.S. adopted vis-à-vis Great Britain in 1940 and 1941. We would have said at the time that despite the supplies we were providing for the British, German bombing of American factories would not have been morally justified (that is, it would have-constituted aggression). The same principle applies with even greater force, I should think, to "little wars" where limitation of the struggle is much more likely than in big ones. Thus the U.S. participated informally in efforts to prevent the French from bombing Morocco and Tunisia during the Algerian war (February, 1958), despite the constructions which French strategists, perhaps quite reasonably, put upon the notion of military necessity. Limits of this sort are very precarious and need to be re-examined in every case. Exceptions are always possible. Allowance might be made for the interdiction of supplies, for example, if it could be carried out with sufficient precision or at the very borders of the battle area. And, of course, a point may be reached when assistance from some ostensibly neutral country passes over into active participation: then the limits have been broken by the other side, and the soldiers must do what they can. Until then, however, decisions are moral and political as well as military, and all of us are involved.

In one sense, however, that is always true, for there are limits to the arguments that can be made from military necessity even after the disappearance of every distinction between battleground and hinterland. The distinction between civilian and soldier still stands, and among civilians that between partial participants in the business of war (workers in munitions factories) and virtual non-participants. In the past, systematic terror bombing of urban residential areas has been defended in the name of military necessity—and it has been carried out, as it probably will be again, even when the defense was none too good. But I find it very difficult even to conceive of circumstances in which such a defense could be good enough to warrant the denial and eradication of these distinctions. For the bar against the systematic slaughter of civilians is of such immense benefit to mankind that it could only be broken by a country absolutely certain not only that the immediate gains would be enormous, but that the shattered limit would never again be of any use. That is why wars to end war (or to end aggression, subversion, or anything else) are potentially so much more brutal than wars fought for realistic and limited objectives. They encourage men to think that *this time anything goes,* for there will never be another time. But there is always another time, and so *jus in bello* is always of crucial importance.

The second argument currently being made relies on the character of guerrilla warfare. By the special use they make of the civilian population, it is said, the guerrillas themselves destroy all conventional distinctions. But it has to be added that guerrillas do this only when they are successful in winning popular support. Failure clearly destroys no distinctions at all. It leaves the guerrillas isolated and subject to attacks which will be horrifying to non-combatants only if the attackers are wantonly careless and cruel. Limited success is a different matter. It can open the way for anything from endemic banditry to actual civil war, with the local authorities never certain just who or how many their enemies are; never certain, either, what actions against the population might be justified. The

problems faced by foreign troops fighting local guerrillas are
different again: their very presence is generally enough to extend the limits of guerrilla success in such a way that the
foreigners must assume that all natives are at least potential
enemies. Foreigners fighting local guerrillas are likely to find
themselves driven to justify, or rather to attempt to justify,
virtually every conceivable action against a hostile population
—until they reach that climactic brutality summed up in the
orders issued by General Okamura, Japanese commander in
the struggle against Communist guerrillas in North China during World War II: "Kill all! Burn all! Destroy all!"

At this point, the questions of morality in war and of the
morality of a particular war come together. Any war that requires the methods of General Okamura, or anything approaching them, is itself immoral, however exalted the purposes in the name of which it is being fought. It is simply not
the case that every war requires such methods or that violence
has some inherent logic which imposes this ultimate brutality
on every combatant. The violence of the guerrillas themselves,
for example, takes a very different form. But any effort to
destroy a guerrilla movement which has won some substantial
degree of popular support is almost certain to involve the indiscriminate slaughter of civilians, the shelling and bombing of
inhabited villages (it may even require the development of
atrocious "anti-personnel" weapons), the burning of homes,
the forced transfer of populations, the establishment of civilian
internment camps, and so on. It is no use saying that the guerrillas bring all this on themselves, or on their own people, by
not wearing uniforms and fighting set battles. Strangely
enough, men seem to prefer to wear uniforms and fight set
battles when they can. They fight as guerrillas only when they
lack the material resources to fight as soldiers. Guerrilla warfare is a means the weak have invented for fighting the strong.
It is not for that reason automatically justifiable: the weak
have no monopoly on morality. Nevertheless, it must be recognized that guerrilla warfare is effective, in part, precisely
because of the moral onus it imposes on the strong. The popularity of the guerrillas (they are not always popular) forces
their powerful enemies either to give up the fight or accept
responsibility for actions universally condemned by the moral

opinion of mankind. I see no reason not to admit that it is almost always better to give up the fight.

Guerrilla warfare is brutal on both sides, though the brutality of the guerrillas is likely to be inhibited by their need to maintain support among the population. The terror campaigns of even moderately successful guerrillas tend to be more discriminating than those of the authorities, partly because the guerrillas have better sources of information, but also because their enemies are forced by their positions to make themselves visible. Under the circumstances, attacks on local magistrates probably constitute legitimate warfare. Such men have consciously joined one side in a civil dispute and presumably know the risks their choice entails. They are, for all practical purposes, combatants. On the other hand, the arbitrary selection of hostages from unfriendly villages, the murder of suspects and "class enemies," the public administration of atrocious punishments—all fairly common guerrilla practices—are illegitimate actions, inadequately justified by some underground version of military necessity. Brutality of this sort must be balanced against the brutality of the authorities or the foreigners.

Let us assume that in a particular case the balance favors the guerrillas. It still might be said that this provides no basis for a final judgment. For what if the guerrillas advocate the establishment of a tyrannical regime, while the foreign troops are defending democracy? I cannot think of any historical case in which these two conditions are met, but they are possible conditions and need to be discussed. The view is common enough that the side fighting a just war has greater latitude in choosing means than does the side fighting an unjust war. After all, war is not a game; crucial issues are being decided; sticking to the rules may well be less important than winning. But this is a very unstable position, since both sides always claim to be fighting a just war and so might argue that the limits don't apply to them. The real issue, then, is not whether the justice of one's cause legitimatizes this or that act of unlimited violence, but whether one's own conviction as to the justice of one's cause does so. The very least that can be said is that most often it doesn't. The maintenance of some internal limits on war-making is almost certainly more important than the military or political objectives of either side. Once again, however, exceptions are always possible. One would have to be morally obtuse to insist that near-certainty is certainty itself. All that can finally be said is that there is an extraordinarily powerful prima facie case for *jus in bello*.

I do not mean to deny the possibility of justifying some degree of wartime brutality by reference to the purposes of the fighting. War is never an end in itself, and so it either can never be justified or it can be justified only by reference to ends outside itself. The resort to war is at best a desperate wager that things will be better, men happier or more free, when it is over than they would be if it were never fought. There are times, it seems to me, when that wager is morally acceptable. Then we fight, and since we hope to finish fighting as soon as possible, and since we are convinced that our cause is just, we resort to the means that seem to promise victory. Yet ends, we all know, do not justify *any* means, both because ends are contingent and uncertain (the results of the war depend in large part upon the ways in which it is fought), and because there are other ends in the world besides the ones we have most recently chosen. Unlimited violence, whatever its immediate effects, compromises everyone's future: for some it is a final solution, for others a warning of things to come.

Obviously, judgments of relative brutality are not the only basis of our political choices. We also pay attention to the purposes that brutality serves or supposedly serves; we may even choose, not necessarily rightly, greater brutality for the sake of greater purposes. So a man may decide that he wants to fight alongside soldiers who burn peasant villages, because he approves of their long-term goals or fears the consequences of their defeat. I have only tried to suggest that such choices ought to be worrying (that they do not simply trap us in the inexorable logic of war) and that they have their moral limits: there come moments when the sheer criminality of the means adopted by one side or another overwhelms and annuls all righteous intentions. One further point should be made: even short of such moments, our political choices do not free us from the business of judging. We judge our comrades and our enemies, in the name of ourselves, our comrades and our enemies. "I have to take part in the struggle, not to humanize it," Jean Paul Sartre has said. That seems to me precisely wrong. If one must take sides, it is not in order to escape having to impose limits on oneself and one's comrades, but (in part) in order to do so effectively.

The same argument holds, I think, in the interior moments of war, when officers sometimes face the most difficult and agonizing choices. They, above all, have a clear responsibility to uphold the limits. But it may be the case that only some act of brutality against the enemy will save the lives of the soldiers under their command, to whom they have an even clearer responsibility. Prisoners are sometimes killed, for example, because there seems no other way to guarantee their helplessness and protect one's own men. Whatever one thinks of such acts, when they are literally *incidents,* they are at least understandable. And when the exigencies of each incident are taken into account, they are possibly justifiable: here the end may justify the means. But it is something else again when brutality becomes a settled policy. Then it is probably true that officers ought to disobey, or at least to protest, the commands which follow from that policy (and which are unrelated to the exigencies of some particular situation). They ought to do so even if they still approve of the ends for which the war is being fought. Protest and disobedience are now the necessary consequences of their judgments, the only way they have to "humanize" the struggle.

Even if the lives of one's own troops are spared by a policy of unlimited violence, and even if more lives are spared than are lost on the other side, the policy is not justified. Morality in war is not settled by any single measure; it is a matter of long-term agreements and precedents as much or more than of immediate arithmetic. Here the rigorous "law of violence" comes into conflict with what are more loosely called the "laws" of international society. With regard to these laws soldiers must keep two facts in mind: that war is only a temporary rupture in international society and that it is a recurrent rupture. For both these reasons, it ought never to be a total rupture.

It is never the case that wartime actions are limited only by the force available to one side or to the other. Not that such limits are no limits at all; the second is especially effective. Fear of the enemy often has a wonderfully moralizing effect. We must all pray that we never find ourselves at war with an utterly powerless country, deprived of every retaliatory capacity. Still, many wars will be fought between states of radically unequal strength. In such cases, more than in other types of war, it is enormously important that the moral opinion of neutral nations and of all mankind be mobilized to uphold those precarious barriers, distinctions and limits which stand between conventional warfare, ugly as it is, and criminal brutality. Rather than accept the "logic of war" we must judge every military act by another logic.

It is, to be sure, disturbing to see a few men seize upon this other logic and make it the basis for hysterical and self-righteous denunciation. Moral judgment, like moral choice, is highly vulnerable to distortion. Both can become occasions for the shrill expression of personal malaise. The tensions and ambiguities implicit in the very idea of *morality in the midst of war* are all too easy to ignore. And then moral judgments are made in bad faith. But it is, I think, only another kind of bad faith to refuse altogether to total up the gruesome balance, to apply one's moral reason even to the business of war. Let us judge with due hesitation, judge without certainty; and then defend our judgments with all the passion we can command.

KEITH BOTSFORD

Venezuela: Revolution and Counter-revolution

KEITH BOTSFORD is a native of Brussels, Belgium, and is presently director of the National Translation Center, a Ford Foundation agency to encourage translation into English. A teacher of Romance languages, he is author of the novels *The Master Race, Eighth-Best-Dressed Man in the World, Benvenuto,* and is currently working on a new novel, *The Index.*

Central and South America are a laboratory for modern politics; but not so the new states without indigenous political traditions, where leaders search for utopias in a vacuum. Latin America is as old as we are; its nations came to national consciousness not long after we did. Their social and cultural unity is considerable and their political destinies have been a matter of concern to them since the days of liberation; to us, alas, only recently. In speech, religion, education, culture, manners, the similarities among them are greater than the differences, which are mostly ethnic or economic. The first separates the "Indian" countries along the western littoral and in Central America from the "white" European triangle in the south, and both from the more "Negro" Brazil and the mixed populations of the Caribbean complex, including Venezuela. The second divides the relatively industrialized, such as Brazil, Argentina, Chile, Uruguay, Mexico, and Venezuela, from the more backward economies.

Yet Latin America shows a bewildering variety of political systems, a variety which we, in our perpetual desire to find an "image" for what we do not understand, have reduced to a most elementary schema: on one side, military juntas and mustachioed officers, corrupt dictators hidden behind sunglasses, wild revolutionaries; and on the other, the "good guys"—among which, obviously, our "democratic revolutionaries." The best of these, once, were the Venezuelans. No régime in Latin America ever enjoyed as enthusiastic United States support as the Betancourt "democratic" revolution. This, to define matters as they were defined then, was what the Alliance for Progress was then peddling as an alternative to the Castro revolution, a determined effort to transform the social, economic, and political structures of a nation without passing through a violent upheaval or getting involved in the Cold War. It was rather like having your cake and eating it too.

The true range of Latin American systems was, even then, far less simple than we claimed. There were demagogic and sentimental dictatorships such as Perón's; thugs—Somoza, Batista, and Venezuela's Pérez Jiménez; Getúlio Vargas' corporate *dirigisme*, with its foundations in Brazil's adopted philosopher Auguste Comte and its model at least partly in Mussolini's Italy. Then, among the military régimes, the present-day Brazilian junta's save-the-country-for-democracy, cautious, semi-scrupulous, semi-careless custody of that nation's political institutions; Ecuador's quasi-technocratic officers' corps; Guatemala's and Honduras' bandying of power between rival groups within the armed forces; the division within the Dominican Republic between "progressives" and "die-hards." Or, among elected democracies, the various "formulas" to provide the one precious ingredient that democracy has always lacked in Latin America—stability—ranging from Uruguay's oligarchy to Colombia's system of alternating the executive power between the two major parties; from the attempt to forge broad, popular-based "movements," such as Muñoz Marín's *Populares* in Puerto Rico, Betancourt's *Acción Democrática* in Venezuela, or Belaúnde Terry's in Peru, to the extremely promising development of basically "leftist," socially oriented Christian Democratic parties, such as Frei's in Chile and the rudimentary beginnings in other countries. Or finally, the two "authentic" revolutions, the Mexican and the Cuban, with their totally opposed developments, the first becoming a political system in which one party detained all the power and yet resolved all conflicts (with some, if a limited, democracy) within itself; the second seeking to open up some "original" brand of the classic Communist society.

Why did a continent that started out with a far more homogeneous culture and political ideal than we in the United States did seek so many different solutions for what are, in simplified form, the same social, political, and economic problems? And here is one of the areas in which we least understand our neighbors. When I say "we," I mean, of course, the United States Establishment—headed, in respect to Latin America, by what is probably the least promising team ever assembled. In fact, by now, it would be safe to say we appear to have lost all interest in the place. This may, ironically, be all to the good. "We" think that these various political formulae are not a "search" for a viable system of government, but simply a reflection of an innate inability to govern at all, to which there are certain notable exceptions: those, for instance, who most closely resemble us, or most readily accept our lead in hemispheric affairs. Nothing could be further from the truth. Even the most histrionic military junta is an assault on the problem of politics in Latin America, and what this maze of systems should teach us is that it is not the *form* of government that defines societies in Latin America, but the *substance*.

First, some questions of context.

A) *The basic context:* poverty, poorly articulated economies, backward societies, populations unabsorbed into the life of the nation, population explosions, illiteracy, malnutrition and disease, deficit budgets, faulty balances of payments, undiversified crops and industries, economic dependence on foreign capital, latifundiary or minifundiary agriculture, obsolescent cadres, overdeveloped military establishments. *Problem:* Do you attempt to solve these questions *before* or *after* devising a politics?

B) Under the conditions described in *A*), *who is involved in politics in Latin America?* Obviously, a very limited number of people, derived, in general, from the Establishments. The Establishment consists of those who have escaped from that morass: broadly speaking, the élites, educated, economically independent, professionally trained, and both

emotionally and intellectually aware of politics in the larger
sense. This is a relatively small group (10 per cent would be
a rough guess). Under this group hierarchically, and some
as dependent on it for thought and leadership as for social
or economic survival, exists a diverse mass, in varying
states of disaffection (which is already a beginning of political consciousness) or totally unconnected to politics at all.
Problem: How to get the 10 per cent to participate more
intelligently, and the 90 per cent to participate, period?

C) What does "politics" mean? Generally, it is synonymous with the person, the group, the movement that holds
power at any particular moment, and hence usually irrespec-
tive of the desires or needs of the citizens. *Problem:* To
distinguish "power" from government. Particularly as "power"
in Latin America has often meant simply power to exercise
personal authority for personal profit; easy enough when the
group of the politically conscious is so small and the mass
of the inert so great, when there are no fundamental "pressure groups" sufficiently institutionalized or coherent to
resist. *Problem:* How to create a political and economical
infra-structure sufficient to resist the abuse of "power"?

*D) Even supposing power to be used on behalf of the
nation, what guarantees exist that it will continue to be so
used, once acquired?* Particularly in Latin America, where
the active society is small. The mass accepts direction and
the élites always find their niche. Alternatives seldom exist,
and governments (and leaders) exert more power than
they ought to simply because no one else will. *Problem:*
How to create support in the nation for consistent and
effective power?

*E) To what extent are the nations of Latin America
nations at all?* An important question, considering that the
days have not passed when Chile and Argentina can quarrel
over a few acres of pasture in the Andes—the ridiculous end
of the scale—and, more sublimely, Mexicans, Brazilians, and
Cubans, among others, can propose to define their ideologies
as "national," to the exclusion, almost, of all the more difficult questions. *Problem:* To what extent does real sovereignty
exist, and how much should it be restricted by common problems and needs?

F) If "liberty" is desirable, what does this word mean in Latin America? Latin-American élites claim that what we mean by individual liberty is a luxury for them and exists in the more advanced democracies because economic and social liberty has preceded political and individual liberty. The masses, they claim, have bread, not liberty; and anyone who has spent any time in Latin America recognizes that there are vast masses of people to whom the word "rights" means little or nothing. *Problem:* Can a government defend individual liberty where there is no desire for such liberty, no expectation of obtaining it?

G) What is the political tradition in Latin America? Either government by force or, in many countries, the attempt to define a constitution. The worst nations have the most model documents. The moderately good ones are constantly suspended, amended, or disregarded. *Problem:* How to get around the disillusionment of history itself, the record of failure?

H) To what degree are the various solutions proposed relevant to their societies? Here again, not much hope, and generally less so with each turn of the wheel. Latin America, like ourselves, and perhaps every nation since Andorra and Monaco, has become a factor in the international pattern of power. Native ideology supinely reflects international ideology. Exceptions: the form of *indigenismo,* or racial consciousness, usually by or on behalf of the Indian, elaborated by Mexico, and later rather woolily by Haya de la Torre; the facile verbiage of "self-determination" and "nonintervention" used to conceal basic anti-Americanism, and indigenous economic ideologies such as "state monopolies" and hybrid "nationalization." These exceptions have traces of originality, but few of relevance. *Problem:* How make ideology relevant?

I) What rôle does the concept of "revolution" play in Latin America? Obviously, a dominant one. Every country in Latin America, with the possible exception of Paraguay and Haiti, has had its periods of "democracy"; these haven't become a way of life, and revolutions of one form or another remain the traditional means of access to power in at least two thirds of Latin America: But the word has more powerful connotations: it has come to mean a change in the basic structures, a break with history, and hence a means to escape the long record of failure. Its outcome is always indecisive, sometimes for more than a generation. It contains, therefore, the essential ingredients of a "happening," to many, the vague hope of a beginning anew, a *tabula rasa* followed by an unknown quantity. *Problem:* Is "revolution" in this sense the best means of effecting a radical transformation? Can the word be upgraded to include more than a change in the ownership of power?

To these problems, the Betancourt régime gave these answers:

A) Betancourt never resolved the question of priority between "problem solving" or political form; he held, quite rightly, that one did a bit of both, because the two were intimately linked. As a young man, he would have tried to create forms of political action to resolve national problems, but nothing changes a man like responsibility, and when Betancourt assumed office he found the problems to be so overpowering that defining the nature of his government had to wait.

B) Participation. Betancourt came to power, after the overthrow of Pérez Jiménez, on a basis of mass support expressed through trade and agricultural unions. If the masses, Betancourt (and others) reasoned, could be brought into contact with the political process at this lowest level, that which affected their own working conditions and material well-being, they might be led, by stages, to higher spheres. In short: put down organizational roots, tie them to *local* situations, and local power structures will support the national structure.

C) To distinguish personal power from government, Betancourt insisted on due constitutional process, and non-re-election. In short, he borrowed the Mexican PRI's motto: "Effective suffrage, no re-election." His main object was to survive his term of office and to hand on power to a legally elected successor, Leoni: which he did. He sought and obtained the presidency in open elections; his régime is notorious, in Latin America, for being honest. He retired from office with what he brought with him: practically nothing.

D) How to create support for *effective* power? Betancourt thought it was a matter of effective action; effective action and, perhaps, visible and dramatic action.

E) Even though a nationalist, Betancourt was more aware than most Latin-American political leaders of the need for joint action on hemispheric problems. He repeatedly sought to assert: (a) the indissolubility of national sovereignty; (b) the absolute primacy of non-interference with the affairs of other states; and (c) the need to establish hemispheric machinery to guarantee both of these, and resolve common problems.

F) Betancourt recognized limitations on individual liberty. It is possible to say that he did so reluctantly at first, then indecisively; but when he finally did, he sought to do two things. First, to inculcate in Venezuelans a desire to fight for their "rights," which he sought to define, both legislatively and ideologically. Second, when he was threatened, he had the courage to admit that Venezuela did not live, as a nation, in the best of all possible worlds, and to state that governments were sometimes forced to act in ways that might be repugnant to their leaders, but which were, ultimately, for the common weal.

G) To get around the record of historical failure, Betancourt thought, was a matter of applying sufficient critical energy to break the cycle. If enough were done during his tenure, and that enough were sufficiently seen and appreciated throughout Venezuela, there was hope.

H) Betancourt's means of making ideology relevant was to base himself, though cautiously, on its nationalistic content. In his younger days, Betancourt had been a close student of a Venezuelan "reality" to which he sought Venezuelan solutions; this meant, of course, excluding "foreign" ideologies, a step Betancourt at first hesitated to take, but eventually did, with rigor.

I) Betancourt thought of his movement and his government as "revolutionary"; he defined it quite specifically as an alternative to the traditional Latin American definition of "revolution." That is, he proposed to make his "demo-

cratic revolution" more than a mere change in government
and to effect through it basic alterations in the nature of Venezuelan society. A natural talent for self-deception enables
politicians, and even their ideas, to survive against all evidence. The real questions are: to what extent were the
Betancourt answers effective in his own country? and, how
relevant are they to the rest of Latin America?

A) To the question of which comes first—pressing problems or political form—I beg off.

Betancourt's pragmatic approach was right for Venezuela
in every respect: right, because there was nothing else he
could do, and right because I hate people who dream up
paper governments and can't even tell you how many
people die every year in their own cities, or what the poor
actually eat, or how many on the average live in one room.
The best approach is the one that works, and I would
rather have imperfections that let me breathe than exquisite
mechanical models.

B) Betancourt was undoubtedly correct in seeing that
effective infra-structures, whether political (through *Acción
Democrática*), economic (through industrial and agricultural
unions), or even social and cultural, are the key to extending awareness of national problems and goals downward into
the supposedly inert mass. The PRI in Mexico functions as
a model: there is not a village, however remote, that is not
in periodic or constant contact with the party or the government, which, in Mexico, are nearly synonymous. Vargas
sought to achieve the same thing in Brazil, and Goulart
wished to extend the Vargas domain.

In fact, nearly every government in a less-developed
country has been tempted (without, I fear, taking into account the sinister precedents offered by the fascist or Communist states) to multiply the effectiveness of its national
government by extending influence into as many spheres
of collective action as possible. What more beguiling picture
for a politician in an unstable, relatively new country, than
the spectacle of the National Nurses marching in starched
white pinafores; the Union of Actors passing motions and
perhaps doing a little agitprop on the side; the trade unions,

hundreds of thousands strong, marching with banners—and all these variously, subtly, intimately blended with the ruling apparatus?

This can be done with sinister or noble aims. To divert organizations from their stated aims to other purposes is to invite limitations on each member's freedom of choice, to put pressures on him which he is ill-equipped to resist, and to introduce into such organizations matters that are irrelevant to their *raison d'être*. To play with the building blocks of democracy, on *whatever* behalf, to make them less effective instruments, if need be, against the government, and certainly, always, against the Establishment, is to vitiate the political process. It serves to weaken the freedom of precisely those groups making their first step toward political consciousness. And, if Mexico is any example, it is to create, in the leaders of such organizations, ambitions relevant first to power for themselves, and, only then, to the general good of their members. Betancourt's successor, Raul Leoni, who had long connections with such movements, would undoubtedly argue that, as the central government becomes stable, these building-block organizations lose their political dependence and begin to act as legitimate substructures. I claim, and particularly for Latin America, that, once politicized, *no* organization (Latin-American universities are a case in point) ever escapes the essential diversion into politics of its basic functions. Universities should be universities and trade unions, trade unions.

C) That Betancourt remained in office for the constitutional period and passed on the reins to Leoni after honest elections is a triumph and an example. *Passons*. That he should have remained honest and not abused his office, or his party and his officials, or theirs, is an astounding adventure. Anyone who has lived in Latin America will recognize the improbability of this situation. Nor does this improbability depend on whether the government is strong or weak. Frondizi and Kubitschek both presided over shaky governments and did very well by the use of imagination and by implicating as much of the national Establishment as they could corrupt.

The remaining problems (*D* to *I*) can be dealt with together.

Both Muñoz Marín and Rómulo Betancourt, who sat at his feet as an exile in Puerto Rico, achieved one great thing: they defied despair and got away with it. They did so under special conditions. Muñoz because of Puerto Rico's economic links with the United States; and Betancourt because Venezuela is, both actually and potentially, a rich nation, and so, for the present, exceptional in Latin America.

I don't think it would be exaggeration to say that to defeat history in Latin America is to win the battle. And to defeat history, two things are necessary to a political leader: first, the necessary charisma, a sense of himself, because the place is *personal;* and second, the ability to make change stick and to make change visible—in short, since we are talking about "revolutions," democratic or otherwise, even if your revolution is very slim pickings compared to a real upheaval (and democracy always gives slow, and often intangible, results), to make certain that these changes bear all the appearance, guise, and trappings of revolution with a capital "R." It also helps to have the blessings or the damnation of Uncle Sam: that way, you know where you stand.

The use of personality in politics is not always bad. In the context of Latin America, anyway, the president who exercises his authority has at least one great virtue: he tends to eschew the abstract, and he expresses himself like the second-generation immigrant mayors of our cities used to, by building bridges, hospitals, roads, and the like: good and public works that will bear his name. And everything he achieves pushes his opponents into the abstract. The "far left" during Betancourt's régime could only oppose progress in housing, sanitation, economic conditions, and land reform by referring to the classic abstractions of Marxist theory. These, fortunately, are less well understood by the masses than a new refrigerator or school. Personality helps defeat the legacy of history. It is dangerous, too: Leoni is no Betancourt, Sanchez Vilella no Muñoz Marín. Age catches up and the best-laid parties and movements begin to rot.

How good was Betancourt? Charisma is the lubricant

that can make social reform work: a good president in
Latin America has to persuade the privileged to give up some
of their privilege and the underprivileged to demand their
rights. Then, by agile footwork, he has to maintain a balance between these two. Even then he may fail unless he
lends it an imaginative fiction. For the Latin is often un-
convinced by the evidence of his eyes; he would often rather
believe he lives in El Dorado than actually have the streets
paved with gold. Betancourt was a "democratic" revolutionary; he had to act by "democratic" methods, and chose in
this to follow Muñoz, whose great lesson was that progress
is a matter of persuasion, an inch at a time. An unglam-
orous method of defeating history! How much easier to wipe
the slate clean with a revolution and start up afresh! But
Betancourt belongs to what is called the democratic "left,"
to whom such easy solutions are taboo.

But a "democratic" leader can't make a habit of demagoguery. The reasons are obvious. Unless you come to power
through a mass revolution, your support is not broad enough
to run the risks involved in demagoguery. You depend on
élites, the moneyed and middle classes: to last out your
time and perhaps to achieve something. And then, demagoguery feeds on demagoguery. You have to get wilder and
wilder (as Jango Goulart did) or lose your audience. So your
opponents get wilder and wilder.

In defeating history, publicly, for all time—and nothing less
is required in most Latin American nations for them to
become nations—modesty is unbecoming; and democracy
seems a chaste, modest maiden.

This was where Betancourt felt the crunch. His enemies—
the Enemy—say that what he did, and what his successors
do, and what all democratic leaders do in Latin America,
whatever their good will and piety, is not enough; not fast
enough and not complete enough.

It is a perpetually exposed flank. For the center is an unnatural position for a Latin American; and the gradual is
an unnatural speed.

On this question of the center and the slow, gradual
approach to change I am fairly sure of my ground. The
Latin American may adopt it for a while, but he is fickle

and can dump it as easily as he takes it up. He uses it while it seems to work, but is dismayed by the first reverse and distracted by the first alternative that comes along. Like a sound marriage, the center and reform come to bore him. He may never actually leave his wife, but the swath he cuts in society is marked more by the mistresses he keeps.

Yet, for all these élites and their talk of revolution, the barricades they storm are imaginary: just fantasies of leaving their wives. Rare indeed is the revolutionary in Latin America who would give up a safe job, a little influence, the comforts of home, or his social standing (preferably on the heads of others). The only change the "revolutionary" wants is that the present government be out and he in.

It is always possible that a whole experiment, like Betancourt's, may fail on a matter of feeling, on a vague desire to go further. Or as some would say: Betancourt and Frei and the experiment in democratic revolutions came just a bit too late.

To make the content of a revolution "nationalist" is to play on words. In the sense in which Latin Americans mean the word all classical revolutions have been nationalist. All I see in this, in Latin America, is an assertion of independence vis-à-vis the United States, which we would do just as well to declare vis-à-vis the Latin American nations. Naturally enough, Betancourt had to pay lip service to Venezuelan national susceptibilities; on the one hand, making stringent regulations governing our investments in Venezuela, and on the other, conjuring up or discovering caches of Cuban arms on Venezuelan soil. The inner contradictions of Betancourt's nationalism (never, after his youth and first attempts at politics, very strong) are apparent. His nationalist heart beat in close tempo with the United States even though in his heart of hearts he despised us as much as he loved us and wanted to imitate our success. All Latin American leaders share this ambivalence: they are middle-class blacks eying Charley. Betancourt's ambitions also lay well beyond Venezuela. He and Frei both share an ancient dream of Bolivar's, at the time when South America was first liberated: that this liberation should lead to union. Bolivar's refusal to take the leadership of that second phase of the struggle was the first and fatal tragedy of Latin American history.

What Betancourt tried to do in Venezuela seems to me a counter-revolution.

First, the attempt to create an alternative to classical revolutions (of which the model at hand for Betancourt was the Cuban) was explicit, a declared part of Betancourt policy.

Second, this alternative can be described as a counter-revolution in the same way one understands the Counter Reformation to be a reaction to the Reformation: that is, as a stocktaking, a close examination of a traditional position menaced by a new and more radical one, and a decision to adopt part of what the new movement offers while preserving what are considered essential elements of the tradition. In terms of revolution, I take this to mean: first, pre-empting some of the goals of a more radical revolution; second, taking firm measures to see that these goals are effectively and imaginatively implemented. Only thus can a counter-revolution forestall the possibility that the more radical revolution will still take place.

Third, I find no difficulty in believing that during the Kennedy Administration, and at the end of Betancourt's, this was official United States policy; and that our goals in this were quite openly *counter*-revolutionary: designed to stop any further revolutions that we could not control or influence or that might turn against us, such as Castro's. We hoped the example might spread.

Fourth, this seems to me perfectly sensible, and well within the limits of what democracies can do to defend themselves against attacks of irrationality. So far as I am concerned, Latin Americans who opt for other solutions are either ignorant (in which case they should go and learn the results at first hand, and not just in Cuba, where, as Cubans themselves say, all is just a *pachanga,* a great ball and a mess); irrational (because they don't know what they're getting into and still want to; or do know and don't care); or, which is most common, venal and generally vengeful against society: in short, carrying on an old Latin American tradition—the easy play for power.

Fifth, I am not convinced that this counter-revolution has many chances of success if it follows the anodyne roads to political progress that might be suggested to it by the representatives of the Great Society at home or abroad. I don't think you take up the hard tasks of reform and revolution, no matter how democratic, with a little band of well-wishers, a few loans, and a tidy middle class scared to death of change of any kind. These, like all members of an élite, sitting, or rather lying lazily sprawled in a perpetual siesta across the recumbent, docile populations that sweep their streets, curl their hair, and bring them their drinks out to the patio, see a greater possibility of loss than of gain. Nor do I think it can succeed in recruiting its leadership out of its own ranks, as Betancourt did, and the Mexican PRI does, in a kind of self-perpetuating sausage roll of ever less charismatic leaders.

Sixth, while these problems are getting themselves sorted out, I am convinced that the Betancourt régime was no isolated phenomenon; and that the counter-revolution is no accident. There are too many elements in common between, for a short list, and with significant differences among them, Betancourt, Muñoz, Figueres, Belaúnde Terry, Frei, and, for that matter, John Kennedy.

Among the points in common, the most important is that they are all what I would call "democracies of the majority"; that is, as governments or as movements or parties, they all seek to speak *for the whole nation.* They wish to be, politically, the filter through which the *vox populi* can be heard.

Quite unlike ourselves, however, Latin American movements are quite uninterested in the notion that it is an opposition, loyal to be sure, that makes an effective democracy. Dissent they will tolerate, as long as it does not challenge their rule.

The counter-revolution wishes, in each country, to be *total,* to include everyone, if possible, and hence to be stable; to be stable and hence endure; to endure and hence to put forth, like roots descending from a tree, all sorts of substructures that will nourish the state and politics itself.

Seventh, to my mind, such concordances, pressed into action

with such vigor and elaborated with such care during the Betancourt régime, smack of policy, not happenstance, and quite justify the term counter-revolution. I will go further, I think they mark a turning point in Latin American history, and, since they have their vague counterparts elsewhere (in the "enlightened" socialisms of Yugoslavia, Algeria, Egypt, etc.), possibly mark a new step in the evolution of politics.

It is surely not coincidental that the counter-revolution should begin at a time when it was becoming increasingly self-evident to most élites, even the least developed, that the great "Reformation"—in the Russian and Chinese revolutions, and for Latin Americans, the Cuban—had its defects? Just when it began to be seen in its true colors? Shall we not mark 1957 and Khrushchev's speech on Stalinism as its beginning? And note, in the years following, how it became increasingly evident that these so-called great revolutions were both degrading to individual liberty and manifestly unsuccessful economically and socially? After this time, one could still push forward on behalf of Moscow, Peking, or Cuba; but it took more effort. And, more important, the waverers, who might have been gathered into the fold earlier, could now seek an alternative with some honor.

To conclude, what is the substance of this counter-revolution? Its probable form? I think most of it is visible in Venezuela. Briefly:

(a) an eclectic attitude toward older political models, adopting elements from many systems: bits of old-fashioned socialism mixed with sophisticated techniques in mixed economies;

(b) a recognition, in all its crudity, that where the basic political material is backward or inert, politics can't survive or function without a monolithic structure of power to protect it; and that this means, in some form, however moderate, one-party rule;

(c) a liberalism that is limited by permitting opposition *within* the structure of power, but none from *without*, thus recognizing that factions may split off from the monolith but that as they do, they lose real power, and hence quickly die in isolation;

(d) a tendency to embody the power of the movement in

the person of a powerful chief executive and a corresponding realization that the chief danger to its stability arises from personal ambition, so that the problem is less one of succession (there is *always* a successor in the ranks) but of keeping the ship of state stable and making the transition from those who made the revolt to those who inherit it;

(e) the use of a certain form of primitive nationalism, more usually directed against something outside rather than for any positive national goal, as the basic cement of societies in transformation—this is where the United States has unconsciously pushed along faltering national revolutions all over the world, by sheer presence and naïve bravado;

(f) the impossibility of allowing politics to run picturesque riot when there are no well-balanced checks and pressures available to regulate the various forces at work;

(g) understanding that the extremes are not the natural home of the modern citizen, and that the ideological passion wanes, with many still left to mourn it, as material benefits increase;

(h) doing something about the various extraneous particles in the national blood stream that so far have stubbornly refused to become absorbed—the very poor, the Indians, those that lie beyond, or outside, the law; and

(i) inventing various names for all these tendencies and forms and mutations, names that will indicate purpose and planning and nothing so dull as mere democracy or a political party—the word "revolution" will do very nicely, and the "democratic" won't hurt, either.

Should we fear, as democracies have traditionally feared, the development of one-party states? With all the dangers we know are implicit in the form? Do we abet this counter-revolution and see it through to its logical end, or try, once again, to impose our own brand of democracy where, as I believe, for technical and contextual reasons, it is largely irrelevant? Do we even *think* about such questions today?

Personally, I cannot breathe the air in such a place. It is like asking me to acquiesce in the liquidation of my own will and my own capacity to act. If I were a Latin American, it would require me to take my position in the machinery of government and deprive me of the greatest gift freedom ever gave us, the right to privacy. Even with our own guarantees in the United States, I find the degree of state control and my powerlessness to change what I disapprove humiliating and intolerable.

But I know that state to be inevitable, as the church once was; and before that, god; and before god, the gods; and before the gods, nature. We live in the shadow of the state because the state also protects us and regulates our prosperity. And we have to approve of it in some way because if it uses its resources properly, it is a great leveler of injustice, inducing its citizens to reason and quietly muffling the voice of unreason, the primitive anarchy, the almost willful self-destruction that still lurks in most of us.

If I had to live in Latin America, I would find this line of reasoning more than logical; I would find it overwhelmingly necessary and desirable. I think most Latin Americans will make this choice, now or later. The first steps have been taken, and taken in Venezuela and elsewhere. Out of all the confusions and experiments has come, at last, some semblance of order. Perhaps. The only change I see, from the hopeful birth of Betancourt's revolution to the present, is that starts of sorts have been made (without us) among Latin Americans. One of the most extraordinary phenomena of that continent is the degree to which each country remains ignorant of the problems, politics, and potential of the others: ignorant, and often callous. I couldn't get Haya de la Torre to talk about parallel conditions in Colombia; he wanted Parisian gossip or literary chitchat.

Yet surely the first step toward putting your house in order is to know who you are. Then you can stop trying to be someone else: Washington, Moscow, Peking, or a cavalry officer in the wars of liberation. Then you can create what works in your own context. And despite the variety of political experiment, the context in Latin America is largely the same, though discrete, disunited. If they were less provincial, Latin American leaders might stop listening to us and look to each other. That would be a first step.

GEORGE LICHTHEIM

Ideas of the Future

GEORGE LICHTHEIM, who lives in London, was visiting professor in modern European history at Stanford during 1965–66. He has taught at Columbia and is a contributing editor of *Commentary*. Mr. Lichtheim's articles appear regularly in *The New York Review of Books*. He is the author of *Marxism: An Historical and Critical Study*.

It is a commonplace that there is today widespread fatalism with regard to the probable outcome of the nuclear race between the major powers (not to mention the minor ones who are just beginning to enter the game). This mood clearly does not depend upon the acceptance of anything worth being called a "philosophy of history." On the contrary, it feeds upon lack of confidence in a discernible direction of the historical enterprise. Contemporary liberalism no longer disposes of philosophical categories which transcend the immediate experience of a society given over to technological rationalization. This loss of perspective is hailed as intellectual maturity. The sinful attempt to think about history in philosophical terms having been abandoned—at any rate by the empiricist school, which today is virtually synonymous with academic liberalism in the Western world—the policy-makers and the public are left with a set of purely pragmatic doctrines which do not amount to more than an injunction to "muddle through." As for the Soviet camp, there is no need to describe its disarray, consequent upon the discovery that the "march of history" is taking the world ever further from the union of Marxist theory with the practice of a revolutionary proletariat destined to reshape society. Liberalism and Communism in fact have both run

Reprinted, in part, from "Ideas of the Future," *Partisan Review,* Summer 1966, Volume XXXIII, Number 3. © 1966 by *Partisan Review.*

aground, and it is precisely this stalemate which enables their
spokesmen to score polemical points at each other's expense.
In this respect the current intellectual situation is a faithful
mirror of "coexistence" in the sphere of politics. Coexistence is
of course preferable to suicide, and tolerance to the sort of
mindless abuse that was still the fashion a few years ago. But
there is little to be gained from an armistice which merely
helps to petrify the erstwhile combatants in the postures they
took up at the start of a contest which has now clearly ended
in a draw. If these frozen positions are to be transcended, it
will be necessary to go behind the assumptions from which
liberalism and Marxism originally branched off. My purpose
here is to suggest that this is going to impose a strain upon all
concerned. On the doctrinaires first of all—but those writers
who in recent years have complacently celebrated the "end of
ideology" may also have to revise some of their assumptions.
It will no longer do to take shelter behind detailed studies of
voting habits in suburbia, or eating habits among the primi-
tives. Such academic exercises will doubtless continue to pay
dividends, but their scarcity value is bound to decline, and one
may suppose that their prestige will diminish accordingly.

What then are the tentative projections which can be undertaken at the present time, in the light of what this generation
has come to know about the relative success or failure of earlier attempts? The next phase, it seems to me, can be approached under two main headings: (1) the race between
modernization and barbarism, and (2) in the developed industrial countries, the retreat from utopia to technocracy.
These topics are internally related, but for convenience they
may be taken separately.

To start with rationalization or modernization, currently so
fashionable a theme that it is difficult to say anything new
about it. There is at least one aspect which has not received
adequate recognition, and that is the evident failure of genuine,
as distinct from spurious, rationalization, both in areas which
officially count as members of the "free world" and in regions
which are usually reckoned part of the Sino-Soviet bloc. In the
first group I would mention Latin America and India; in the
second China itself. It is plain that if, instead of thinking in
political terms, one operates in terms of culture, the West has

very little in common with some of its political or economic dependencies. Conversely, the U.S.S.R. (or at least European Russia) does not have much in common with China. In the short run this may be politically irrelevant, but it is a pointer to what may conceivably happen in the not so very distant future, if the nations should decide to regroup along historical and cultural lines, instead of continuing the present East-West split. This after all is more than mere guesswork. There are indications that such a realignment is becoming a practical possibility. Here I am only concerned to suggest what seems to me a possible approach which has the additional merit of reflecting a distinctively "European" attitude. The real question then is no longer who is going to win the Cold War, but whether the United States and the Soviet Union can be trusted to continue Europe's traditional role in the world. Depending on how one stands on this issue, one may be classed as a "Westernizer" or as something else. One may also form significantly different conclusions about the probable survival of what it is conventional to describe as civilization.

I confess to some slight impatience with historians who keep reminding us that the European age in world affairs is over. The fact itself is indisputable. Differences arise at the point where some of these writers—Professor Geoffrey Barraclough comes to mind—seem to imply that the displacement of Europe from the central position it occupied in the spread of civilization was both inevitable and in some sense desirable. No sensible person is going to deny that as the world's power center, Europe has indeed committed suicide. Nor, with memories of the "final solution" and other horrors still fresh in our minds, are we likely to assert that the loss of esteem Europe has suffered is unmerited. The fact remains that the moral values in whose name the crusade against Germany was waged were themselves of Western origin. Significantly, they evoked no marked response in the Orient. Let me also recall a small but relevant circumstance which was brought home to me by conversations with survivors of the Armenian catastrophe in Turkey half a century ago. What struck them was the conspicuous difference between postwar German "restitution" and the callous attitude of the present generation of Turks to the record of their then national leaders (who included some of the later founders of the Turkish Republic). So far as I am aware, it has never occurred to anyone in authority in present-day Turkey to voice regret at the Armenian massacres. Similarly, in the well-publicized mudslinging that goes on daily between Delhi and Karachi, it seems to be tacitly taken for granted that no words need be wasted over the respective share of Hindus and Moslems in the events accompanying the partition of India in 1947. Yet that upheaval, and the ensuing civil war and "religious" massacres, cost the lives of some two million people, while tens of millions were driven from their homes. Admittedly human life has traditionally been cheap in Asia, and who are the Westerners to blame Indians for trying to retain some calm in the face of a catastrophe for which they were not wholly accountable? It remains a striking fact that such human loss is endured with a composure which Westerners have not yet learned to muster. Is it mere cultural chauvinism that inclines some of us to suspect the existence of a deeply rooted difference in our respective attitudes to the worth of human life?

The material foundation of what looks like passivity in the face of disaster—to put it no higher—is indeed evident. Statisticians tell us that by the end of the present century there will be one billion people in India and an even greater number in China. One does not have to be conversant with the precise state of Indian agriculture, or the prospects of industrialization elsewhere, to realize that—even without nuclear war—there may be catastrophes in the offing, of a sort which Europe has learned to forget, and America has never had cause to remember. And since the scale is so great—what is the Irish famine of the eighteen forties, or even the Ukrainian disaster of the nineteen twenties, by comparison with what may happen quite shortly in India and China?—there is a natural tendency to shrug and pass on. A tendency, I might add, shared by some of the better situated and better educated fellow citizens of the prospective victims. But this too has to be taken into account when it is casually asserted that the East may be about to make a historic comeback. It is easy to say that the West has been privileged by history and geography, and has not uniformly made the best use of its good fortune. The truth of this observation is not in question, merely its relevance. After all, the original rise of Mediterranean culture is partly attributable to favorable geographic and economic features. We owe it to these fortunate accidents, whatever they may have been, that the Greeks were able to break away from the pattern of Oriental despotism and to produce those distinctive achievements on which Europe and the West have lived ever since. We do not question their significance by relating them to their material substratum. In passing let me remark that cultural relativism is itself an aspect of that loss of the philosophical dimension to which I have referred. Its current popularity rests upon the not very startling discovery that every culture has its own norms and values, which enter into the perception of what is called "reality." The norms—so we are told—are binding only upon those who accept them, but this does not invalidate them, since it is their fate to be "subjective" and "objective" at the same time. We are all conditioned by the culture to which we belong, and there is no way of escaping from this situation, for empirical research can never get beyond the point of clarifying the origin of the norms we happen to call our own. As for the Hegelian idea that the nature of man, and the logic of history, can be grasped by philosophical reflection, we are presumably too wise to entertain such extravagant hopes. What remains when this illusion has been discarded is the conventional procedure whereby we treat our own moral values as though they possessed absolute worth, though as good empiricists we are of course aware that such intellectual and moral absolutism is illegitimate. In principle—so it would seem—we have no business rating our civilization above that of the Aztecs.

Is this a caricature of the reigning academic fashion? One would like to think so, but there is evidence that some such muddled notion does subtend the "pragmatic" solutions urged upon us by the spokesmen of the new orthodoxy. Without attempting to go into the underlying philosophic questions— space forbids, and I have tried my hand at it elsewhere—I propose to indicate the relevance of these considerations to the choice between barbarism and Europeanization.

I am going to state dogmatically that no other alternative exists, and that the proponents of cultural relativism are fooling themselves if they imagine that what we and they call "civilization" can go on existing if Europe goes under, or if America and Russia fail to preserve the European inheritance. You will notice that I classify the U.S.A. and the U.S.S.R. with reference to their cultural inheritance, not their current political structures and ideologies. I take the view that, so far as those two are concerned, the Cold War has ceased to represent a conflict between different civilizations, and has become an ordinary political struggle over spheres of influence. This fortunate development was made possible by the partial extrusion of the Asiatic element from the Soviet system, consequent upon the demise of Stalin and the weakening of the "Eurasian" aspect of Soviet totalitarianism. The present regime in the U.S.S.R. remains an autocratic police state, but it is no longer the mortal threat to European and Western civilization which it was under Stalin, and might have become permanently if the "Eurasian" synthesis, which was Stalin's peculiar contribution to Leninism, had been legitimized by his successors. These successors, in a muddled fashion, show a tendency to revert to the European sources of Russian civilization. It seems to me that this trend should be encouraged—not merely on political grounds, but for deeper reasons. It is going to be difficult enough to avert the danger of total nuclear war. If in addition there is also a permanent East-West antagonism along lines which threaten us all with cultural retrogression and eventual barbarization, the tendencies making for a collapse, on the scale of that which in the fifth and sixth centuries of our era overtook the Hellenistic world, may become overwhelming. Even as it is, the tone and content of the ideological pronouncements coming out of Pyongyang, Ulan Bator, and similar centers of light and learning, suggests the possibility that parts of the globe may be fated to undergo an artificial rebarbarization, or at best a kind of pseudomorphosis comparable to the early Islamic period. I do not wish to be misunderstood. I am not overlooking the existence of an ancient Chinese civilization. And doubtless it is in some sense a tribute to the pervasive element in our own culture that Chinese scholars should now be studying those curious Western philosophers, Hegel and Marx. Just so did the learned men of Central Asia in an earlier age make the acquaintance of Aristotle. But one does not look forward with any hopeful anticipation to the advent of another Middle Age. It is not our business to promote it, or to entertain any illusions about its probable character. We can find out quite easily what such an age would be like: we need only contemplate Anatole France's picture of it in *Thaïs*: unwashed hermits from the desert assembling in conclave, under the rule of barbarian chieftains, to dispute theological points in dog-Latin, or in the Greek spoken by runaway slaves, while the last surviving representatives of the older culture wandered about among the ruins. Anyone who imagines that a similar catastrophe is no longer possible ("the world has been unified, we all speak the same language") had better study the ideological pronouncements coming from Peking, and then try to imagine what it would be like having to live under semiliterate schoolmasters equipped with dictatorial powers. I have no desire to sound alarmist. I merely observe that barbarization is a real and present danger. The road from Maoism to Mau-Mauism is not as long as M. Sartre would like us to believe.

It is indeed a question whether the West still has the assimilative power it once possessed: whether, in other words, it is capable of revolutionizing not merely the economies of the premodern peoples, but also their cultures. Certainly Europe is no longer equal to the task. The burden must now be shouldered by America and Russia: jointly if possible, in a carefully controlled posture of rivalry, even enmity (by all means short of major war) if they cannot or will not act together. If one wants to be cynical, one may say that it is perhaps an advantage for them to maintain their current mutual animosity: on condition that it does not get out of hand. Who knows, if the Big Two were seen to act in conjunction, the poorer people of the world (most of them colored as well as starving) might begin to lend credence to the litany coming from Peking. Whereas if Washington and Moscow go on affirming by all the gods that they are and will remain mortal enemies. . . . But one must not carry cynicism too far. Let me simply conclude this part of my discourse by suggesting that the U.S.A. and the U.S.S.R. are beginning to look somewhat similar, and that it is desirable (as well as probable) for them to become more alike still; though doubtless this will not eliminate the built-in differences between East European and genuinely

Western attitudes. One hardly expects the Soviet regime to carry its so-called "liberalization" to the point of actually permitting genuine individual freedom. Yet if in this generation the rule of law is installed, that alone will represent a cultural advance sufficient to reintegrate Russia within the fabric of European civilization. And this, in the short as well as in the long run, is vastly more important than any economic changes. All of which, incidentally, corresponds to the traditional Marxian view of Russia's relation to Europe: a relationship defined very precisely in terms of civilization, not of class. It cannot be called Marx's fault that his Russian followers (or those of them who came to power in 1917) lost sight of these distinctions.

When one ascends from the level of our current political preoccupations to the higher realms of thought, the atmosphere becomes perceptibly thinner and the traveler needs a constant supply of oxygen to restore his mental faculties. The air has to be fed into his system by political scientists and sociologists who somehow manage to combine professional expertise with an awareness of relevant changes in the material environment. It is in this intermediate range, midway between politics and philosophy, that one encounters concepts such as "technocracy," "bureaucratization" or "the industrial revolution." The latter term indeed is pretty old, having emerged in the eighteen thirties and forties out of the complex of ideas and preoccupations which also gave rise to the schools of Saint-Simon and Comte, to the early socialist movement and to the Marxian doctrine of class conflict. The world still lives on the intellectual heritage of this eruption, most of which took place in the second quarter of the nineteenth century. Currently it is the fashion to assert that we have outgrown these ancestors, but the writers prominent in holding this view are foremost in employing the above-mentioned vocabulary, so that one does not quite see what exactly it is that we are supposed to have left behind: unless it is the more democratic and libertarian aspects of nineteenth-century socialism. Moreover, the same theorists (I had almost described them as "ideologists") who are so positive in affirming that traditional socialism is outmoded appear quite innocent of any notion that the same fate has overtaken the classical liberal system, of which socialism was and is the theoretical and practical counterpoint. To hear them one would think that it was possible for socialism to disappear while leaving its old antagonist quite unaffected. This seems to be another variant of the belief that capitalism would be perfect if only there were no proletariat. Unfortunately capitalism is defined by the existence of a proletariat, so that if one wants to get rid of the latter, one has to transcend the social nexus which produces it. I apologize for recalling these truisms, which until recently few people would have questioned, though they might have doubted the practical feasibility of the operation. It is only the academic industry of Marx-baiting—a minor though flourishing by-product of the Cold War—that obliges one to rehash these elementary verities.

There exists, however, an alternative line of reasoning which undercuts both the traditional liberal and the conventional socialist approach, and thus deserves to be taken seriously. It may be conveniently summarized by saying that bourgeois society has in fact disappeared, that the class struggle is over, and that the more advanced Western countries have entered a stage to which the nineteenth-century categories no longer apply. Capitalism and socialism are to be regarded as rival subspecies of what is called "industrial society," and the problem facing us—at any rate in the West, where the industrial revolution has been more or less completed—is to work out the appropriate political and intellectual concepts suitable to the post-bourgeois age. As for the so-called Communist countries, their particular form of state-controlled planning appears in this perspective as a mere variant of the "technocratic" society of the future. Lastly, the backward regions of the globe are seen as the battleground of a contest in which nothing more (or less) is at stake than the form of industrialization. In the long run, so it seems, the whole world will present pretty much the same picture.

I have considerable sympathy with this analysis. I only wish its exponents could bring themselves to agree that it subverts the conventional assumptions of liberalism as much as those of communism. It really is no good trying to pretend that one can have one without the other, or that classical liberalism may yet triumph in the long run. On the "technocratic" as-

sumption, liberalism and communism are both threatened, in
their theoretical formulation as well as in their "existential"
hold over their followers, and it may not be long before these
traditional antagonists are obliged to form a defensive alliance
against the common enemy: the technocracy and the ideologists of scientism who are busy putting the new viewpoint
across. This viewpoint will, of course, be described as "socialist." Indeed it is so described by the Soviet theorists, as well
as by the more left-wing planners and "technocrats" in Western countries, and by the radical nationalists in backward societies on the threshold of industrialization. We are all socialists now. Just as in the nineteenth century it was common
form for even the most benighted autocrats to employ the
language of constitutional liberalism, so today every regime
intent on modernization tries to be in tune with the socialist
fashion. The more retrograde the country, the more up-to-date
the terminology. It is partly a matter of catching up and skip-
ping the intermediate stages. In part the fashion springs from
the evident exhaustion of liberalism: now rightly seen as a
post-revolutionary creed, inappropriate to a situation where a
radical break with the past has to be made. One may question
the communist assumption that liberalism is always and everywhere synonymous with *bourgeois* individualism. That it is
synonymous with *individualism,* I do not believe anyone seriously doubts. And it so happens that individualism is a post-
revolutionary, or post-totalitarian, sentiment quite unrelated
to the decisions that have to be made at the peak of a revolutionary crisis. It is only when the tribunes of the people, the
terrorists and the dictators, have left the scene, that individualism can hope to flourish. So today there is a wave of "revisionist" sentiment in Eastern Europe quite plainly related to
the longings of the newly emancipated intelligentsia—a group
which accepts the system but wants to "humanize" it: in different terms, to bring it back to the West European origins of
the communist faith.

This too is a post-revolutionary sentiment, the counterpart
of that older liberalism which crept out of hiding in Western
Europe after the Jacobins and Napoleon had vacated the historical stage. It is a way of saying that one may have one's
cake and eat it, continue the Revolution (democratic in the

one case, communist in the other) and yet preserve personal liberty and the decencies of civilized life. And clearly under favorable circumstances this may actually occur. If democratic liberalism turned out to be historically possible in the nineteenth century, why not democratic socialism in the twentieth? The question can only be answered empirically. It is foolish to deal with it on a priori grounds, starting from a few abstract propositions about the "nature" of this or that system. At most one might argue that under modern conditions the State has become too strong for society to be as autonomous as it was in the liberal nineteenth century. The growth of centralized planning must inevitably circumscribe the effectiveness of the new liberalism, now making its first tentative steps in the guise of "revisionist" Marxism. But that it should be *impossible*, under so-called communism, to preserve an area of personal freedom, seems to me an unwarranted assumption. It may be very difficult, for reasons having to do with cultural history, but it is surely not impossible in countries whose way of life is rooted in the traditional civilization of either Eastern or Western Europe.

But having said this, one is bound to qualify one's comparatively hopeful prognosis in at least one important respect: it does seem necessary to introduce a distinction between the "revisionism" of the intelligentsia and that of the technocracy. The former group is genuinely concerned with humanist values. The latter desires efficiency rather than liberty, and is quite willing to cooperate with an authoritarian—even a totalitarian—regime, as long as its own privileged position is guaranteed. One notices signs of such a cleavage in the U.S.S.R., and doubtless we shall have further occasions to differentiate between "modernization" and genuine "liberalization." As intellectuals, needless to say, we are concerned only with the latter. Mere bureaucratic rationality is not enough. The technocracy is an important ally against the irrational tendencies of a totalitarian regime; but not a very reliable ally. Being the predestined ruling stratum of the new planned and centralized order, now arising before our eyes in East and West alike on the ruins of the old bourgeois society, it has the self-confidence characteristic of every socially privileged group: it can afford to wait. Unlike the humanist intellectuals

who spearhead the "revisionist" movement, the true technocrats are not impatient, nor are their aims precisely those of
their intellectual allies and outriders.

Above all, they are concerned to safeguard the essentials of
their rule before embarking upon the perilous experiment of
personal (let alone political) freedom. I refer to the countries
of the Soviet bloc. In the West, the problem presents itself differently. Here it is not a question of instituting individual and
political freedom: both exist and will presumably continue to
exist. It is rather a matter of defending certain democratic assumptions against the slow, almost imperceptible, growth of
authoritarian attitudes quite compatible—this needs stressing—
with individualism, constitutional liberty and the rule of law.
None of these need be threatened. I do not believe they *are*
seriously threatened. What may be in danger is something
else: the conventional democratic assumption that there is no
area of decision-making which ordinary citizens cannot and
should not, in principle, control and make their own. It is here
that the new technocratic society poses its challenge: a challenge wrapped up in the soothing language of the benevolent
autocrat: certain complex matters, it appears, are too difficult
for the ordinary citizen to resolve, though they may be debated
ad libitum. Thus the area of effective democratic control
shrinks, though the principle may never be questioned. In con-
tradistinction to the Eastern nations, we shall retain our liberties, but shall no longer care to exercise them. In the end, of
course, the liberties will atrophy. With the best will, Caesar
cannot keep the Republic alive if there are not enough Re-
publicans to go round.

Where then are we to look for a counterweight to the triumph of managerial technocracy? Quite clearly we can no
longer make the assumption that the historical burden is going
to be shouldered by the industrial working class: a class which
has, in fact if not in form, become the foundation of the new
industrial order. In a certain fundamental sense the class struggle is over, and with it the material basis of those radical-
democratic movements which in the age of the bourgeois revolution provided an automatic check upon all attempts to
constitute a unified and irremovable ruling elite. It is a truism
that the aims of Marxism, and the actual character of the

organized labor movement in the Western world, have become discontinuous. The "union of theory and practice" has dissolved, leaving in its wake a reformist mass movement, and an academic critique of society which increasingly represents the intelligentsia's rejection of the modern world. Does it follow that socialism as such has lost its relevance? Not if the term is understood in its original sense, as the vision of a planned society taking the place of an unplanned one. There is little doubt that the Saint-Simonians would feel at home in our world. What has been shaken is the confidence that the new industrial order would be mastered by the collective action of the actual producers: the workers. With a slight exaggeration one may say that Europe—East and West—has by now almost completed the road leading from Utopia to technocracy. No one any longer doubts the feasibility of a socialist order. What has become doubtful is its democratic and egalitarian character. It is an open question whether this situation represents a temporary defeat, a permanent dissolution of the union between socialism and democracy, or the germ of a stable compromise whereby the working class will permit itself to be led by the technical intelligentsia, and the latter will incorporate labor's traditional democratic and syndicalist aspirations within its own political consciousness. I am inclined to think that such a compromise is the best one can hope for. The alternative presumably is some form of corporate authoritarianism.

In saying all this one is of course making some quite large and possibly unwarranted assumptions about the probable future course of development, as well as about the upheavals of the past half century which have landed us on the threshold of the new society. These assumptions, which I am not going to defend but shall simply take for granted, include the following:

(1) Our age has seen the collapse of the unregulated market economy and the bourgeois society built upon it. The resulting gradual changeover to a planned and state-controlled economy is the counterpart of the more dramatic upheaval in Russia and Eastern Europe which—for ideological reasons—goes under the name of "Communism." As for the ancient cultures about to enter upon the process of modernization, they have before them two different "models" between which

to choose. It is going to depend very largely upon accidental political factors which of these alternatives—or what eccentric combination of traits taken from both—they decide to adopt. In all probability, most of these countries will go through a "national-socialist" phase, though it need not be as totalitarian as is currently the case in China.

(2) In our own Western or Atlantic world (I abstract from the subordinate quarrel between "Atlanticists" and partisans of an autonomous Europe) the dominant feature of the post-liberal age, i.e., the half century since the 1914–18 war, has been the gradual displacement of bourgeois society by a new social formation, for which at the moment we still lack the appropriate intellectual nomenclature. All one can say is that the current intermediate stage corresponds neither to the traditional picture of capitalism (defined as a market economy with private property in the means of production) nor to the historic anticipations of the socialist labor movement. In consequence, liberalism and Marxism have both been found wanting, as "theories of action" if not as general philosophies.

(3) The lineaments of the new society are still rather indistinct, but the combination of centralized economic planning, modified authoritarianism in politics and the social predominance of a new "technocratic" stratum (in the place of the ancient bourgeoisie) suggests that, in the long run, the picture will not differ very radically from the corresponding state of affairs in the *soi-disant* communist bloc: subject to those historic differences (rule of law, individual liberty) which have always distinguished Eastern from Western Europe (and, one might add, Latin America from North America).

(4) In the U.S.S.R. and the Eastern bloc countries, the technocratic stratum lacks an adequate self-consciousness, and *a fortiori* an ideology that links it to the masses and enables it to rule without the constant employment of fraud and force. The attempt to constitute "communism" as such an ideology has failed. Communism is historically the ideology of a revolutionary working class. This class having exhausted its mission and been subjected by the technocratic stratum which evolved from the ruling group of the Communist party, the latter employs the traditional vocabulary for the purpose of

legitimizing a new form of inequality. In principle this state of affairs might stabilize itself, but under the conditions actually prevailing in the U.S.S.R. and its satellites, there is just enough latent tension to make an experiment in controlled democracy seem perilous to the rules. Moreover, the official ideology needs to be reformulated, so as to serve at once as a rational guide for the ruling elite and as an ideology for the masses. This cannot be done consciously, in Machiavellian fashion: it must come about as a result of genuine debate and conflict. Hitherto this has not happened, and in the near future does not seem likely to happen.

(5) In the West, the changeover from liberal democracy to socialist (or quasi-socialist) technocracy is proceeding in haphazard fashion. In Western Europe it is furthest advanced in France and Italy. In Northern Europe it is mediated by reformist socialism. In Latin America it will probably come about under the banner of radical nationalist, or national-socialist, movements. In the United States it has hardly begun. North America, notwithstanding some elements of welfare-state economics, remains wedded to bourgeois economics and the corresponding liberal-democratic ideology. The U.S.A.'s relationship to the Atlantic world may be compared to the position of mid-Victorian England in relation to the European continent. This applies both to its current economic role, its predominance in the fields of technology and applied science, and its politico-ideological conservatism. Like Victorian Britain in the nineteenth century, the United States is currently the guarantor of the established order in the Western world, and the repository of liberal-democratic traditions, in this case inherited from an earlier era. Paradoxically, it is at once the most advanced and the most conservative of all the Western countries. This accounts for the ineffectiveness of its foreign policy in areas where the struggle against the rival totalitarian bloc has to be waged by political and ideological, rather than military, means. An ideology still bound to Lockean liberalism and empiricism is useless in this area, though it acts as a guarantor of political and personal liberties at home.

(6) While the United States is handicapped by the antiquated character of the official liberal ideology inherited

from the eighteenth century, the U.S.S.R. suffers a corresponding disadvantage in being tied to the Marxist-Leninist interpretation of history. Yet neither side is willing to let go of its ideological legitimation. Liberalism and communism are alternative ways of rationalizing a state of affairs which in actuality does not correspond to the claims made on behalf of either, though the discrepancy is more glaring where an official creed has been clamped upon the whole society. Both represent the historical incorporation of a universal idea within a particular national context, so that in each case the national sense of identity, and the naïve patriotism of the individual citizen, becomes entangled and confused with absolutist doctrines. Although these doctrines have a common source in the rationalism of the eighteenth century, the pretense is kept up that the contestants are separated by an impassable gulf, when in fact it is only the Cold War that prevents public recognition of the existing parallelism. This state of affairs is not perceived as such because the universal creeds—liberalism in the one case, Marxism in the other—have become ideological: they are employed to defend national traditions and imperial rivalries, or at best alternative ways of organizing the world after its hypothetical unification. This unification in turn is rendered impossible by the inability of the contestants to escape from their ideological straitjackets. The short-run consequence is a tendency for the "third world" of emerging countries to seek an escape through a revival of cultural nationalism and parochialism. The long-run effect may be to promote a series of catastrophes, for which each side will then blame the other.

If one ignores the immediate political perspectives and assumes the long-run continuance of present trends, one must suppose that the technological unification of the globe will at some stage give rise to a kind of planetary organization which will do away with the unrestricted sovereignty of the nation-state. This desirable goal is, however, unlikely to be reached by the straight path of international agreement. If history is any guide, the world will have to traverse an intermediate phase of predominantly regional and continental organization. The racialist deformation of Chinese Communism is a danger sign. One sees here how a universalist faith can be perverted at its very core by an upsurge of primitive emotions stemming from an earlier cultural stratum. Of the various African and Asian nationalisms it is unnecessary to speak. They are both historically legitimate and intellectually sterile. Nations which have the misfortune to arrive on the historical scene after the age of nationalism is past cannot help presenting a tragi-comic spectacle, however well-founded their claims to sovereign independence. The delusions of grandeur which are a necessary part of their mental equipment—indeed a condition of their emergence from the prehistoric stage—must be shed before they can see themselves and the world in a true light.

This cancellation and destruction of self-generated illusions is the work of history, which is no bed of roses but rather that slaughterhouse Hegel described in terms which have recovered their meaning for our generation. We who during the Second World War saw entire nations hurled from the Tarpeian Rock have acquired a better understanding of the conception of history as a concrete totality determining, and being determined by, the movement of its parts. If it is necessary to guard against the temptation to treat history as an independent entity operating "behind" the actual empirical process, it is no less important to grasp the logic of the process, as it unfolds through its various local and parochial manifestations. World history is not a suitable topic for nominalists who deny the possibility of valid generalizations not verifiable in private experience or controlled experiment. To the charge that such statements are at best mere guesswork, and at worst poetic nonsense, the answer must be that it is impossible in human affairs to dissociate factual analysis from an imaginative grasp of the total situation in which men are involved. In reality such an understanding is always implicit, if only because we approach every problem with a theoretical equipment which carries the burden of its own past. We cannot, in the present instance, abstract from our concrete position as individuals who are concerned about the fate of a particular civilization: that of which we are the heirs. The question what sort of future lies before us is quite specifically the question whether our civilization

will survive. In a sense this is obvious, but one needs to
see the implication: if we identify the continuance of civilized
existence with the survival of *our* civilization, we are making a statement about European and Western history as
being in some sense unique. Such a claim is implausible unless it can be shown that the "Westernization" of the world,
now going on before our eyes, is more than an accident due
to passing historic advantages. This is an instance of what
may be called "grasping the logic of the process." It calls
for something more than the weighing of pros and cons.
Either our categories—which, needless to say, are themselves
historical—equip us for a proper understanding of the concrete totality known as "history," or they do not. If they
fail, we in turn shall fail to influence the minds of people
belonging to other cultures. That, so far as I can see, is the
only pragmatic test possible in the matter.

Concretely, then, it is here affirmed that Western history
possesses a paradigmatic value in virtue of certain traits
which are currently in process of being imitated by the
remainder of the world. Sociologists and economic historians
are unlikely to find such a statement surprising. They may
even regard it as the kind of truism that is hardly worth re-
peating. The relativistic mode of thought, which treats Western history as a singularity among others, is more common
among cultural anthropologists than among scholars whose
professional work is centered upon the material process
whereby the globe is currently being unified. They know
to their cost that Westernization is both urgently desired and
actively resisted: desired for its economic benefits, resisted
because it involves the radical uprooting of archaic cultural
patterns and traditional ways of life. From a strictly European
viewpoint it may be doubted whether the transformation now
in progress is worth all the bother, since it is unlikely to
produce any very exciting cultural conquests. But that is
water over the dam; the decision is out of our hands. We
have let the genie out of the bottle (if I may vary the meta-
phor) and must take the consequences, however disagreeable
or unnerving. And after all it is only right and proper that
the European laboratory should be thrown open, especially
now that the period of experimentation is over and done

with. In future the Europeans will take a back seat and watch
the others at the perilous game of employing the material and
intellectual tools that have been fashioned for them. Let us
hope they will not blow themselves up.